JEWS AND THE OLYMPIC

JEWS AND THE OLYMPIC GAMES

Sport: A Springboard for Minorities

PAUL YOGI MAYER

Foreword by Sir Martin Gilbert

VALLENTINE MITCHELL
LONDON · PORTLAND, OR

First published in 2004 in Great Britain by
VALLENTINE MITCHELL
Crown House, 47 Chase Side, Southgate,
London N14 5BP

and in the United States of America by
VALLENTINE MITCHELL
c/o ISBS, Suite 300
920 NE 58th Avenue
Portland, Oregon 97213-3644

Website: www.vmbooks.com

British Library Cataloguing in Publication Data

A catalogue record for this book is available from the British Library.

ISBN 0-85303-451-6 (paper)
ISBN 0-85303-5164 (cloth)

Library of Congress Cataloging-in-Publication Data

A catalog record for this book is available from the Library of Congress.

Typeset in 11 on 13pt Palatino by FiSH Books, London
Printed in Great Britain by MPG Books Ltd, Victoria Square, Bodmin, Cornwall

This book is written in memory of my late friend and mentor Hajo Bernett and also in honour of all those who could NOT participate in the modern Olympic Games because of their faith, nationality, race, sex, class or disability. I also dedicate my writings to my friend Hans Joachim Teichler.

Contents

Illustrations

Foreword

Yogi Mayer has written a book of utmost fascination. Many people have been curious about Jewish participation in the modern Olympic Games, and many rumours have circulated – such as the number of Jews who participated in the 1936 Berlin Olympics – but until now there has been no authoritative account. Not only is this book authoritative, it is written in a lively style that will engage the reader from the outset. Above all, it shows how a minority group, in this case the Jews, can rise through sport to a fulfilment of their national destinies, and break free from the prejudice and restrictions of the societies in which they live.

This is a topic that has engaged Yogi Mayer for many years. Angered when members of the Jewish sports clubs in Germany – of which he was an active member – were expelled en masse as 'non-Aryans', he began even then, in this first year of Hitler's rule, to collect the names and details of Jewish sports champions of that time. In 1935, shortly before the Berlin Olympics, he published, in Berlin, a list of those champions. Coming to Britain shortly before the outbreak of war, and working after the war as the sports instructor and rehabilitator of many survivors of concentration camps, he has always encouraged other authors not to neglect the aspect of Jewish sports. I answered his call in my book *Letters to Auntie Fori: 5,000 Years of Jewish History and Faith*, in which several of the letters were devoted to Jewish sports.

Yogi Mayer now sets the Jewish sportsmen and women of the modern Olympics on a triple pedestal: one of research, learning and affection.

The first Games of the modern era were held in Athens in 1896, when a Hungarian Jew came third in the marathon. At that same Olympics another Hungarian Jew won two of the three swimming events. Two German Jews – they were cousins – were in the first winning gymnastic team; one of them achieved a gold in the parallel bars. Of the forty-four events, Jews won nine. Yogi Mayer points out that had these Jews competed as a nation they would have been placed fourth, ahead of both France and Germany.

Two other Jews, one British (he was then the world champion weightlifter) and the other American, were among the judges at Athens. This remarkable roll-call of Jewish achievement in the Greek capital was to be repeated in many variants by Jewish sportsmen and women in each succeeding Olympic Games. Yogi Mayer's account of this is gripping; at the end of the book he lists all Jewish Olympic winners, a table of endless fascination, which can be used in conjunction with his index for a remarkable voyage of historical discovery.

Yogi Mayer – who was present in 1936 when Hitler opened the 1936 Olympics, and who was tested as a commentator for the BBC at the 1948 London Olympics – writes that he hopes that his work will inspire other minorities to publish similar works. This is a worthy aspiration. 'All sport', he writes, 'can serve as a springboard towards the emancipation of all minority groups, as I believe it has been for the minority to which I belong.' This book is a model that could well serve other minorities in their quest for recognition and self-worth.

SIR MARTIN GILBERT
August 2003

Preface

When the German National Olympic Committee meets to select its team for the Olympic Games, the sole criteria for the selection process are those of sport. Considerations of an athlete's sex, origin, colour of skin, political orientation, religion or race have no part to play. Everything takes place in an atmosphere of fair competition.

It was not always so in the history of the Olympic Games. At the 1936 Games in Garmisch-Partenkirchen and Berlin, Jewish fellow-athletes were discriminated against. That discrimination against German-Jewish sportsmen and women was the motivation behind this book with its investigation into the achievements and successes of Jewish athletes at the Olympic Games. This report by eyewitness Paul Yogi Mayer on the fate in the Holocaust of Jewish participants in the Olympic Games, brands the criminal race-policies of the Third Reich, and highlights the contributions made by Jewish athletes and sport administrators to the success of the Olympics and Paralympics – contributions which are indisputable today.

In order that none of these facts be forgotten, Paul Yogi Mayer's book is an invaluable resource.

PROFESSOR WALTHER TRÖGER
President, German National Olympic Committee
August 2003

Acknowledgements

My special thanks and gratitude go to my wife Ilse and our children Thomas, Monica and Carol, my family in England and Australia. All of them gave me their unstinting support and tolerated my shortcomings while I researched the book in Britain and abroad. Their understanding and encouragement made it possible for me to devote much of my retirement to this work.

In addition I should like to thank my editor, Jonathan Manley, and my copy-editors Leon Rogers and Paul Beasley. Ludwig Berlin assisted with the statistics and Henry Kuttner with translation from German into English.

Finally, I extend my gratitude to Sir Martin Gilbert for his generous foreword and to all those who assisted me in my research since I began it in Berlin in 1935.

I am grateful to all those who gave me their permission over so many years to use quotations and pictures from their publications.

P.Y.M.

Abbreviations

The criteria for inclusion in the lists of medal winners at the back of this book are explained in the section headed 'Jewry' (see pp. 25–31).

F = Female; D = Disputed; WR = World Record; OR = Olympic Record

The statistics are drawn principally from publications by Stan Greenberg and David Wallechinski.

Throughout the book, names of Jewish medal winners, officials and authors are given in italics on their first mention in the main body of the text.

Part I

Prelude

My Reason Why

In 1935, shortly after Hitler had seized power and just before the Olympic Games were due to be staged in Berlin, I wrote about Jews and sport and published lists of Jewish champions of the time in *Das Jüdische Sportbuch*.[1] Many years after the war the publishers reprinted *Das Philolexikon* in its original form and rejected requests for corrections to be made.[2] In 2000 I wrote *Jüdische Olympiasieger: Sport – Ein Sprungbrett für Minoritäten* to assist those involved in research on German Jews before the Games.[3] To gain the right balance I extended my research worldwide. I was delighted with the reception and numerous reviews the book received.

I am now presenting this English version of my research in an improved and enlarged edition. I hope to be able to prove that we Jews in the sporting world are neither inferior – as Jewish artists, writers, musicians and scientists have long demonstrated – nor superior to others.

As a *Zeitzeuge*, or witness, I have presented the achievements of Jews at the Olympics for the inspiration of the young and in order to oppose anti-Semitism wherever it is manifested. I hope, too, that this presentation will inspire other minorities to publish similar works. After all, sport can serve as a springboard towards the emancipation of all minority groups, as I believe it has been for the minority to which I belong.

On the advice of my late friend and mentor from Bonn University, *Hajo Bernett*,[4] and, after him, Hans Joachim Teichler from the University of Potsdam, I refrained from attempting an

1   Sidi Goldschmidt, Paul Yogi Mayer and Martha Wertheimer, *Das Jüdische Sportbuch* (*The Jewish Sportbook*) (Berlin: Atig Verlag, 1936).
2   Paul Yogi Mayer, *Das Philolexikon, Handbuch des Jüdischen Wissens* (*Handbook of Jewish Knowledge*) (Berlin: Philo Verlag, 1935) (Suhrkamp: 1992); reprinted as *Jüdischer Verlag im Suhrkamp* (Frankfurt and Mainz: 1992).
3   Paul Yogi Mayer, *Jüdische Olympiasieger: Sport – Ein Sprungbrett für Minoritäten* (*Jewish Olympians: Sport – A Springboard for Minorities*) (Kassel: Agon Sportverlag, 2000).
4   The names of all Jews mentioned in the text are italicised on their first mention in the text.

academic dissertation, for which I have neither the required qualifications nor the resources for full-time university study.

Based on my background as a *Zeitzeuge*, I approached several national Olympic committees in the hope of obtaining information about the participation of Jewish athletes and organisers in each national team. I am aware that in so doing I was trespassing into an area protected by the ethos of the Olympic Movement and which was encapsulated in 1974 in the rule that no discrimination was to be allowed 'against any country or person on the grounds of race, religion or politics'.

It was in the spirit of the Olympic Charter[5] that several national committees expressed their regret at being unable to help me, since, on principle, they had never registered either the race or the religion of their team members. I was first disappointed to receive these replies from such countries as France, Belgium and the Netherlands, but am now the more grateful to all those who later wrote to me privately to assist with their first-hand information or to express their good wishes for my undertaking. A number of these correspondents were sports historians or journalists or had themselves taken part in sports competitions.

My work has naturally been coloured by my having grown up in Germany and now having lived for over 60 years in England. I have revisited Germany frequently since my retirement to speak to young audiences at schools and universities about Jews and sport, often linking my words to my own life before emigration.

I was born two months after the 1912 Games in Stockholm ended; I am sure that none of my family was aware of them then or could have foreseen my own future involvement with the Olympics. Years later, I was expelled from the universities of Berlin and Frankfurt because I was a Jew and was also deprived of any further financial support from my late father's business, which had been liquidated by the new state. At the same time, other Jewish members of sports clubs, or so-called 'Nichtarier', were expelled.

---

5   For the full text of the Olympic Charter – the codification of the Fundamental Principles, Rules and Bye-laws adopted by the International Olympic Committee (IOC) – go to the 'Organisation' section of the official IOC website, www.olympic.org, and follow the links; alternatively, go directly to www.multimedia.olympic.org/pdf/en_report_122.pdf. The website also features further information about the development of the ethos and rules of the Olympics. A good printed source of information about these topics is Lord Killanin and John Rodda (eds), *The Olympic Games: 80 Years of People, Events and Places* (Highbury: Barrie and Jenkins, 1976); see pp. 12–22 and 258–64 in particular.

All of this angered me so much that I began to collect the names and details of the achievements of Jewish champions. I was lucky in that I could combine my hobby with my professional activities: I always liked to work with young people and to write about and report on them.

I stayed in Germany working as a journalist and teacher within the increasingly restricted life allowed to Jews. I narrowly escaped arrest during the pogrom of 1938, thanks to the help of our house-keeper. But, on 9 November, the flames of burning synagogues signalled what was to come and I finally understood that there was no longer a life for me in Germany. Luckily, my wife and baby son Thomas were able to emigrate with me to England. When the Second World War began I volunteered for military service, first in the Auxiliary Military Pioneer Corps and then with the Special Operations Executive (SOE).

After nearly six years I was demobilised and started to teach art and sport in the East End of London. I then accepted a call to form a centre for young people who had been rescued from concentration camps. Situated in Hampstead and called the Primrose Jewish Youth Club, the centre represented probably the most rewarding period of my working life. Finally, when my task was done and these boys and girls were able to stand on their own two feet, I returned to the East End and became the youth director of the Brady Clubs. After 15 years I ceased Jewish youth work and became the area Youth and Community Officer for the Inner London Education Authority in the borough of Islington until my retirement. Having qualified also as a track and field coach with the Amateur Athletic Association, I assisted as deputy leader and team coach the British team at a number of Maccabioth in Israel before starting to write about education and sport in England and Germany and becoming involved in the history of the Olympic Games.

In recognition of my writings in Germany I was granted an honorary doctorate from the University of Potsdam. In 1997 I was awarded The Membership of the Order of the British Empire (MBE) for services to youth.

Olympia – Defined

The terms 'Olympus', 'Olympia', 'Olympiad', 'Olympians' and 'Olympic Games' have so frequently been misused and interchanged that some clarification may be helpful.

Olympus is a 3,000-metre-high snow-covered mountain often shrouded in clouds over 150 miles north-west of Athens. It is claimed to be the seat of Zeus and the other Greek gods. Olympia is a plain and one-time sacred grove in Peloponnesus, roughly 120 miles west of Athens. Now largely excavated, it provides an amazing display of former temples and sculptures connected with the ancient Games. I was overwhelmed by the whole area and, when I later visited the Greek National Museum in Athens to see further exhibits, fell in love with a sculpture of a little rider, a reminder that horseracing was already a well-established sport some thousand years ago.[1]

There are also many written accounts of the ancient Games – the four-year period between them being called an 'Olympiad' – but none tells us of any Jewish participation. What we do know is that competitions traditionally took place with athletes in the nude and that whenever Jews did take part they tried to have their circumcision reversed in order to look like the other athletes. In any case, some form of Games also took place in Jewish areas, such as Jerusalem and Alexandria.[2]

Unlike the ancient Games, the modern Olympic Games are certainly not a form of offering to any deity. However, the Olympic Movement has now become a religion – or at least a substitute one with its rituals and deities – for its most devoted followers.

Before legislation was introduced, the word 'Olympics' was often misused, the 'Workers' Olympics' organised by the International Workers' Sport Movement is just one example. Even

---

1   Some of the sculptures on display at the museum date back to the eighth century BC.
2   Manfred Lämmer.

in the years preceding Baron Pierre de Coubertin's initiative, festival organisers in many countries were adding the name 'Olympics' to their competitions. Now both the name 'Olympic Games' and its associated logo of five interlocking rings in different colours are protected in order to prevent such abuse.

An Early Jewish Involvement

Baron Pierre de Coubertin visited England on several occasions and attended many sports festivals, some with histories going back to the eighteenth century.[1] These included the Manchester and Saxon Games and the Shropshire Games. While there, he met and was much influenced by Dr William (Penny) Brookes, the founder of the Much Wenlock Games, and soon became a firm Anglophile. He also most probably visited the games organised at the Crystal Palace by *Ernest Ravenstein*. Ernest was the son of *August Rabenstein*,[2] who, as a follower of 'Turnvater' Jahn,[3] had founded the 'Turnverein' (Gymnastics Association) in Frankfurt and the Feldberg Taunus (festival).[4] Today, when I drive along St Pancras Road in central London, I can still see the inscription 'Turnhalle' (gymnasium) on the portal to a large hall where the Turnverein used to meet and where *Ida Ravenstein* gave her first classes for women.

The Crystal Palace games were supported by competitors from many countries and were regarded as a kind of Olympic Games. Among the participants was a former German gymnast, *Karl Blind*, who had been imprisoned in Germany for his revolutionary activities in Baden. Having escaped, he found refuge in Ernest Ravenstein's club on St Pancras Road. In due course, Blind became a renowned public speaker. Ravenstein got together with John Hulley and Dr Brookes to form the British Olympian Association and later, in 1905,

---

1   The British Olympic heritage is referred to in 'Minds, Bodies and Souls', a manuscript written by Dr Don Anthony – to whom I am indebted for a copy. He also supplied information on athletes, officials and organisers who were, to the best of his knowledge, Jewish.
2   Ernest changed the 'b' in his father's name to a 'v'.
3   Freidrich Ludwig Jahn (1778–1852) founded 'structured' gymnastics (Turnen) in Germany in 1810.
4   It is well worth noting that the German Gymnastics Association (Deutscher Turnverein) had an international membership that included Jews.

the British Olympic Association. This had 16 members – including *E. Lawrence Levi*, a teacher, author and former weightlifting champion who represented the British Gymnastics Association.[5]

---

5   Levi taught at the Hebrew School in Birmingham and later became Principal of Denbigh Lodge School. Strange as it may sound, he was also the English international weightlifting champion of 1891. His writings include *Jews in Birmingham 1870–1929: The Autobiography of an Athlete* and *A History of the Birmingham Athletics Club*. Within two years of the inaugural meeting in Paris concerning the revival of the ancient Games, the 1896 Athens Games welcomed Levi and Sir Charles Walston, a lecturer and author: both acted as judges at the Games and, in addition, Walston took part in the pistol-shooting competition. Walston was an American by birth who had changed his name from Waldstein and was to be known – once knighted – as 'Sir Charles'.

Minorities, Sport and the Olympics

Since their revival, the Olympic Games have been of special value to the aspirations of minorities. Many of the competing nations have become increasingly multiracial and multi-ethnic. I have chosen a few minority groups, with particular emphasis on the unique situation of my own – the Jews, through which to examine the roles of class, socio-economic structure, sex, belief systems, race and ethnicity, and paraplegic disability in relation to the Games and their extension, the Paralympics. I shall refrain, as far as possible, from discussing political minorities and their special problems – as with the continuing conflicts in Northern Ireland, the Balkans, Africa, Asia and, of course, the Middle East – and concentrate on the indigenous Aboriginal peoples, the Maoris and Afro-Americans. As a starting point, it will undoubtedly be helpful if I try to explain the term 'minority' and provide an example pertinent to the subject of this book of the consequences of being a member of a minority, regardless of one's sporting abilities.

'Minority' – A Definition

Alfred Adler, the father of individual psychology, claims that the individual member of a minority has 'a general feeling of failure *vis-à-vis* the demands of the environment, a feeling of inferiority, insecurity and weakness in reference to the achievements of [his] fellow men'.[1] If transferred from the individual to the behaviour of the group, in my opinion Adler's psychology not only highlights a collective inferiority but in most cases a superiority complex also, which leads black Americans to proclaim that 'black is beautiful',

---

1   Alfred Adler (1870–1937).

the Nazis to claim the superiority of the Nordic races and the Aryan superman, and Jews to be the 'chosen people'. If one, for example, follows K. Günther's description of the Nordic races as quoted in J.A. Mangan's *Shaping the Superman: The Fascist Body as Political Icon*, then there is no doubt that even within the German people supermen are also a minority.[2]

All of us belong to one or, more often, to a number of minorities due to the fact that we live in increasingly multicultural societies. International law demands that 'a minority has the right of recognition as well as of protection, and that not only when facing the law', and the *Encyclopaedia Britannica* states that 'only individual liberty and tolerance can solve the minority problem in a form acceptable to the conscience of civilised humanity...'[3]

Ironically, it was German pressure in 1922 – the year that its Foreign Minister, *Walther Rathenau*, was murdered – that persuaded the League of Nations to formulate and recognise the rights of minorities. Years later, moreover, it was Hitler's Germany which withdrew from the League when his excessive demands for the recognition of 'Volksdeutsche' ('German groupings') were not accepted. Yet Germany remained as a member of the IOC – there being no difference between the statuses of nations within the Movement – as 'The practice of sport is a human right'. This applies to any minority and thus to Jews, too.

Yet what about those minorities who had no recognition or representation, either nationally or internationally, and little relation to sport at all, let alone the Olympics? When the Nazis assumed control of sport in Germany they also excluded other minority groups, including the 'Gypsies' (a word often used abusively and now often replaced by 'Romanies') and homosexuals.

The fate of one person will illustrate the situation minorities encountered in Nazi Germany. In his book *Leichtathletik im Geschichtlichen Wandel* (*Athletics in the Historical Change*), Hajo Bernett recounts the story of Germany's famous middle-distance runner Dr Otto Pelzer,[4] holder of four German and two world records and victor over the famous Paavo Nurmi. Pelzer was a teacher at a residential co-educational and rather progressive school at Wickersdorf. He was

2 J.A. Mangan (ed.), *Shaping the Superman: the Fascist Body as Political Icon* (London: Frank Cass, 1999), p. 30.
3 'International Law', *Encyclopaedia Britannica*, 1768–1964, vol.15, pp. 564–75.
4 From having spectated at various athletics events, I remember Pelzer as a lonely figure wrapped in a blanket, waiting for his race.

a typical non-conformist who still had Jewish friends and lived in the flat of a Jewish woman. As he, together with some other leading German athletes, was occasionally critical of the policies of the Reichssportführer (Reich's sport leader), he was arrested by the Gestapo under the pretext that he was homosexual and had been involved with boys at his school and sentenced to 18 months in prison. As this happened in 1935 he was released early because of the approaching Games and allowed to travel abroad. When his visa expired he had to return home and was rearrested by the Gestapo on landing. He was taken for interrogation in the notorious basement of the organisation headquarters in the Prinz-Albrecht Strasse in Berlin and afterwards sent to the quarries of the Mauthausen concentration camp. He survived the war, a broken man. His badge had not been the yellow Star of David but the pink square for homosexuals.[5]

Concept of Class

Although the modern Games have ultimately been the springboard for a new type of star performer largely free from negative minority-related issues, the revival of the Games initially owed an obvious debt to classicism and soon drew criticism from some quarters that the structure of the organisation was itself class-based.

In 1890 the French government asked Coubertin to draw up a questionnaire and to send it to a large number of countries to ascertain the extent to which they provided for physical education. Three years later, at a conference held in Paris at the Sorbonne, Coubertin first declared his interest in reviving the ancient Olympic Games. By 1894, 21 countries had indicated their support for such a restoration to be held in Greece.

Interest in a revival was already in the air in various countries several decades before Coubertin's guiding hand became evident: in 1852 a Greek, Evangelis Zappas, had already organised the first Pan-Hellenic sports festival, and German archaeologist Ernst Curtius had continued the excavations started by the French at Olympia.[6] The excavations revealed parts

---

5 Hajo Bernett, *Leichtathletik im Geschichtlichen Wandel* (*Athletics in the Historical Change*) (Schorndorf: 1987), pp. 279–80.
6 Curtius was assisted by another German, Alfred Schiff, who had spent many years in Rome and Greece. See the chapter on the 1936 Olympics for further information about Schiff.

of many ancient temples and other buildings and statues, all of which added to the interest.

Encouraged by so much support and by the impressions he had gained during his visits to England, Coubertin then proposed at a conference in Paris in 1894 that the first Games of the modern era should be celebrated in Athens in 1896. The Greek poet Demetrius Vikelas was to be president of the new International Olympic Committee and Coubertin saw to it that he himself would be its first general secretary. Membership of the IOC was by 'invitation and self-recruitment' only – thus ensuring its freedom from any outside political influence – and consisted of aristocrats, senior military officers and academics, while messages of support came from several royal families.

Meanwhile, the International Workers' Sport Movement resented the formation of the IOC and criticised the first modern Games with its award-seeking competitions as being capitalistic, bourgeois, elitist and chauvinistic. Support for such socialist workers' groups came from east Berlin, Austria, Poland and neighbouring countries to the east. Strong anti-elitist support also came from 'Bund' in Poland, the Jewish socialist workers' association, and 'Morgenshtern' (Morning Star), the Bund's workers' sports organisation, in spite of there also being Jewish involvement in the formation of the IOC. In this manner Bund and Morgenshtern between them opposed any Jewish participation in the first Games. Even in 1931 over 100,000 workers, with a strong participation by Morgenshtern, marched through Vienna, with, according to reports, 250,000 jubilant spectators in support. But when the 1932 Games were held, it became apparent that a democratic process had occurred during the preceding three decades and that the Olympic Movement had evolved into a classless organisation.

A few years later Hitler's invasion of Eastern Europe destroyed the socialist workers' movement, and especially the Morgenshtern organisation. Few such Jewish clubs survived the Holocaust. Where workers' sports bodies were restarted after the war they soon diminished in importance and size, until finally all opposition to the by now well-established Olympic Movement ceased. At the same time, partly because of economic developments in Europe and the wider world and the social changes brought about by the war, the modern Games emerged free from any prejudice based on class, gender, faith or ethnicity.

Apart from the close relationship with the media, and particularly radio and television over the years, the Games were becoming ever more closely linked with commercial enterprises, such as the manufacturers of sports goods (Nike, Adidas, Puma, etc.), lotteries and other money-spinning activities, and so could provide countries in need with free equipment, sponsored training facilities and sports scholarships. Such advantages for athletes have combined with full professionalism to create a new class of star performer who linked up with the media and commerce.

When the first professionals were allowed to compete in the Games there was apprehension that monetary prizes would soon be added to the awards of medals. But, surprisingly, the star athletes were as keen to participate without direct financial reward for the honour and the medals as the ordinary athletes who only had a very small chance of winning. Many sportsmen and women may have returned home empty-handed from the Games to what was now nearly all of the world's 200 countries, but they were proud to have competed under their own flag and to have taken part in the greatest of all sporting competitions. Only later would they have learned how the stars had profited financially at the many sponsored events that followed. And still the Games remain free from any monetary prizes and financial awards, thus avoiding the frequent wage- and incentive related issues of many modern professional sports. Instead, a spirit of friendship continued among the competitors, including the stars themselves.

'Ladies' Become 'Women'

Since the days of the suffragette Emmeline Pankhurst, women have played an increasingly important role in British political life, culminating in Margaret Thatcher becoming the first woman prime minister. In the world of sport, a similar contribution has been made by women such as Princess Anne, who was president of the British Olympic Association and also a member of the IOC. There is still, however, a discrepancy between men and women in sport. Men tend to dominate on committees and in administration, coaching and management. Men receive higher rewards in prize money (as at Wimbledon), more sponsorship and wider media coverage. Women golfers, for example, may still be excluded from the 'nineteenth hole' – the club bar, and, until recently, women were also banned from membership of the Marylebone Cricket Club (MCC), the national governing body of the game.[7]

Many years before the reintroduction of the Olympic Games, social organisations for women already existed in continental Europe and North America. Some provided opportunities for health-centred recreation while others supplied a wider programme, including artistic and other cultural activities.[8] In Britain at the time of the first modern Olympics, women who participated in sport were mostly from the middle classes and would sometimes play games such as tennis or croquet as social activities. Many sports, and particularly those described as 'contact' sports, were considered to be socially and physically inappropriate and, ultimately, unladylike.

Influenced by such thinking, Coubertin did not consider women in his ideology for the revived Olympics, opposing their participation as being 'against nature'. His vision was strongly influenced by what he saw in British boys' public schools, where the emphasis on sport and 'muscular Christianity' enhanced the qualities required of a gentleman: leadership, courage, self-discipline, physical fitness and the spirit of friendship, understanding and cooperation. All of these qualities prompted his conception of what the Games were about. In the ancient Games, where men competed in the nude, women were not only barred from participating but could not even attend as spectators: the ultimate penalty for transgression was death.

The early Olympic villages accommodated male competitors only; women lodged in hotels. Subsequently, camaraderie and the nurturing of team spirit were later enhanced by the inclusion of women in the villages.

In the 1900 Games the IOC invited ladies to play golf and tennis; archery was introduced for them in 1904 and figure skating in 1908. The first Olympic swimming competition for women was in

---

7 Most sports clubs in Britain are private and can therefore select their membership as they wish. However, if a club is dependent on funding from its local authority or a governing body, it may find that this is restricted if there is any evidence of a policy of discrimination being applied. This occurred at a golf club in Hampstead, north London, where membership had been refused to Jewish applicants and women. When financial penalties were to be imposed on the club this deplorable policy was revised.

8 Gertrud Pfister, formerly of the Freie Universität in Berlin, although not herself Jewish, has written more about the physical activities and organisations of German Jewish women than any other Jewish writer. See Bibliography.

1912, fencing followed in 1924, but gymnastics and athletics were not contested by women until 1928. However, the first three of these sports were soon dropped, so that by 1936 there were only four sports left for women: swimming, fencing, athletics and gymnastics. There were still only five sports by 1948 and a mere six 20 years later. By 1996, though, the programme had expanded to 23 sports. This clearly reflects the changing perception of the role of women in society generally and it is now widely accepted that women are entitled to take part in any sport they may choose.

Although most sports now have competitions for men and women, the events may differ. In gymnastics, for example, the men's apparatus includes the rings, horizontal and parallel bars, the pommel horse, and a long horse for vaulting, all of which require the slow build-up of strength of an adult male, whereas young women and, more often than not, teenagers compete on the asymmetric bars and the beam. Both have floor exercises but only the women's programme is accompanied by music, with both male and female competitors assessed for their quality and the content of their individual sequences. Generally speaking, women's performances require additional grace and flexibility as well as the strength and agility demanded of men. This may be why gymnastics is one of the few sports where the quality of performance and the charisma of young women attract wider support, greater media coverage and larger audiences than the more powerful performances of men.

The place and standing of women as minorities in the societies of member states have also contributed to developments within the Games. The inclusion of the USSR – as it was then – in 1952 increased pressure on the IOC to open up many events for women since women in Russia had sporting opportunities comparable to those available to men, both as part of their education and through their work. More recently, we have celebrated the achievements of women from Muslim countries, recognising the role model they represent for women around the world who might thereby be encouraged to challenge the boundaries imposed by their own cultures. It was recently reported that the daughter of a former president of Iran had pointed out that women were not admitted as spectators at soccer matches but could, on the day when they were allowed to participate as players, real progress towards their emancipation in other fields would follow. This is another indication that sport can become a springboard for minorities and other disadvantaged groups to improve their situation in society.

However, since the revival of the Games in 1896, no woman has ever been president of the IOC and women have been largely ignored both as athletes and administrators, as the *International Journal of the History of Sport* points out. The cover of this issue shows the outgoing – now honorary – president, Juan Antonio Marquéz de Samaranch, with his 11 fellow IOC executive committee members: there is not one woman among them.[9] Will his successor, Dr Jacques Rogge, be able and willing to give the biggest minority group of all fair representation?

Jewish Women and Sport

In Europe, most Jewish sports organisations were for both sexes. West Central in England, the first Jewish girls' club in the country, was set up in 1896 for workers in the textile industry whose parents had emigrated from Eastern Europe. In America, single-sex clubs were more common, examples being the Young Men's Hebrew Association, the Women's Association and the Young Men's Christian Association in America. *Charlotte Epstein ('Eppie')*, for example, founded the National Women's Life-Saving League in America, which had a strong Jewish following, and later the Women's Swimming Association. Eppie was the first chaperone for the American girls' swimming team at the Olympics and successfully coached medal-winning teams. She also became the first woman judge of swimming at the Games.[10]

Most Jewish clubs remained single sex throughout the first half of the twentieth century. Later, they became more mixed in response to changes in Jewish society. Regional competitions in athletics, swimming, football and netball were, and still are, organised by the Association of Jewish Youth in England and by Maccabi worldwide. Although there were separate competitions and leagues for boys and girls, sport was significantly more important for the former. As an illustration of this, several male

---

9 *International Journal of the History of Sport*, 16, 2 reported that: 'The IOC is striving to promote a larger participation of women in sports activities and the Olympic Games. A working group was established to advise the IOC on the policy to be implemented in the field of the advancement of women in sport. The IOC also supports the view that women should play a larger role in the administrative structures of the Olympic Movement and established as a goal, to be achieved by 2000, that at least 10% of all positions in all their decision-making structures (in particular legislative or executive agencies) should be taken by women and that such percentage should reach 20% by 2005.'

10 Eppie refused to attend the 1936 Games and died two years later.

Jews have competed for Britain at the Games, but so far no Jewish women.

There were certainly women, though, who had the ability to compete for Britain at such a level. One young woman, *Joan Belasco*, demonstrated an amazing high jump potential when, in the early 1920s, she cleared a height of 5ft 4in (1.65m) over a bamboo cane rather than the more customary tightrope bar. However, her Olympic potential was never realised for two reasons: firstly, women's high jump was not introduced into the Olympics until 1932, and, secondly, Belasco's Orthodox father refused to allow her to compete on the Sabbath. Had she been born ten years later and been given the same opportunities to train and compete as other athletes she might have become the first – and still the only – British Jewish woman to win an Olympic gold, but as an Orthodox woman continued participation in top-level sport would have been difficult.

Gertrud Pfister, who has written extensively about the physical activities and organisations of German Jewish women, considered that in Orthodox Judaism women were largely 'defined by religious practices in order to reduce their sexual attractiveness and to safeguard men from women's potential uncleanness.' This protection was to be achieved by women taking purification baths – both before and after menstruation, by wearing a wig after marriage to hide their hair and by avoiding activities that were not in keeping with those of an Orthodox woman. In addition, male and female social activities were to be kept separate from each other.[11] The impact of religious orthodoxy, whether in Judaism or any other belief system, will limit sporting opportunities for women. Only occasionally can sport become a step for Orthodox girls to move beyond the confines of their own community.

Pfister, furthermore, identified 15 per cent of the Berlin Jewish population as Orthodox and maintains that up to 30 per cent of girls in some high schools were Jewish.[12] There were Jewish sports clubs in Berlin, although they were not common elsewhere in Germany, where Jews lived in small towns and where the community was not strong enough to support such clubs, whether

---

11 Taken from lectures about Jewish Sport by Gertrud Pfister, *Die Rolle der jüdischen Frauen in der Turn- und Sportbewegung, 1900–1933* (*The Role of Jewish Women in the Sport Movement, 1900–1933*) (Berlin: Academik Verlag-Saukt Augustin, 1989), p. 65.
12 Ibid.

they desired to or not. Therefore, those with an interest in sport joined the local association. This situation was probably equally true in other countries where Jews joined sports clubs and their religion was considered to be a private matter for them.[13]

In spite of these obstacles, the list of Jewish women who have excelled as champions, and particularly in the Olympic Games, is impressive and therefore warrants more attention, as we shall see. An example, though, of what is more likely for Jewish women comes from my own family. No family members – going back at least three generations – showed any interest in or aptitude for sport. When I committed myself to competitive sport, my family considered me 'aus der Art geschlagen' ('the odd man out'). My maternal grandparents from Hesse, who were Orthodox to a limited extent, sent their three daughters to a finishing school near Frankfurt. Only one of the daughters' children – other than myself – went on to university. Moreover, none of the 15 cousins on my father's side stayed on at upper school. Like any other children, they swam, cycled, hiked and played games with their mainly non-Jewish friends and never considered joining an organised club for sports or other activities, Jewish or otherwise. However, my younger daughter Carol furthered her interest in sport at the Dartford College of Physical Education, the first such college in England, which was founded by Bergman Osterberg in 1896. After teaching physical education in schools, she moved into further education, where she now lectures on physical education and the sociology of sport.

The Disabled as a Minority

When considering the disabled as a minority and their journey to full Olympic-level representation I am happily obliged to tell the story of one man whose contribution to this journey is perhaps greater than any other: *Dr Ludwig Guttmann*.[14]

---

13 It's certainly worth noting that, until 1933, German Jewish women lived in a modern, democratic country, very different, for example, from the way women were treated under the retrogressive regime imposed by the Taliban in Afghanistan. This treatment is, of course, entirely at odds with the progress toward sexual equality in the Olympic Movement.

14 Guttmann's efforts illustrate the personal contributions that many Jews have made to sport through their work with individuals and groups. In this unique case, an individual from one minority furthers the cause of another.

In 1943, the British government approached Guttmann, a neurologist and former refugee from Nazi oppression, to open a rehabilitation centre for the treatment of disabled ex-servicemen. The Stoke Mandeville Centre (later the National Spinal Injuries Centre) was situated in a village in the Chiltern Hills, north-east of Aylesbury in the south of England.[15]

Guttmann was aiming to use physical activities as a way of further rehabilitating those of his patients who responded enthusiastically to treatment. He included the playing of games in his schedule, starting with archery and then progressing to wheelchair basketball. From these active beginnings, the centre soon progressed to arranging competitions with a nearby centre called 'Star and Garter', which had a similar ethos. Dr Guttmann discovered that, apart from physical disablement, some of his patients also had to overcome physiological disturbances. To foster further integration with the able-bodied, he also added fencing, table tennis, snooker and even weightlifting as part of the treatment.

Long after the Second World War, Guttmann published a book entitled *Sport and the Disabled*,[16] which summarised his work, an undertaking in which he was assisted by his secretary, Joan Scrutton MBE. She sent me material which was still unknown at the time. In it he stated: 'If I ever did one good thing in my medical career, it was to introduce sport into the treatment and rehabilitation programme of spinal cord sufferers and other severely disabled...'[17] This 'good thing' was not without the rewards of immediate personal recognition: Guttmann's caring approach and his searching for ways and means to increase their mobility incited his patients to address him as 'Popa'.

When I was the senior area youth and community officer for the rather advanced-thinking Inner London Education Authority I was approached for grant aid for wheelchair basketball matches. At that time, I was astonished when watching former Stoke Mandeville patients and others. In play, no pardon was given, but foul play had to be punished, and players did not shirk from

15　Dr Guttmann came from Breslau (now Wroczlaw), where my wife Ilse was born and went to school; he had been her mother's physician. Dr Guttmann then went to Oxford to continue teaching and research into the treatment of spinal injuries, and – like myself – became a founder member of the 'Association of Jewish Refugees', which is when I had contact with him.

16　Dr Ludwig Guttmann, *Sport and the Disabled* (London).

17　Joan Scrutton, *Paraplegia*, publication of the British Wheelchair Association, 1970.

turning over an opponent's wheelchair; so wheels were subsequently adjusted to ensure that this could not happen.

With the increase in events for the disabled having received international support, the Ministry of Pensions financed the provision of an indoor pool and the Queen opened a 400-metre running track. Not only did Guttmann make full use of these facilities for his patients, he also invited local able-bodied young people to join in the activities. His patients gained from the contact and so did the visitors, who were able to overcome their inhibitions about the disabled.

Games were soon organised in coordination with the IOC at venues where the Olympics had taken place, events that the Americans were quick to dub the 'Paralympics'. It was the Dutch, though, who took the initiative to meet and compete against other countries in a new indoor games hall, a venue Guttmann was invited to name: he chose 'The Lady *Else Guttmann* Hall' in honour of his wife. He also had the honour of being awarded a Knighthood by Queen Elizabeth. After the Games following the 1960 Olympics in Rome, Sir Ludwig was invited to meet Pope John XXIII, who welcomed him with the greeting 'You are the Coubertin of the paralysed'. This was particularly fitting: the Games were now supported by 23 nations and over 400 participants. Rome was followed by Japan and then Israel, at Ramat Gan, as Mexico could not cope with hosting additional Games after the 1968 Olympics had ended. The wheelchair basketball at the Israel Paralympics was watched by 25,000 spectators, who went into a frenzy when their national team defeated the Americans 49 to 40. The one-eyed war hero *Moshe Dayan* presented the medals.

It was regrettable that in Munich, four years later, the Olympic village had been sold prior to the commencement of the Games. Therefore, immediately after the Games a former USA Army camp in Heidelberg had to be used for over 1,000 Paralympic participants; the provision for women was still based on separate accommodation. As the Americans had helped so much in looking after the needs of the disabled at these games a victory of one point over the Israelis in the wheelchair basketball was taken as a fair recompense.

Not all the countries sponsoring the Paralympics could house all participants in an Olympic village, but the Seoul Games managed to accommodate over 3,000 in 1988, and when the wheelchairs began to roll into the stadium they were greeted by over 70,000 enthusiastic spectators.

The millennium 2000 Games in Sydney was where the Paralympics reached a height which had never been dreamed of, not even by Sir Ludwig Guttmann. He died in 1980 and at the closing ceremony of the Paralympics the flags of 40 nations were lowered in his honour to fly at halfmast, a tribute unique in the history of the Games.

Race and Sport[18]

Long before Hitler, there had been a so-called 'Rassenforscher' ('Race researcher') in Western Europe in the nineteenth century who proclaimed the superiority of one part of the human race above all others. He was Joseph Arthur Gobineau (1816–82). Others, such as the Englishman Houston Chamberlain (who became a German) and de Gobineau supplied the basis for the beliefs of men such as Henry Ford in the USA and Richard Wagner in Germany, both aggressive anti-Semites.

Closer to home, the *Völkischer Beobachter* (*Racial-National Observer*), the official organ of the National Sozialistische Deutsche Arbeiter Partei (NSDAP), declared shortly after Hitler's Machtergreifung (seizure of power) that 'there is no place for Negroes in the Olympics... otherwise it could be that the free man would have to compete with the unfree black, with Negroes, to win' and, finally, 'the next Olympic games will take place in Berlin in 1936. It is hoped that those responsible will know their duty: the black must be excluded. We expect this.' And, as far as the Jews were concerned, there were pages of anti-Semitic outbursts in *Mein Kampf*, to which *Dietwart*, the organ of the Reichssportführer, Tschammer-Osten, added, 'we keep the Jews at a distance from our own organization... The Jew is a parasite... The elimination of the Jews from our community... is an emergency defence measure.'[19] These derogatory comments followed slogans such as 'the Jews are our misfortune'.[20]

As part of this anti-Semite propaganda in Germany, a series of pictures were published showing people of different skin, hair and

---

18 In this section I have limited myself to the discussion of questions of race and the differences of opinion that it provokes in relation to the Olympics and the rejection of racism in the ethos of the Movement.

19 Hitler in various speeches and publications.

20 Proclaimed by Stöker – a leading nineteenth-century German churchman.

eye colour, hair form, cranium shape and physique, as well as certain character traits which were used to project the Nordic peoples as the Aryan superiors of all other 'races'. For many years, scientists, anthropologists, sociologists and historians have tried to assess the significance of these differences as regards performance. The performances of athletes from Kenya, Ethiopia, Morocco, Tunisia and Algeria over the longer distances have tempted sports journalists to develop new claims of the superiority of particular racial groups. The fact that basketball player Michael Jordan, the golfer Tiger Woods and heavyweight boxers such as Mike Tyson and Lennox Lewis are among the highest paid sportsmen at present can be used to augment these claims. For many years, the all-black Harlem Globetrotters, trained, promoted and owned by *Abe Saperstein*, were the forerunners of the 'Dream Team', which enthralled spectators at the Barcelona Olympics. From time to time, racial and physical characteristics were also invoked to explain the performances of Finnish athletes such as Nurmi, Kohlehmainen and Ritola, and of the British middle-distance runners Sebastian Coe, Steve Ovett, Steve Cram and Peter Elliott. There is no doubt, though, that factors such as tradition, nutrition, social conditions and training were significant elements in the quality of their performances. Research into ethnicity continues. More recently, the length of muscle fibre has been suggested as an explanation of the differing achievements of East African middle-distances runners and Afro-American sprinters.

However, studies have also taken place that contest the assertion of such special racial and physical characteristics. For example, *Ernst Jokl*, a sports physician, undertook tests on children in South Africa before the introduction of the Apartheid policy. He concluded: 'After tests on physical skill, strength and endurance of a... cross-section of South African children, English, Afrikaner, Jewish, Bantu, Cape-coloured and Chinese, we are impressed with the similarity between the standards of physical performance found in different racial groups.'[21] When racial differences were used to segregate communities in South Africa, it was the nation's cricket captain, *Ali Bacher*, who fought for equality between them and for the representation of blacks in the national team. Now equality in sport has spearheaded moves elsewhere for the emancipation of all the country's citizens.

21 *Journal of the American Medical Association*, 116 (May 1944).

Whatever the physical and racial factors behind the sporting successes of minorities, it is clear that success itself has led to positive recognition. Colin and Paul Tatz, for example, tell of the achievements of 129 Aborigines displayed in a special Hall of Fame in Australia. No doubt Evonne Goolagong, the Wimbledon, French and Italian tennis champion and, more recently, Cathy Freeman, the star of the Sydney Olympics, have also advanced the cause of the Aborigines.[22] In New Zealand the Maoris have bridged the gap between the original inhabitants of the islands and the emigrants; rugby has played a great part in this. In Britain, too, black sportsmen and women are becoming ever more apparent. Colin Tatz concludes *Black Diamonds* with the words: 'they have discovered that their strength in sport has given them a passport into the world of the whites and their respect and friendship'.[23] Whether we call sport a passport or a springboard towards equality for minorities, the result is the same.

Yet theories into why racial minorities 'overachieve' in relation to their demographic representation continue to be propounded. The American writer Jon Entine expresses the following in his book *Taboo*:

> In other words, champions are born not made. Diet, skill and training make little difference if you are the wrong colour. Thus European whites are over-represented in some sports such as weightlifting, wrestling, hammer-throwing and the shot put, because they have the strongest upper bodies in the world...likewise athletes with West African ancestry have a near-monopoly on sprinting because of their inherent speed... Blacks form just one-eighth of the world's population, yet make up 70% of players in the US National Football League and 85% of basketball professionals. In England blacks are just 2% of the population but form 20% of the League footballers.[24]

From such data, Entine argues that it is different population groups, rather than entire races, that have different physical and psychological attributes which can help to make them either brilliant or hopeless at particular sports.

22 Colin and Paul Tatz, *Black Diamonds* (Sydney: Allen and Unwin, 1996).
23 Ibid., p. 24.
24 Jon Entine, *Taboo: Why Black Athletes are Better and Why We're Afraid to Talk About It* (New York: Public Affairs, 2000).

When reviewing *Taboo*, the *Observer* quoted Sir Roger Bannister, who said that 'the combination of genetics, biology and the ancestry of black athletes had certain natural anatomical advantages over whites', and Carl Lewis, who stated that 'Blacks, physically in many cases, are made better', but in opposition to this view Tessa Sanderson, the black British Olympic javelin champion, said that 'hard work, determination and the will to win are what make an athlete'.[25] In my own view, the picture is not the same in women's and men's sports as the former appear to be much more multiracial to the extent that any claims of racial superiority cannot be maintained.

Jewry[26]

For many years, various sports historians have continued with their research in order to improve earlier findings with up-to-date information and to strengthen the continuing debate on Jews and sports history, a debate which underlines my own research about Jews and the Olympics. For example, several contributions were made in a report of an international seminar on 'Physical education and sports in Jewish history and culture' held at the Wingate Institute in Israel in 1972. Among the contributors were *Harold Harris* and Manfred Lämmer, who gave an account of their studies on Jews, sport and Greek culture, *Uriel Simri* and the late *Arthur Harnak*, who presented papers on Jews and sport during the Middle Ages, and Hajo Bernett, who presented an assessment of Jews and the Olympic Games that focused on the 1936 Berlin Games.

These contributions add their insights to a rich and extensive lineage of writings on Jewish history. *Josephus Flavius*, the Jewish historian from the first century of the Roman Empire, traced Jewish history from the second century BC onwards, and Philo of Alexandria (15 BC–AD 50) wrote in detail of the synthesis of Greek culture with existing Jewish concepts. They also maintained that, at that time, more Jews lived outside the kingdom in countries bordering the Mediterranean than in Israel. Wherever they lived, Jews had aligned their culture with that of the indigenous

---

25 See Denis Campbell, 'Genetics "The Key to Black Success"' in the *Observer*, 23 Jan. 2000.

26 It is not my intention in this section to attempt to provide a formulated answer to the perennial question 'Who is a Jew?' but to report on Jews in their relationship to the Olympic Games and to maintain that this relationship shows Jews to be a different minority to the others I have discussed above.

population. In Israel itself there existed conflicts between the Jewish orthodoxy and a large number of the less law-observant citizens – who had been greatly influenced by Greek culture.

Many centuries later, the uprising of the Macabbees and Bar Kochba against the Greek and Roman occupiers were the inspiration for *Max Nordau* to introduce the watchword 'Muskeljudentum' ('Muscle Judaism') at the first Zionist Conference (Basle, 1987) and to demand that this concept, which was based on physical fitness and political input, be applied to some of the already established Jewish sports clubs as well as those to come.

Jewish participation in organised sports must, of course, take place within a broader framework of values, a necessity set forth as early as the Middle Ages by rabbis – including *Moses Maimonides*, who was also a physician – who supported some forms of physical recreation such as sports provided they were pursued under the observance of written and spoken law. This is no mean feat as it is said that there are over 600 laws – 'as many as bones in the human body' – which govern the daily lives of Jews, and, in addition, there are 40 or more stipulations connected with the Sabbath and High Holydays. (I must confess that to try and relate these demands to my own lifestyle is awkward, especially as I already find it difficult to observe all of the Ten Commandments!)

Jewish laws, rulings, observance and traditions with their detailed schedules for daily prayer, work and travel, along with traditions about wearing distinctive clothing and other rigid stipulations, undoubtedly make it rather difficult for many Orthodox Jews to participate in physical education and competitive sports. In Israel, moreover, proportional representation has enabled a minority of Orthodox members in the Knesset to curtail recreation and sport, especially, of course, on Shabbat (the Sabbath) and High Holydays.

These restrictions, though, are by no means exclusive to Judaism. Many law-abiding believers in other religions such as Buddhism, Islam and Hinduism, face similar problems regarding their participation in the Olympics. In the past, devout Christians were also subject to restrictions. The Scotsman Eric Liddell refused to run on the Lord's Day at the 1924 Olympics. Much closer to the present day, at the beginning of his career the triple jumper Jonathan Edwards – who went on to be world record holder and Olympic champion – would not compete on a Sunday owing to his Christian beliefs. From a Jewish viewpoint, the strict observance of the Sabbath was an additional reason for the formation of segregated Jewish clubs.

The history of Jewish segregation in sport leads to the question of what the phrase 'Jewish sports' actually means. The American George Eisen, whose opinions on Jews and sport I shared until I heard him at a recent seminar in Berlin, stated the following in an introduction to a special edition of the excellent aforementioned *International Journal of the History of Sport* devoted to Jews and sport:

> Jewish history with its infinite religio-ethnic nuances and sheer complexity, compounded by a given host-nation's cultural value system, national aspirations and sensibilities and its relationship to sport and the Olympic Movement would prove too complex...I must immediately put a disclaimer on the term 'Jewish sport'...I am more convinced than ever that 'Jewish sport', unlike Jewish music or literature, did not come from the 'psyche' of a people. Neither could 'Jewish sport' emerge from a generic Jewish culture because a uniform concept as 'Jewish culture' never existed...Thus good compromise would be to retain such an expression as sport in history, culture and society. We might except through the notions that there are easily identifiable attitudes towards and rationales and desires for engaging in, relating to and even rejecting sport.[27]

I found this comprehension of Jewish sport rather misleading and too provocative in its implicit claim that such a thing as 'Jewish sport' does not exist.

A view different to both Eisen's and mine was put forward in the new German periodical *Sport Zeit* (*Sport Time*), which involves sports historians such as Hans Joachim Teichler and Arnd Krüger as advisors. As a clear indication of these differences, the first issue of *Sport Zeit* was devoted to 'Jewish sport'. My understanding remains that 'Jewish sport' is not the same as 'sport and Jews': they are two entirely different concepts. Obviously, there is a difference between the Jewish individual and his own love for sport for sport's sake and the collective involvement of a group of Jews in physical education, sports and games that restrict membership of 'non Jews', thus 'ring-fencing' the activities. If 'Jews only' is a governing principle or has been brought about by an outside power and its anti-Semitic influence we are forced to use the term 'Jewish sport'. The converse is where Jewish athletes and players join a specialist sports organisation which may assist them to become a champion or even represent their country in the Olympic Games: in this case the term 'Jewish sport' is inappropriate for them. Where, for purely social reasons, a group of Jews form a club for their specific group, the organisation may be considered Jewish even without an affiliation to an existing Jewish association as its Jewishness is of secondary importance. Where a special aspect is added to sport so that it is no longer 'sport for sport's sake' but serves as a vehicle for political education as well, one faces an entirely different situation. Surely where – as in the Diaspora – Jewish sports organisations are confining their membership and where sport is linked with Jewish political aspirations, then the term 'Jewish sport' prevails either with a positive or negative valuation.

When the Nazis politicised sport and excluded Jews from German sport they created an isolated organisation for Jewish athletes by law, who in response created 'Jewish sport' for Jews only and demanded facilities for 'Jewish sport'. In other countries, where Jews and others were refused membership – as in some British and American golf and tennis clubs, they created a justification for segregated Jewish sports clubs for social or 'national reasons'.

When the new state of Israel was formed in 1948, sports organisations such as the Zionist Maccabi – a worldwide Jews-only sports organisation, the religious-orientated Elizur and Esra and the right-wing Betar all joined the socialist Hapoel, all transferred the leadership of Jewish sports organisations to Israel. The Hapoel was already well established as a workers' sports organisation operating mainly in the Kibbutz movements and factories. After some time all of the associations started to work together and subsequently formed a national Olympic Games committee for Israel.

Besides Olympic objectives, there were also moves to create a truly international sports event open to Jews worldwide. After some initial protest, the Maccabi succeeded in making the Maccabiah an international event, one that transcended its origins as a members-only event. Originally (in 1932 and 1935), the Maccabiah were only open to members of the Maccabi World Union, but after the Second World War it was decided that the Maccabiah should welcome worldwide Jewish participation, irrespective of affiliation.[28] This was a particularly inclusive move as the majority of Jewish sportsmen and women who excelled in sport were nearly always members of specialised elitist clubs and not restrictive Jewish associations. Some, moreover, in representing their home country in Olympic Games, had won medals; the opportunity to bring such sportspeople together soon led to the obsolescence of the original Maccabi-only concept of the Maccabiah.

I participated in the first three Maccabiah Games after the Second World War as the deputy leader of the British team, with special responsibility for athletics. As with other teams, we had difficulties in deciding who was Jewish in accordance with the 'laws of return' as stipulated by the Israeli government and enforced by the Maccabi as the organiser. *David Ben-Gurion*, the first Israeli prime minister, approached a number of prominent Jews in the Diaspora for their advice on this matter, including *Sir Isaiah Berlin*. The responses he received differed greatly and were so involved that Ben-Gurion decided that the time was not yet right to amend the 'laws of return', which gave all Jews, wherever they were, the right to become Israeli citizens. For our part, we of the British team had accepted a black sprinter, *Prince Jacobs*, who had a Jewish parent, as a participant in the first post-war Maccabiah. When our team assembled for departure, I heard some astonished voices ask 'Why a Schwarzer?'[29] This was a question we also had to face and answer when we arrived in Israel. Today, there are many non-whites in the country and, as a result, that question is not now asked, but the question 'who is a Jew?' undoubtedly continues to be problematic.

At the same time as the Maccabiah became more inclusive and welcomed Jews from outside, not just Maccabi members and any Israelis, the young state of Israel had made strides in the opposite direction by using sport as a springboard to international recognition and greater inclusion on the international stage. When Arab and Asian sports organisations refused to admit Israel to competitions, Israel consequently became a member of various European Sports Federations and gladly accepted as a solution the European status such affiliations bestowed in the field of sports, even though the country is, geographically speaking, situated in

---

28 It was also decided that the Maccabiah should always be held the year after the Olympic Games.

29 A 'Schwarzer' was a pejorative term for a man of Afro-American origin.

Asia. The results of these affiliations have not been without
individual and team success: there are already Israeli players in
football, basketball and other sports who are among the best in
Europe. And, from a broader perspective, the total number of
medals won in international contests has increased steadily in its
first 50 years and a small but increasing number of qualified
participants have reached finals in many Olympic sports and even
won medals.[30]

Israel has also been the springboard for many Jewish athletes
who were initially of other nationalities to compete in the Olympic
Games. When during the cold war some of the top Soviet Jewish
athletes were aware that they would not make the Soviet Olympic
squad but might be able to obtain Israel citizenship after a short
period of residence, they agreed to join the Israeli team. The hope
of athletes from the former USSR to represent Israel so soon after
their immigration was also the desire of the Israeli National
Olympic Committee. A related modern-day case is that of *Zhanna
Pintusevich-Block*, one of the world's top female sprinters. When
Pintusevich-Block wanted to compete for Israel, the Ukraine, her
home country, demanded financial compensation for the funds
they had invested in her development. Subsequent negotiations
failed and she agreed to compete again for the Ukraine.

A short time ago, the London *Jewish Chronicle* reported that the
Israeli government had stated that 60 to 70 per cent of immigrants
from the former USSR were Jews in accordance with the 'laws of
return' and the present constitution of Israel.[31] There may be as few
as 600,000 Jews left in Russia today, where once an estimated 2.6
million lived before 1930 and 1.45 million after the Second World
War. According to the 2001 *Jewish Yearbook*, Israel's population has
grown – mainly through immigration – to 4.87 million, of whom 90
per cent are Jewish.[32] Taking a global view, the total number of Jews
living in America is 5.8 million and another third of world Jewry
lives in Europe and half a million in the southern hemisphere.
Together, there is a world Jewry of over 13 million – 3 million less
than prior to the Holocaust.

---

30 An ideal climate – one that is comparable to California's – is a great asset for the
    development of sport in Israel.
31 *Jewish Chronicle*.
32 Stephen W. Massil (ed.), *The Jewish Yearbook 2001 (5761–5762), A Record of the
    Organisation, People and Events in the Contemporary Jewish World* (London: Vallentine
    Mitchell, 2001).

This coexistence of Jews with other peoples in Israel and other countries around the world raises certain 'laws of return' issues that have been acknowledged at governmental level. For example, an Israeli minister who was responsible for immigration has stated that 'there is nowhere in the world, a pure Jewish community', while *Ehud Barak* declared in his prime ministerial victory speech: 'Tonight, we wish to extend a warm and firm hand to the secular, religious, ultra orthodox, settlers, Sephardim and Ashkenazim, Ethiopians and Russian immigrants, Arabs, Druze, Circassians and the Bedouins. All are part of the Israeli people.'[33] Does this mean that the conditions of the 'laws of return' apply to immigrants only, or also to others living as Israeli citizens, whether they are a child of a Jewish mother or a Bedouin woman? Is that what Ben-Gurion had in mind when, before independence, he wrote in the leader of the *Misrachi Journal*: 'we do not intend to establish a theocracy, nor do we enforce an affirmation of a religious belief from our citizens in our State, which will have non Jewish citizens as well.'[34] Does this mean in a future peaceful Asian continent, the Israeli people could be an accepted minority in a Muslim, Hindu, and Buddhist region, and that Israel will become recognised as a state like any other nation in the area? This would be in accordance with the Olympic ethos but remains, at present, a desirable dream *vis-à-vis* the present situation in the Middle East.

Speaking about a Jewish minority, Barak noted the 'generic mix of Israel's population' and Ben-Gurion said that 'the country is also a religious mix'.[35] Maybe, then, it is too early to talk of an 'Israeli culture'. Surely all this underlines that we Jews, at least those in the Diaspora, the Galuth, remain a minority and one that is different to other groupings. Finally, I do believe in the dual form of existence for us Jews, whether in Israel on a social and national basis or in the Diaspora, wherever we are accepted as an integral and equal part of a nation and as its citizens. Here, in the Diaspora, lies my own involvement, encompassing any contribution I can make in the field of sport and to the well-being of young people – Jews and others. I am, and remain, a convinced Diaspora Jew.

33 Quoted in the *Jewish Chronicle*.
34 *Misrachi Journal*, a monthly publication.
35 Quoted in the *Jewish Chronicle* and *Misrachi Journal*.

Part II

The Modern Games

1896: Athens – Jews at the First Modern Games

When, in 1894, the IOC was formed to revive the Games, its very name implied that the modern Games would return to their original home in Greece, and the first modern Olympic Games were accordingly awarded to Athens.

The ancient stadium is said to have had a track with sharp bends. Over time this fell into ruins and so it was decided to rebuild it for the 1896 Games, with financial support from a Greek philanthropist living in Egypt. The Games were watched by 45,000 enthusiastic spectators in the newly constructed marble stadium and by many more from the surrounding hills.

The Jewish community of Greece can trace its origins back 2,200 years. At the time of the 1896 Games, Jews formed about 5 per cent of the total population of Greece, many living in Salonica (better known these days as Thessalonika) and employed in commerce, as tradesmen or in the docks. It is not known whether any Greek Jews took part in the Games since the names of only the first three successful competitors in each event were recorded and then not always reliably, and only the first two were awarded medals (silver and copper, plus an olive branch and a diploma – every competitor received the last; the names of competitors in third place were discovered only recently).

Thirteen nations took part in the Games; 75 per cent of all the competitors were Greek and the USA was the only non-European nation to participate. The competitors were a very mixed group: there were university and club teams and even private individuals.

The highlight of these Games was the run from the tiny village of Marathon, north-east of Athens, over a distance of 42km (26 miles), to commemorate the events of 490 BC when the Greeks fought the Persians and a Greek soldier ran to Athens to report the Greek victory – then promptly collapsed and died. The winner in

1. Members of the International Olympic Committee in Athens (1896). Standing (left to right), W. Gebhardt (Germany), Guth-Jarkovsky (Czechoslovakia), F. Kemeny (Hungary), V. Balck (Sweden); seated (left to right) P. de Coubertin (France), D. Vikelas (Greece) and A. de Butovsky (Russia).

2. Germany's gymnastic team, 1896 gold medallists. Gustav Felix Flatow (first left) and Alfred Flatow (third right).

4. *Alfred Flatow (Germany) gold, gymnastics 1896.*

5. *Baron Pierre de Coubertin prior to the first Games in 1896.*

3. *Alfred (Hajós) Guttmann (Hungary) won two gold medals in swimming in 1896.*

6. *Edward Lawrence Levi (Great Britain), world champion weightlifter and judge at the Athens Games.*

1896 was appropriately a Greek, Spiridon ('Spyros') Louis, as was the third-placed runner, who was later disqualified for having had a ride for part of the course; his place was given to the next man to finish, the Hungarian Jew *Gyúla Kellner*.[1]

Some parts of the Habsburg Empire were allowed to compete as nations in their own right. In Hungary, for instance, Jews were far more integrated into society than was the case in either Russia or Poland. The population of Budapest was 5 per cent Jewish, many having a professional background and connections with sport.

The Hungarian Jew *Alfréd Guttmann* (also known as *Hajós* or *Häyosch*) was, at just 18, the youngest competitor in Athens and won two of the three swimming events. These took place in the open, and in stormy spring weather Guttmann won the 100-metre freestyle against 12 opponents; the Austrian *Otto Herschmann* finished third. The storms were so bad that both the rowing and the sailing events had to be cancelled. Boats were used, though, to take the participants through Phaleron Bay into the open sea to the start of the 1,200-metre freestyle event. The waves by then were so high that these same boats on their way back from the start had to pick up some of the swimmers. Guttmann was not one of them: he had greased his whole body and won by a three-minute margin over the second-placed competitor. There were then no restrictive regulations in the swimming events and competitors could use any style they wished, hence the description 'freestyle'. *Paul Neumann* won the 500-metre event.

Two German cousins, *Alfred* and *Gustav-Felix Flatow*, both members of the Berliner Turnerschaft, took part in the gymnastics competitions. Alfred won the parallel bars and, together with Gustav-Felix and others, went on to win the team events for both the horizontal and the parallel bars. We shall return to these athletes later.

Jewish Olympians were also to be found among the officials at the Games. *Ferenc Kemény* of the Hungarian Games committee became one of Coubertin's secretaries in the IOC. The then world champion weightlifter, the Englishman E. Lawrence Levi chose to act as a judge, as did the American *Charles Waldstein*, although he also competed in the pistol shooting; we have met Levi already.

---

1   Throughout this book I have occasionally had difficulty in deciding who qualified to be
    included in my list of Jewish Olympic medal winners. When in doubt I have added a
    letter 'D' in parenthesis after the relevant names on the list. In most cases, though, I have
    received reliable information. See list of winners in the Appendices, pp. 209–26.

No Jews from Eastern Europe took part because of the pogroms which had taken place there. Rather, these persecuted people either went westwards to Austria, Germany, Britain and the USA, or to Palestine. Some of their descendants became Olympians in the course of time.

The success of the Jewish athletes in 1896 – nine medals from 44 events – is a ratio which has never since been equalled. Had they competed as a nation they would have been placed fourth in the unofficial national table, ahead of both France and Germany.

1900: Paris – Failure

George I of Greece and his son Crown Prince Constantine had hoped that the success of the first modern Games in 1896 would permanently secure the Olympics for their country and be recognition of the enthusiastic support of the participating athletes and the admiring public who had turned out in such large numbers to watch. But Coubertin and the IOC hoped that, through a link up with the planned World Exhibition, the Baron's birthplace of Paris would gain special recognition for the Games, in which 1,235 competitors from 25 countries participated.

Not all of Coubertin's efforts came to fruition, though, and other aspects of his conception of the Games appeared to be under threat. His efforts to copy the practice of the ancient Games and exclude women were soon rejected by the IOC – which felt that to continue to exclude women would be harmful to the future of the Olympic Movement – and 19 women arrived for the golf, tennis and yachting events. All competitors in the Games were given certificates and in some events valuable prizes, too; there were suggestions that money was sometimes involved, thus threatening Coubertin's conception of the amateur ethos of the Games.

Since the Games stretched over five months, they became a kind of sideshow to the exhibition. The nature of the failure was that this format prevented the Games from appearing as a separate entity with its own unique identity. As an example of the ambivalence that ensued, it had been arranged for there to be races for cars, speedboats and even balloons but these were later regarded as having been a part of the exhibition. Additionally, the showpiece of the exhibition, the recently constructed Eiffel Tower, overlooked the events, which took place in the nearby Bois de Boulogne. There, the running events on a grass track attracted only a small crowd when compared with the attendances in Athens – and this in spite of the fact that three-quarters of the competitors were French.

Nevertheless, these first modern Games in France were of

particular interest to French Jews. In spite of the Revolution, the first Grand Synhedrion and the policies of Napoleon I, the hope of increasing emancipation suffered under a persisting anti-Semitism. As in Germany, the proportion of the population who were Jewish was only 0.5 per cent. Yet Jews hoped that their co-religionists' successes at Athens would change widespread attitudes, but it was only after the 'Dreyfus affair' that change developed.[1]

There were a number of Jewish competitors who gained honours in the Games, but only one Frenchman, the footballer *Jean Bloch*, whose team won a silver medal. The most successful Jew was the American *Myer Prinstein*, competing with a team from a university with a Methodist foundation. This banned its team from competing on Sundays, and, although Prinstein was not a Christian, he too was banned from the long jump finals, which took place on a Sunday. But his performance in the preliminaries won him a silver medal, which – according to the rules of the time – counted in the final placings, and he subsequently won the gold in the triple jump.

Otto Wahle tried to follow in the wake of the Hungarian Guttmann in the 1896 Games, but he finished only second in the 1,000-metre freestyle swimming and also in the obstacle race, an event that was later discontinued. The Austrian *Siegfried Flesch* won a bronze medal in the sabre fencing; he was one of the first of many successful Jewish fencers. Also of note is that *Helga Hedwig Rosenbaumova* was the first successful Jewish woman to compete in the Olympics. She represented Bohemia at tennis and won the bronze in both the singles and the mixed doubles events.

---

1   Alfred Dreyfus was a Jewish captain on the French General Staff who was accused of treason and sent to Devil's Island in 1894; he was released and his honour restored in part through the efforts of Émile Zola's campaign 'J'Accuse' in 1906.

1904: St Louis – The American Games

Following the failure of the Paris Games, the IOC was concerned about the future of the Games and it was hoped that American enthusiasm for sport would help to sustain their revival. The then President – Theodore Roosevelt – was also president of the American Olympic Committee and this fact was thought to be additional assurance of strong support from both the competitors and the public.

The IOC felt that to link the Games to the World Fair in St Louis would be the ultimate guarantee of success. But this was not the case, and only 687 competitors from 13 countries came to the opening on 1 July, or later, since events were staged in sequence until the end of October. Although Americans had competed in the earlier Games in Europe, athletes seemed reluctant to undertake the equivalent long and costly voyage in the other direction. When the Games were opened, no fewer than three-quarters of all the participants came from the home country. Once more the assumption that an association with a major international exhibition would be beneficial was disproved beyond all doubt.

The low turnout meant that a number of events were contested between American clubs and university teams, which inevitably led to walkovers. Furthermore, runners from overseas found it difficult to adapt to the unusual dimensions of the track, which was one-third of a mile long, with a straight of 200 metres for the sprints.

Myer Prinstein had learned his lesson in Paris and now competed for an Irish–American association; he won both the triple jump and the long jump, the latter with a new Olympic record. In second place in the long jump was *Daniel Frank* (USA). Another fellow American, *Samuel Berger*, was only 19 when he won a gold medal in the heavyweight category of the Olympic boxing tournament.

Lacrosse featured in the early revived Games and *Philip Hess*, together with *Albert Lehman* of the St Louis AAA, gained silver medals. Otto Wahle of Austria was again successful in the swimming pool, this time winning a bronze in the 400-metre freestyle.

Once more the marathon had its problems. One runner was in the lead only to be disqualified for having been offered a ride over part of the course. Another took a mixture of strychnine and brandy, but the taking of drugs was not yet an official reason for disqualification.

In spite of the relatively small number of competitors, the Games continued in parallel with the exhibition for over five months – too long for the athletes and also too long to keep the attention of spectators. By the end of the Games the USA had, not surprisingly, won 242 medals; of the remaining 38, 4 were won by Cuba.

Had Coubertin attended in 1904 he would surely have objected to the special 'anthropology day', which comprised events for Native Americans, blacks and African pygmies; Ainu people from Japan even had a day to themselves. Deplorably, such events might have been thought more appropriate for the international exhibition than for the Olympics.

By the time the Games ended, it was obvious that the ideals of the modern Games were being compromised and, reluctantly, Coubertin agreed that the next Games should once more be in Greece, in 1906. He did not want to wait for another four years before re-establishing the ethos of the competition.

1906: Athens – Back to the Start

Coubertin and the IOC were much concerned about the failure to promote the Games in conjunction with an international exhibition. Finally, after considerable pressure from members of the IOC, Coubertin reluctantly agreed to plans for an interim – or intercalated (as they have also been called) Games, but still insisted that these were not to be counted as official games in the sequence of the Olympics and that the four-year interval between the Games (which should be in different countries to retain the international flavour) should be adhered to in future. The decision that these 'interim' Games would not be included in the numbered sequence of Olympics has been a cause of difficulty to sports historians. *Dr Ferenc Mező* declined, as a loyal member of the IOC, to include any results from them in his definitive history of the Games, and it was not until years later that the results were included in the official Olympic lists.[1]

And so, as ten years previously, the Greek king took the salute at the opening ceremony. Then, with the USA having agreed to participate as a national team rather than as a group of university and club deputations, 886 competitors – but only 6 women – from 20 countries marched into the stadium. Once again, the spectators were out in force. For the first time there was an Olympic village for male competitors in nearby Zappeion. To allow new competitions to be held others had to be curtailed since the Games lasted for only ten days.

Among the Jewish participants representing their national teams there was once again Myer Prinstein from the USA, winning his third Olympic gold and fourth Olympic medal overall by taking the long jump title; compatriot *Hugo Friend* came third.

---

1   Ferenc Mező, *The Modern Olympic Games* (London: Collet Holdings Ltd, 1956).

Otto Scheff (Austria) could not repeat the success of the Hungarian Alfred Hajós Guttmann over the 1,500-metre race across Phaleron Bay and came only third, but he recovered to win gold in the 400-metre freestyle. That successful Hungarian swimmer from 1896 had since increased his achievements by playing not only for leading Hungarian football teams but also for the national eleven. Guttmann had also won national titles at sprinting, 400-metre hurdles and discus, and his younger brother *Henrik* followed in his wake by winning gold as a member of the Hungarian 4 x 250-metre swimming relay team.[2]

In a sign of great things to come for Jewish fencers, *Edgar Seligmann* won a silver medal as part of the British épée team. Overall, Jewish competitors won 11 medals. The king presented not only medals to the winners but also a variety of trophies, some donated by private individuals.

---

2   1906 was the only Olympics in which a 4 x 250-metre relay was held; from 1908 onwards
     the 4 x 200-metres has been a regular event.

1908: London – The Place of Sport

These Games were originally awarded to Rome, but the eruption of Mount Vesuvius in 1906 caused enormous financial problems for the Italian government and so the Italian Olympic Committee had no choice but to withdraw their offer to hold the Games. London stepped in and offered to host them. In the space of two years a new stadium with a capacity of 68,000 was built for them at Shepherd's Bush and became known as 'White City'.[1]

Encouraged by the achievements at Athens, 22 countries sent national teams comprising 2,035 participants, of whom 36 were women. The Games stretched over nearly six months since they followed the seasonal pattern of sports in Britain. Edward VII opened the Games on 13 July when all the participating teams marched behind their national flags (the Americans adhered to their tradition of refusing to lower theirs – even to a king).

The president of the British Olympic Committee was the all-round athlete Lord Desborough, who obtained the aid of the Hungarian impresario *Imre Karalfy* to organise the Games, and especially the opening ceremony in the new stadium. This had a running track of three laps to the mile (1,609 metres), which was surrounded by a banked cycling track. The inner oval had a temporary swimming pool, but many of the 21 competitions were held at already established venues. Tennis was played at Wimbledon, home of the All-England Club; Henley-on-Thames was used for the rowing; Cowes for the sailing; and the Solent (the stretch of water between Southampton and the Isle of Wight) for the power-boat racing (an event later discontinued). The first true winter Games competition, comprising only four events – men and

---

1   White City was demolished in the 1990s to make way for a new BBC Television Centre.

7. *Hungary's fencing team, 1908 Olympic champions: (left to right) Lajos Werkner, Oszkár Gerde, Jenö Fuchs and Deszö Földes.*

8. *Richard Weisz (Hungary), 1908 gold medallist in heavyweight Greco-Roman wrestling.*

women's individual and pairs figure skating and ice hockey – was held in central London at the Prince's Rink.

As in the earlier Games, the host nation took the majority of the medals – the British winning almost as many as all the other nations combined. But there were some team events in which Britain was the only entrant; one example was the tug-of-war: the USA refused to compete when they discovered that a police team were wearing spiked shoes to give themselves extra leverage.

Jewish athletes gained 21 medals, their highest total so far. Many of these were in the fencing events. *Jenö Fuchs* (Hungary) won the gold in the individual sabre competition and was also victorious as a member of his national sabre team (the other members of the team were *Oszkár Gerde, Lajos Werkner* and *Deszö Földes*). Most of the Hungarian fencers were academics since the sport was so closely linked to student fraternities, and especially in Germany. *Alexandre Lippmann*, representing France, took the silver in the individual épée and gold, along with *Jean Stern* and *Eugène Olivier*, in the team event; the latter also won the bronze in the individual épée. *Paul Anspach* (Belgium) – at the start of what was to prove a great Olympic career – was in the Belgium épée team that came third and *Edgar Seligman* won silver with the British épée team.

The Hungarian heavyweight wrestler *Richard Weisz* took the gold in the Greco-Roman style event. *Harald Bohr* was a member of the Danish football team that took the silver medal.[2] *Otto Froitzheim*, representing Germany, lost in the tennis final to the Briton Major Ritchie. Two years later he was again to be the runner-up at Wimbledon. He was, however, to become one of the world's leading players before the First World War but, returning from a competition at the beginning of the war, he was interned by the British on Gibraltar for the duration of the war. He returned to England in 1927 but lost at Wimbledon to Brugnon, one of the French 'Musketeers', and went on to become chief of police in Wiesbaden where I went to school.

Other Jewish medallists included *J.C. 'Barney' Solomon* and *Bertram Solomon*, who were members of the second-placed English Rugby team, the American *Harry Simon*, who won the silver medal in the 300-metre free rifle shooting competition, and his colleague

---

2   Both Harald and his brother Niels played at home for the Akademic Boldclub; the latter
     achieved fame as a Nobel laureate for physics (1922). Their mother, Ellen Adler,
     belonged to a well-known family of Danish scientists.

Charles Jacob, who took the bronze in the pole vault.[3] In the 4 x 200-metre freestyle swimming competition *Jozsef Munk* and *Imre Zachár* won silvers as part of the Hungarian team that finished second to Britain. And, finally, *Otto Scheff*, an Austrian who changed his name from *Suchachewski* when he was baptised, won the bronze in the 400-metre freestyle swimming.

---

3   On the track, John Taylor – competing as a member of the American 4 x 400-metre relay team – was the first black athlete to win an Olympic gold medal.

1912: Stockholm – A Model for the Future

The Stockholm Games lasted from 5 May until 22 July and were the largest Games yet to be held, attracting 2,547 competitors, including 57 women, from 28 countries. It is not known whether there were any Jews in the Swedish team as it marched past Gustav V in the opening ceremony; certainly, their number in the country was small – about 15,000 – with a history going back to the eighteenth century. There were Jews in other teams.

Two innovations were of great help in making the Games a success: the introduction of electrical timekeeping, thus avoiding the unfair judgements that had marred previous Games, and of a public address system, enabling spectators to be kept informed of what was happening.

As in earlier Games, Jewish fencers distinguished themselves, with the Hungarians again taking the major honours. The sabre team including Jenö Fuchs, Oszkár Gerde and Deszö Földes took the gold; Fuchs also won the individual sabre event. In the team épée competition the Belgians took the gold. Again, this team was entirely Jewish in composition: Paul Anspach, *Henry Anspach*, *Gaston Salmon* and *Jacques Ochs*. Other successful fencers were Edgar Seligman, who took the silver in the épée team competition for Great Britain, and *Ivan Osiier*, who won a silver in the individual épée; Osiier continued his remarkable sporting career by representing Denmark for the next 40 years. Otto Herschmann of Austria added a silver in fencing to the bronze he had won in swimming 16 years previously in Athens.

Other Jewish successes were gained in athletics, gymnastics and swimming. *Abel Kiviat* won the silver in the 1,500 metres for the USA; *Alvah T. Meyer*, also American, won the silver in the 100 metres; *David Jacobs* was a member of the gold-winning British 4 x 100-metre relay event; *Jenö Réti-Rittich* and *Imre Gellert* were members of the

Hungarian gymnastic team which took the silver; and *Josephine Sticker* was in the Austrian 4 x 100-metre swimming relay team that won the bronze. In total, Jews won 23 medals at the Games.

Two non-medal-winning Jewish participants, *Gottfried Fuchs* and *Julius Hirsch* – both FC Karlsruhe players, played in the German football team. Even though the former scored ten goals in Germany's 16–0 defeat of Russia in the Games (an Olympic record held jointly with Sophus Nielsen of Denmark that has only recently been beaten), Germany ended up only seventh in the competition. In 1933 Fuchs was expelled from his club because of his religion, but managed to travel to Canada. In 1936 he was invited to attend the Berlin Games as a guest of honour but he declined to accept. Hirsch had joined Karlsruhe club in 1902; 31 years later he, too, was expelled. But he did manage to see Karlsruhe play when a groundsman allowed him to watch through a gap in the surrounding fence. He had great difficulty in supporting his non-Jewish wife and their children. In order to help them to escape the Nazis, he divorced his wife, but to no avail; both children were sent to the camp at Theresienstadt. They survived the war, but the fate of his wife is unknown. When a former admirer of Hirsch offered to hide him in his 'locomotive' to get him across the border, he refused and he subsequently died in Auschwitz. A number of successful German football teams, such as Werder Bremen, FC Nürnberg and Bayern München, had Jewish presidents until the mid 1930s, when the Nazis expelled all Jewish sportsmen and women from public life.

These Games saw the first individual gold medals go to a member of a minority group other than the Jews: Jim Thorpe, an American, who was without doubt the greatest athlete of his time. He was of mixed Irish–Native American descent. His Indian name Wa-Tho-Huck means 'Bright Path'. His outstanding achievement was to win both the pentathlon and the decathlon in Stockholm. Gustav V presented him with his medals with the words, 'You are the greatest athlete in the world', to which Thorpe replied, 'Thanks, King.' Apart from the medals he was lavished with many other gifts, one of which, an 'art nouveau' gold and silver bowl, is on display in the Olympic Museum in Lausanne.

Thorpe's exploits, though, were later to be steeped in controversy. After returning to the USA as a national hero, the story appeared that he had been paid for playing minor league baseball as a semi-professional in the summers of 1909 and 1910. He was

9. Wa-Tho-Huck (Jim Thorpe) won the decathlon and pentathlon for the USA at the Stockholm Games.

ordered to return all his awards and gifts. It took many years of campaigning by his family to have the medals returned and his records restored; the IOC finally relented in 1982 – 70 years later. The film 'Jim Thorpe, All-American' appeared in 1951, starring Burt Lancaster, another athlete.

There were three other athletes in the decathlon who later came to prominence: Avery Brundage, who became president of the IOC; George S. Patton served in the First World War, continued as a professional soldier and was a successful but controversial general in the Second World War; and Karl Halt, who won a medal for gallantry in the Bavarian Army and the title 'Ritter' (the equivalent of a knighthood), and became president of the German National Olympic Committee after the 1936 Games.

1914–18: The First World War Interrupts the Games

When the IOC chose Berlin to host the 1916 Games little did they realise that their plans and the aspirations of the world's athletes would be shattered by the start of the Great War.

The war began in August 1914 and by the following February it was obvious that the Games could not take place. The IOC had no choice but to cancel them. Victor von Podbielski, president of the German organising committee, and Carl Diem, general secretary, saw their hopes of Berlin being the focal point of the world's greatest sporting event disappear. Young men on both sides of the conflict rushed, full of enthusiasm and patriotism, to enlist. Those who had once been friendly rivals in sport now faced each other in combat. This was a far cry from the ancient Games when hostilities between enemies were suspended so that the Games could proceed.

Jews were promoted within the German Army, but not above the rank of captain. Such discrimination did not, however, apply in the Austro-Hungarian K&K Army of the Habsburgs. Nor did it apply to the Allied side, an example being the Australian general Sir John Monash. But there was another sort of discrimination among the Allies: irrespective of their achievements in sport or elsewhere, black Americans served in separate units and, when sent to Europe, fought alongside Moroccans, Senegalese and Spahis (Algerian cavalry) who were also fighting separately in the French armed services. Furthermore, at the beginning of the war the British employed their Indian troops only in labour units.

In 1916, when the Games should have been taking place, the patriotism of the Jews was questioned. The High Command gave way to anti-Semitic pressure from several quarters to have the Jews at the front counted (Judenzählung), on the grounds that they were not 'pulling their weight'. The truth was somewhat different: not only did Jews contribute fully to the war effort, but by 1918 more than 12,000 had been killed in action in the German Army, and many more in the Austro-Hungarian Army, not to mention the Allied forces.

Such attitudes persisted after the war. Jewish ex-servicemen in Berlin, excluded from the Stahlhelm (Steel Helmets) and other national ex-servicemen's associations, took up unarmed combat in the form of ju-jitsu to protect Jews from the attacks of right-wingers in the Berlin Scheunenviertel. In time, some became German champions in a sport which eventually became an Olympic event, but too late for their participation.

10. *Julius, Adolf and Hermann Baruch. Julius and Hermann were German champion wrestlers. Hermann became European weightlifting champion after the First World War. As they had fought for Germany in the First World War, they were excluded from the Games from 1916 to 1928.*

Among Jewish soldiers who returned after the war were *Julius* and *Hermann Baruch*, who came from my home town Bad-Kreuznach. They were the local odd-job men who regularly worked for my parents. Julius and Hermann became German champions in wrestling; Hermann also became a European weightlifting champion. Since Germany was excluded from the Games in 1920, he could not represent his country in peace as he had in war.

1920: Antwerp – The Guilty are Excluded

During the war the IOC consulted its members to obtain their opinions about the steps to be taken to find a suitable venue for the next Games to take place after the war had ended. In spite of the damage it had suffered, Antwerp accepted the IOC's call to stage the Games in 18 months' time – this was a tall order given the usual four-year period between successive Games. Nevertheless, a new stadium to seat 30,000 was completed in time, but an Olympic village could not be provided and all the participants were billeted in schools.

Even though the 'war guilty' nations – Germany, Austria-Hungary and Turkey – were excluded, the number of athletes was 2,668, including 77 women. This exclusion of the Central Powers, though, affected Jewish participation in the Games.

The Games began in April with the customary march past and for the first time the Olympic flag was raised. It had been devised by Coubertin himself and showed the now-familiar five coloured rings on a white background. The opening ceremony had changed over the years, and once the new flag had been hoisted and the athletes assembled, an oath was taken by a member of the host country that represented all the teams in the international spirit of the Games.

By staging the Games over a long summer, it was possible to house all the participants and to find venues for all the events; this would not have been easily possible within the 16-day period which became the rule in the following years.

The rising star of the Games was the Finnish runner Paavo Nurmi, who, by the time he retired, had gained more medals than any other athlete. Another noteworthy non-Jewish competitor was the British parliamentarian Philip Noel-Baker, who won the silver in the 1,500 metres (he had also competed in the 1912 Games) and was later awarded the Nobel Peace Prize.

Nearly all the medals won by Jewish competitors were in events involving or derived from combat in one form or another. The American sergeant *Morris Fisher* won three golds in rifle shooting, in the individual three-position rifle and in the three-position and prone shooting team event. His fellow countryman *Samuel Mosberg* added another gold to America's tally by winning the lightweight boxing, while the Canadian *Albert Schneider* triumphed in the welterweight division. Two wrestlers were successful: American *Samuel Gerson* won the silver in the freestyle featherweight competition and *Fredrick Meyer*, the bronze as a heavyweight; middleweight Canadian wrestler *Montgomery Herscovitch* gained a bronze. French fencer Alexandre Lippmann took silver and bronze in the épée and team épée respectively, and Paul Anspach, representing the home country, won a silver medal in the team épée, adding another medal to the personal haul that he started accumulating 12 years earlier.

The only Jewish medals not won in combat-related events were taken by the water-polo-playing brothers *Maurice* and *Gérard Blitz*, who excited their fellow countrymen with a place in the final; Gérard also swam to bronze in the 100-metre backstroke. In total, Jewish competitors won 14 medals, a highly commendable achievement given the unusual circumstances prior to the Games.

1924: Chamonix and Paris

Chamonix

When the winter Games were first presented as a separate tournament they were proclaimed as 'the international winter sport week'. But since these Games followed the ceremonial pattern set by the summer Games (ice hockey and figure skating were already Olympic events) the new Games became 'the Olympic Winter Sports Games'. Sixteen nations sent 254 competitors, of which 13 were women, to Chamonix. The Norwegians were the most successful team, winning 17 medals, of which 4 were gold. There were no reports of any Jewish participants.

Paris – Abrahams – Chariot of Fire

Austria, Hungary and Turkey were now readmitted to the Games, but not Germany, as France, the host, was not yet ready to accept a German presence, even though six years had passed since the war's end.

Coubertin was delighted to have the chance to present the Games once more in the beloved city of his birth. A special stadium, the Stade de Colombes, was built, with a 500-metre track and accommodation for 60,000 spectators.

One competitor at the Games, English sprinter *Harold Abrahams*, was later immortalised in the award-winning film *Chariots of Fire* (1981), which was produced by Lord Putnam and has a signature tune I will always remember. A Cambridge student, Abrahams felt that there was a measure of concealed anti-Semitism among his tutors. This is one theme of the film, which also shows Abrahams employing a professional trainer, *Sam Mussabini*, an approach to training which was not approved of under the University's

11. *Harold Abrahams (Great Britain) 100m champion, Paris 1924.*

12. *Elias Katz (Finland) won silver in the 3,000m steeplechase.*

restrictive rules concerning amateurism. For many years there was a clear distinction between the amateur sportsman and the professional in Britain; this was most obviously displayed in the annual Gentlemen vs. Players cricket match at Lord's, with separate changing rooms and gates. Abrahams, nonetheless, was well coached to beat the three American favourites and won the blue ribbon of the Games, the 100-metre sprint. (His British long jump record of 7.38 metres would, if replicated, have won him a silver medal in that event, but he had declined to take part.) There was a delay, though, in the presentation of medals and, as Abrahams had left Paris by the time the medals were given out, they followed him by post. Injury forced him to give up competing and to concentrate on his professional career as a lawyer, then as an administrator in a number of organisations, and then more and more as a sports journalist and broadcaster. He was appointed vice-president of the British Amateur Athletic Association (AAA) and a member of the national Olympic committee. He acted as the official reporter to the AAA about the Empire (later Commonwealth) Games and the Olympics.[1]

The sensations of the Games, though, were Finnish middle- and long-distance runners, with Paavo Nurmi – the runner who competed with a stopwatch in his hand – the main attraction. Nurmi won gold over the 1,500 metres and the 5,000 metres and led his team to a rather one-sided victory over the 3,000-metre cross-country together with his shadow Ville Ritola. Nearly all the long-distance events were won by either Nurmi or Ritola, the former winning five golds and the latter four golds and two silvers. *Elias Katz* was also a member of the victorious Finnish cross-country team and added an individual silver medal in the 3,000-metre steeplechase. After the Games, Katz moved to Germany where he joined 'Bar Kochba' Berlin and became one of Germany's leading runners. He finally settled in Palestine and was killed in a skirmish with Arabs while making a film.

Morris Fisher of the American Army had distinguished himself in earlier Games. He now increased his tally of medals to four by winning the individual and the team free-standing rifle shooting. Three of his compatriots did equally well: the 16-year-old *John Field* won the featherweight boxing title, *John Spellman* wrestled his way to light-heavyweight gold and *Louis Clarke* was a member of the victorious sprint relay team which beat Britain (Jewish runners featured regularly in sprint relays).

To the jubilation of the French crowd, the home team won gold in the team épée event, assisted by Alexandre Lippmann. *Ellen*

---

1   One of his three brothers (Sidney, later Sir Sidney) had also competed in the Olympics of 1906 and 1912, but without success; he was later chief justice of Tanganyika and Ceylon. The Abrahams brothers wrote a number of books together on athletics. Adolphe (Sir Adolphe) Abrahams was Chief Medical Officer of the British Medical Association (BMA) and for many years medical officer to the British forces at various Games.

13. Stadium designed by Alfred (Hajós) Guttmann.

Osiier, wife of Ivan (silver medallist in Stockholm), secured a gold for Denmark; Ellen was born a Christian but she and her husband decided to bring their children up as Jews.

The Belgian water-polo players Maurice and Gérard Blitz won silver medals with their team, as did their fellow countryman, the fencer Paul Anspach. The Italian tennis player *Umberto Luigi de Morpurgo* reached the semi-finals and thus won a bronze. *Janós Garay* was a member of the Hungarian sabre team which gained a silver and his fellow Hungarian *Sidney Jelinek* was cox of the rowing four which came third.

Once more Alfred (Hajós) Guttmann completed a remarkable achievement: following his two swimming medals at the first Olympics he now won a silver medal (the gold was not awarded) for architecture for the swimming pool he had designed.

Since Germany was still not allowed to take part in the Games a number of Jews were not given the chance to distinguish themselves. For this reason, *Hans Halberstadt* missed his chance in fencing, as did also Hermann Baruch, the European weightlifting champion. *Martel Jacobs*, a student at the Deutsche Hochschule für Leibesübungen (German High School for Physical Education), first a German and then an English and South African javelin champion, missed out as well. It is doubtful whether *Otto Froitzheim*, an earlier winner of a silver medal, would have still been young enough to repeat his previous success.

14. Martel Jacobs, German, English and South African javelin champion.

1928: St Moritz and Amsterdam – Germany Readmitted

St Moritz

The winter Games in St Moritz, high up in the Engadine area of the Swiss Alps, suffered from a sudden and unexpected thaw in February 1928. This rise in temperature affected events which were scheduled to take place on the deeply frozen lake just below the resort. This turned out to be most unfortunate for *Irving Jaffee*, a young American speed skater who had produced the best times in the qualifying round. When the ice started to melt, the referee cancelled the finals and, consequently, no medals were awarded, in spite of protests from the Americans and other participants.

Amsterdam

Prince Henrik of the Netherlands declared the IX Games of the modern era open to the thousands of spectators and the 3,014 competitors – including 260 women – who marched into the stadium, representing a total of 46 countries. The stadium itself had been especially built to house a 400-metre running track, which set the norm for all other stadia built for future Games, and was encircled by a cycling track.

There were enriching innovations to the programme, including the release of doves as a symbol of peace and an 'eternal' flame burning in a bowl on top of a tower 45 metres high. Once more the Games lasted for nearly three months as various competitions followed each other, rather than being staged simultaneously.

15. Lilli Henoch, the best all-round
German woman athlete of the 1920s.

16. Daniel Prenn, German tennis champion
(1932), ranked sixths in the world.

Germany, now finally readmitted to the Olympic Games, sent one of the largest teams, which also turned out to be one of the most successful – finishing as runners-up to the Americans in the unofficial medals table. The American team was led by Douglas MacArthur, who, in the mid 1940s, was to achieve fame as Commander of the Allied forces in the Pacific battles of the Second World War. The Soviets, though, declined to participate in these 'capitalistic' Games, citing ideological and political objections.

Just as the Soviet withdrawal from the Amsterdam Games denied many of its sportsmen and women a chance of Olympic success, so Germany's 16-year exclusion since the 1912 Games in Stockholm had already frustrated and disappointed many German sportsmen and women – as mentioned in the previous chapter. Besides not competing in the most significant international championships, they had also foregone years of specialised training at crucial stages of their careers. Those who lost out included Jewish athletes, some of whom had set world records in the years after the First World War but now had no chance to participate in the 1928 Games.

Among others was *Lilli Henoch*, a winner of ten German championships since the war, making her the best German female all-round athlete of the 1920s. She also shared two world records with the other women members of the Berliner Sports Club's (BSC) sprint relay team. When, finally in 1928, five Olympic athletic events were offered to women, Lilli sadly was past her prime. The same applied to *Daniel Prenn*, Germany's best tennis player at the time. Prenn had shown his ability when beating the Englishman Bunny Austin in a Davis Cup match but was too old when, many years later, tennis finally returned as an Olympic event.

Despite these unfortunate absentees, Jewish participation had increased over previous Olympics, helped by the fact that the Jewish community in Amsterdam was as high as 10 per cent of the city's population. Many of these Jews were Sephardim – some of whom were successful in the trade of precious stones – whose ancestors had escaped the Spanish Inquisition hundreds of years before.

Fanny (Bobby) Rosenfeld, whose parents emigrated to Canada from what was then Russia when she was a small child, developed into one of the greatest all-round athletes of her time. She held a number of national records in track events, jumps and the discus. No doubt she would have done well in the pentathlon, which was only introduced as an Olympic event years later. Rosenfeld won a silver medal over 100 metres and a gold as a member of the sprint relay team. After she retired from athletics she excelled at hockey and softball at national level; after her retirement from competitive sport, she became a sports journalist.

Hungarian fencers were the forerunners of many Olympic successes for their country, first having come to prominence in the 1908 Games. Here, in Amsterdam, *János Garay*, *Sándor Gombos* and *Attila Petschauer* won gold medals, with Petschauer also winning a silver medal. Another silver medal winner, *István Barta*, was the first of many Hungarian water polo players to triumph at Olympic Games.

The greatest Dutch achievement was a gold medal for their women's gymnastic team. Of the twelve participants, five were Jewish: *Estelle Agsteribbe, Elka de Levie, Annie Polak, Judikje Simons* and *Helene Nordheim*. These girls were the best of numerous male and female gymnasts in the Netherlands, but nobody could imagine the tragedy that was to follow, see p. 130. I will also go into more detail about the German fencer *Helene Mayer* in the Berlin chapter. It was here, though, at the Amsterdam Games – where

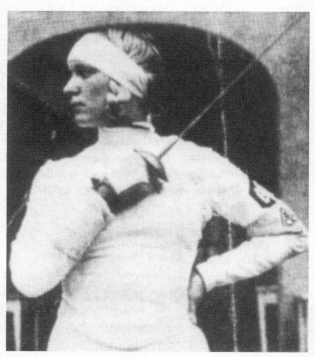

17. 18-year-old Helene Mayer, German fencing champion

18. *'Cavalier Rouge' by Isaac Ïsraëls and 'The Polo Players' by Max Liebermann (Germany).*

Helene won a gold medal in the ladies foil – that her strange Olympic saga began.

For America, *Lilian Copeland* gained her first medal, a silver in the discus. She later became an American national champion in javelin and shot-put, but neither discipline was included in the athletics programme at the Amsterdam Games. Other Jewish medallists included the British wrestler *Sam Rabin*, who gained a bronze medal and later was to be seen in the *Alexander Korda* film *The Private Life of Henry VIII*, the South African bantamweight boxer *Harry Isaacs*, who gained a bronze medal, and the American featherweight boxer *Harold Devine*, who also won a bronze medal.

Altogether, 25 medals went to Jewish participants – the best so far. Queen Wilhelmina awarded the gold medals, Prince Henrik the silver and Coubertin was honoured by being asked to present the bronze medals.

The Arts Contest Introduced in the 1920s

Dr Ferenc Mezö, who was a member of the IOC, gained a silver award (gold was not allocated) for his book *The Modern Olympic Games*. Another Jewish winner was the Dutch painter *Isaac Israëls*, who gained a gold award for his oil painting 'Cavalier Rouge'. Israëls was the son of *Josef Israëls*, a teacher of *Max Liebermann* – who had been given special recognition for his painting 'The Polo Players'. A few years later, *Liebermann* became the president of the Prussian Academy of Arts and was awarded the highest German award in peace and war, the order of the 'Pour le Mérite' (civil division).

However, for many years following the 1928 Games these cultural awards were not included in the programme of the Olympics as it was thought that they could not be judged by any objective measure of excellence, unlike sports events with their stopwatches and tape measures.

1932: Lake Placid and Los Angeles

Lake Placid

Four years after the debacle of the St Moritz winter Games, the snow and ice in and around Lake Placid in the state of New York drew large crowds. At the previous winter Games only the ice hockey and bobsleigh were well attended. Ice hockey had a huge following in the USA and also in nearby Canada. It was the Canadians who won the final by a single goal. Germany lost heavily to both the USA and Canada but still managed to win a bronze medal, to the immense pleasure of their star player *Rudi Ball*. He had become the darling of Berliners whenever he scored at the Sportspalast, where he and his two brothers played for the same Berlin ice hockey club.

The American speed skater Irving Jaffee won gold in both the 5,000 and 10,000 metres but was still claiming that he had been 'robbed' of gold four years earlier when his event was abandoned because of softening ice on St Moritz lake. An interesting 'thumb nail' sketch by the American sports biographer Robert Slater describes how Jaffee was exposed to some unpleasant practical jokes at the hands of some of his anti-Semitic fellow American skaters.[1]

Los Angeles – The Best Games so far

The Games moved across from the east to the west coast of the United States, with Los Angeles doing its best to attract participants. However, the long sea journey from Europe and from elsewhere plus a worldwide economic depression reduced the

---

1   Robert Slater, *Great jews in sport*, New York: Jonathan David, 1992.

number of competing nations and therefore the number of athletes
– in spite of the generous American offer to provide free
hospitality. In fact, 1,408 competitors from 37 countries took part,
only half the number in Amsterdam four years earlier. Five
hundred bungalows were specially built for male competitors,
whilst the 127 female competitors were accommodated in nearby
hotels.

Technical innovation had always advanced from Games to
Games, and Los Angeles was no exception. In addition to
electronic timing devices, the introduction of the filming of
competitions assisted the judges. Moreover, spectators and
competitors alike could see not only the results on the huge
electronic scoreboard but also the message of the Bishop of
Pennsylvania: 'The most important thing in the Olympic Games, is
not the winning, but the taking part... not the triumph but the
struggle... not to have conquered but to have fought well.'

The Coliseum stadium, first opened in 1923, had an amazing
capacity of 100,000 spectators, one that is seldom surpassed even
today. At another venue, the famous Pasadena Rose Bowl – the
scene of so many exciting American football games – a special
wooden cycling track had been built. These two venues along with
all of the others provided spectators with the best facilities for any
Games so far.

Last but not least of the achievements of Los Angeles was their
success in meeting the IOC aims of reducing the number of days
for events to just 16, a duration which now became a firm target for
all future Games.

It was at these Games that Hungarian Jews began to shine even
brighter, especially in fencing and water polo. The Hungarian
sabre team of *Endre Kabos*, Attila Petschauer, István Barta and
György Brody won gold, as did *Miklós Sárkóny* playing for the
victorious Hungarian water polo team – which was once more
trained by *Belá Komjádi*. Another Hungarian medal was won by
Károly Kárpáti, who took silver in the lightweight division of the
freestyle wrestling.

The American Lilian Copeland had already won a silver medal
at the previous Games for discus; now she won gold with a new
world and Olympic record throw of over 40 metres. In the same
competition, Poland's *Jadwiga Wajsowna* won a bronze. Other
Jewish successes under the American flag included the gymnast
George Gulak, who won gold for his performance on the rings,

swimmer *Albert Schwarz*, who won bronze in the 200-metre freestyle, and lightweight boxer *Nathan Bor*, who also won a bronze medal.

Austrian *Nikolaus Hirschl*, a member of Hakoah Wien wrestling club, gained his bronze medals in the heavyweight categories for both Greco-Roman and freestyle wrestling, while the Danish wrestler *Abraham Kurland* was third in the lightweight competition. Ellen Preis, an Austrian fencer whose Jewishness is still in dispute, won gold in the ladies foil, and, finally, British yachtsman *Peter Jaffe* cruised into the silver-medal position in the international star class yachting.

A Personal View

I left school in the same year the Lake Placid/Los Angeles Olympics took place. These Games were barely reported in the German press. The entry on my abitur (matriculation) reads: 'He leaves school to study economics and physical education. Whilst he also had much success leading youth and sports groups, both within the school and outside, and has notably distinguished himself at the National Youth Championships [Reichsjugend Wettkämpfe].'

I went to Berlin and enrolled at the Humboldt University and the BSC, one of Germany's leading athletics clubs, which – like the Sport Club Charlottenburg (SCC) – had many Jewish members. Within a short time, I won a high jump competition at the Sportfest der Unbekannten (Sport Festival for the Unknown). This brought me to the attention of the American coach Hoke at the BSC and also gained me individual help from several German champions and Olympic medal winners. For the first time in my life I was not coaching others using manuals or passing on what I had learned from competitions.

During the months which followed, I had more pressing priorities in Berlin with regard to the political situation than training and competitions. The forthcoming Olympic Games scheduled for Berlin, therefore, hardly occupied my thoughts – especially as one of its foremost sports clubs (the BSC) had just expelled me for being Jewish. Only a season earlier my Jewishness had not bothered anyone – we were all club mates together, but now all Jews, along with their clubs and organisations, had been expelled from German sport.

Part III

The Berlin Games

1936: Garmisch-Partenkirchen and Berlin – Jews Not Welcome (Juden Unerwünscht)

Never in the history of sport has a single event attracted so much publicity as the 1936 Olympic Games in Hitler's Germany, the Games I have described as 'the great deception' on a number of occasions. These Games were, in the truest sense of the word, unique because Hitler used them as a festival of peace to disguise the intensification of Germany's preparations for war. For me, they became the centre-point of this, my very personal presentation of the relationship between us Jewish athletes and the unique part we – as a minority – have played.

In order to give the full context of the events leading up to the Berlin Olympics, it is necessary to briefly consider the antecedents of Hitler's rise to power and the impact that this had on German Jewry before focusing on the Games proper. What follows in this chapter is part history, part personal, as I interweave my own experiences with broader factors relating to the Berlin Games and the escalating mistreatment of the Jewish minority in the early-to-mid 1930s.[1]

---

1   The previous version of this book, which was written in German, had primarily a political message in support of all those non-Jewish friends who are now engaged in correcting the misconceptions of Jewish history from the Nazi past. For the English reader, and I must emphasise this, the message differs. To understand one of the main differences between the two books, I have given information and details about German Jewry in order to assist the reader of this English language version in their understanding and evaluation of what happened before, during and after the 1936 Games.

Prelude to the Games

In 1918, in the months following the First World War, Germany – after great internal upheavals – created its Weimar Republic. It had first to overcome an influenza epidemic, which cost many hundreds of thousands of lives – millions if one includes the losses among the homecoming armies and German allies.[2]

For many years, Germany suffered under the burden of the Treaty of Versailles and its demands for reparation, which not only hampered a national rebirth but also affected the country's infrastructure. Unprecedented inflation followed: my weekly pocket money, for example, 'increased' to one 'milliard' ('billion') Reichsmark! In spite of a successful stabilisation of the country's currency, more than four million Germans were unemployed.

Understandably, Germany had now been refused participation in the 1920 Olympic Games in Antwerp, which had been organised at short notice by Count Henri Baillet-Latour. France continued with this ban of German athletes at the 1924 Chamonix and Paris Games, which was a blow to aspiring young German athletes – including Jews. Now Germany had another opportunity.

The IOC felt that awarding the 1936 Games to Berlin would constitute an acceptance of the young German democracy as well as a special recognition of the organisation's German members, especially Karl Ritter von Halt, Dr Theodor Lewald, then president of the German National Olympic Committee, and Carl Diem, the general secretary.

However, two years later, in January 1933, Adolf Hitler became the Reichskanzler (Prime Minister) of the German republic by manipulating the Weimar Constitution in order to form a coalition government with the conservative parties on the Right, who shared his re-armament aims. Within a few months a further election increased the Nazi Party's number of seats in the Reichstag (Parliament). By barring the Communists from voting, Hitler was then able to dissolve the Reichstag based on a special paragraph of the existing constitution which provided for an emergency situation, thereby facilitating his rise to the position of dictator.[3]

---

2 Among the victims was my mother, who died in January 1919.
3 For the scope of this book I must assume that Hitler's rise to power is general knowledge and therefore forgo the temptation to indulge in an assessment of National Socialism and its influence on the German people. See also various publications by the English historian Martin Gilbert.

19. *'JEWS – ENTRY FORBIDDEN'. What Baillet-Latour saw in Garmisch on his visit to Hitler's Berghof.*

This leads me to the second matter: the 'Jewish problem', in which I became so much involved for the next six years of my life.

The Exclusion of Jews from Germany

I am always surprised when speaking to German universities and schools that an impression exists that there were a few million Jews living in Germany before 1933 and not just half a million. In 1933, the number of Jewish Germans was given as 499,682, with 160,000 of these living in Berlin – a community that dated back to 1295.

The real reason for the registration process undertaken by the Weimer Republic that produced the above figures soon became apparent, with any further, deeper, more heinous reasons not yet foreshadowed. On 1 April 1933, the first boycott of Jewish shops, doctors and lawyers took place, with the SA (Sturm Abteilung – Storm Trooper Division) making certain that no one dared to buy anything from Jews. At the same time, the dismissal of Jews from all areas of the nation's public services continued, and finally affected education and sport.

All German sports organisations were taken over by the State under the direction of a new minister of sport (the Reichsportführer), SA leader Hans von Tschammer-Osten. Hitler's own writings clearly reveal the thinking behind such a move:

> Every athlete and sportsman in the Third Reich must serve the State and contribute to the production of a standard National Socialist human body... All athletic associations must receive instructions in politics and philosophy from the Political Organisation or from the Labour Front... Athletics and sport are the preparatory school of political driving power in the service of the State.[4]

This entailed a major reorganisation of sport: all areas of sport were placed into self-contained sections called 'Fachämter'; other associations, such as the International Workers' Sports Club, were dissolved; and organisations based on a religious persuasion were excluded and German Jews expelled. At the beginning of this process, Jews could train and compete in segregation at public establishments, but later, after the Olympic Games, all such facilities were withdrawn from use by Jews (as non-Aryans).

Some German champions who were Jewish left their home country deeply wounded by these changes. Daniel Prenn, Germany's tennis champion and a Davis Cup player, left to settle in England. *Ilse Friedleben*, who was leading the national tennis rankings, departed for Switzerland. Helene Mayer, the Olympic Champion of 1928, packed her fencing kit and left for America once again to continue her studies (she would be back in time for the Olympics, though). Rudi Ball, Berlin's ice hockey idol, joined

---

4   Extracts from various Nazi publications.

Diavoli Rossoneri in Milan. *Eric Seelig*, a boxing champion, left to continue his professional career in France.[5]

Other Jews or individuals of Jewish origin avoided the fate of being murdered by the Nazis by fleeing the country. Brian Mark Rigg, an American researcher working at Cambridge, has looked into the background of a number of German officers.[6] Some German aristocrats, often for financial reasons, had married a Jewish partner and their offspring followed the family tradition of an army career, some of which distinguished themselves in battle, persuading Hitler to agree to a continuation of their services. The same situation may have been the case where a successful player or athlete's origins were covered up by their comrades. In a corrupt administration of a totalitarian state nearly any 'adjusted' document could be obtained for an inducement.

At this point, it is important to acknowledge that German Jewish organisations did present various petitions to Hitler's government. I now feel slightly embarrassed about the rather servile and obsequious language of those petitions. They can only be understood and evaluated as an attempt to gain time, because German Jews believed that Hitler's 'Third Reich' would only last for a much shorter time than his proclaimed 'thousand years'. This belief was shared by some other sections of Germany's population prior to the Second World War and, of course, many of the so-called former allies abroad.

Jewish organisations, moreover, were not only preparing young people for an aliyah to Palestine but were also helping them to acquire agricultural and other skills in order to gain visas for emigration to other parts of the world. Many others found someone in the USA who would offer help to obtain an 'affidavit' (guarantee), but numbers (so we are told) were restricted to only 25,000 Germans (Jews and others) who were accepted each year, but many died before their number came up. Most of my wife's close family, to give a particularly painful example, had affidavits but did not survive the concentration camps or the war.

In the meantime, a large number of German Jews expelled from their sport clubs often hesitated to join the Maccabi Union because

---

5   There were also other Jewish champions who left Germany, but their fate is unknown to me.
6   Brian Mark Rigg, *Die Welt*, 4 April 1997. Rigg's findings led to headlines in some American papers such as 'Jews fought in Hitler's Army'. Educated as a Christian, Rigg discovered in Germany that he had Jewish forebears.

of its affiliation to the Zionist movement and its national Jewish ideals. They preferred a non-political association – the 'Schild' – after having left clubs (quite a number were classified as 'Mischlinge', see later) where, until a short time ago, class, social status and religious beliefs were treated as a member's private concern. At first, these men and women were unable to comprehend what was happening in Germany and to their clubs after many years of active and loyal membership. Some had been the club founders, others even the presidents and many had been honoured with special awards for services rendered, both locally and nationally.

Having been a member of the BSC I had also lost my affiliation. I switched to the University in Frankfurt in 1934 to continue my studies. From one day to the next I was barred from entering the university by the SA in uniform standing at the entrance doors of the main building. It was at this time I was informed that the firm of my late father, who died in 1924, had been appropriated by the government and that no further funds could be made available to me. Luckily, I heard of a vacancy for an assistant teacher at the Landschulheim at Herrlingen in the Black Forest, a residential school that had interchanged Christian and Jewish pupils, as had others, and so was in search of Jewish teachers. I applied and was accepted.

Within months, though, I was offered the position as the Jugenddezernent (Youth Officer) at the Frankfurt offices of the League of former Reichsbund Jüdischer Frontsoldaten (RJF – Jewish Front Soldiers). After a while I was transferred to their headquarters in Berlin, where I was responsible nationally for various educational schemes for the children of ex-Servicemen and also for their social and educational work. In addition, I was involved in schemes for the preparation of young people for resettlement abroad and contact with the Jewish youth organisations which declined to be involved in competitive sports. I edited the weekly sports pages for the periodical *Der Schild*, which was called 'Die Kraft' ('The Strength'), and, because of my earlier involvement in athletics, I was appointed honorary coach and conducted basic training courses in various parts of Germany. It was while working in this capacity that I was surprised to see Jewish horsemen and women, who formed special riding sections; others continued with fencing, cycling or the more widely spread football, handball and, where possible, athletics, swimming and other sports, at least until the Olympic Games in Berlin. My travels enabled me to pass on certain unofficial information about emigration which could not be conveyed by telephone or letter and was connected with the steadily decreasing opportunities to obtain a visa – even illegally from some Consulate staff.

My friend and mentor, the late Hajo Bernett, a non-Jew, wrote in 1978 a quite unique book with the title *Der Jüdische Sport im Nationalsozialistischen Deutschland 1933–1938*. He, as a sports historian, recorded in chronological order the events between the expulsion of Jews from German sport in 1933 and the pogroms on 9 November 1938. He summed up his findings in the following words:

> Jewish sport in National Socialist Germany has suffered all forms of degradation: dishonourable exclusion from the German sport community; being deprived of self-determination by the Reichssportführer; control and suppression by the Gestapo; collusion with hostile surroundings; the narrowing of one's living space and room for action; the destruction of organisation; the requisition of property and finally expulsion. This process is without parallel in history and in the history of sport. It can only be analysed with a sense of shame and a feeling of guilt. But that a suppressed and persecuted minority did not give up sport in spite of all pressures must be encouraging ... Notwithstanding all differences in ideology, Maccabi and Schild practised in an identical manner sport as it had been shaped by the cultural, political and sociological conditions of Germany and Europe.[7]

With increasing unemployment, mounting difficulties in making ends meet, no support from the outside and the loss of well-wishers, Jewish clubs were now entirely financially dependent on their own members' efforts, which alone enabled Jewish sport in Germany to carry on. These efforts reached the limit of their achievements in 1936, when Maccabi recorded 18,000 members in 79 local clubs and Schild quoted figures of 20,000 belonging to 250 clubs. Both organisations were now overcoming all initial conflicts and working together, and, by order of the

---

7   Alfred Hajo Bernett, *Der Jüdische Sport im Nationalsozialistischen Deutschland 1933–1938*, (Schorndorf: Verlag Karl Hoffmann, 1978), p.119.

Reichsportführer, established the Reichsausschuss der Jüdischen Sportverbände (Central Committee of Jewish Sport Organisations) which followed the pattern of a similar organisation formed by the Jewish youth movement well before the Nazis came into power.

With Maccabi and Schild cooperating closely, there were leagues for football and handball wherever there was enough support to create more than one club in a town. Both organisations, as well as Vintus and JSTV in western and southern Germany respectively, had their own championships. Maccabi and Schild also arranged an athletics challenge meeting in Berlin. Here, the Jewish community had built its own sports ground with a running track and three playing fields, a facility to be used by all clubs as well as youth groups and schools, irrespective of affiliation. Before the Olympics, on occasion it was still possible in larger towns to hire other facilities for exclusive use by Jews as players or spectators.

In 1934, I was taken aback when, without any prior warning, I received a direction to report for Olympic training (Olympia Lehrgang) from Tschammer-Osten, the Reichsportführer. In the past, all preparation for training and the final selection of Germany's Olympic team had been made by the great variety of national sports organisations. Now the State had taken over. My call-up was issued by the Fachamt Leichtathletik (track and field section) to attend a course at Wilhelmshöhe near Ettlingen in the Black Forest, where the National Training Centre for Athletics was situated. The irony was that this call-up entitled Jews to a free railway ticket to and from the nearest station. A few Jews in other sports were also called up to attend training courses at the same time, among them a yachtsman called Baer, the swimmer Bernd Meysel, and weightlifter Max Seligmann.

The Course in Ettlingen

It was here that I met *Gretel Bergmann*, the high jumper from Laupheim near Ulm. Gretel had been in Ettlingen on a number of occasions when Geo Brechenmacher was the director of the centre, who now occupied a high position close to Tschammer-Osten. Amongst us also was a group of sprinters: *Werner Schattmann, Kurt Sternlieb, Eric Lorch, Erich Schild* – all of whom had run the 100 metres in 10.8 seconds on poor cinder tracks. Also present was

Franz Orgler, one of the best German junior middle-distance runners.[8] Most of us had won the championships of our Jewish organisations, but *Schattmann, Orgler*, and *Bergmann* were in a different class and were called up later for further Olympic training.

A year later those of us in charge of Schild were informed that the centre at Wilhelmshöhe could be available to us for another athletic training course, but for athletes of our own selection. At the same time, Maccabi was given permission to take a team to the second Maccabiah in Palestine. As this team consisted of members of Maccabi only, the offer for the second Olympic training course to Schild did not include them, although some of the Schild selection had attended both courses in 1934 and 1935. Only years after the war did we understand from a report that both the second Ettlingen training course for Schild members and the permission to send a team of the Deutscher Makkabi Kreis (German Maccabi Organisation) to Palestine were a token response from the German government to the various attempts from the USA to have the Games cancelled or transferred to another country.

As the Maccabiah was a sports festival restricted to members of the Maccabi World Union and Palestinians, it had a limited participation of world-class athletes who had competed in the 1932 Olympics and could be selected to represent their home country at the Berlin Olympics.

In contrast to the more 'middle-class' competitors at the Maccabiah, the Socialist Hapoel organisation invited 'working-class' sportsmen and women from all over the world to a very differently class-orientated workers' festival of sport in Palestine. Both games, though, had more of the character of a folk festival than an international championship. Maccabeans from Germany did quite well in the Maccabiah in spite of the isolation of Jewish sport in Germany, and, understandably, a number of participants decided to remain in Palestine afterwards.

---

8   There were a few others, but I cannot remember all the names of a group of approximately twenty athletes. Looking back over the years, I remember, among others, young Inge Mello, who represented Argentina in two Olympic discus finals after the war. She had been a member of the JSG in Berlin, and gave me a telephone call while in London in 1948 suggesting a training session, as once we had in Berlin. Another young athlete, long-distance runner Henry Laskau, who won many American championships as a walker and represented the USA at the Olympic Games and later became a track judge, trained together with the Israeli Shaul Ladany, the holder of the 100km walking world record. I am sure that under different circumstances and with better training and competitions other young athletes would have equally distinguished themselves.

Unexpectedly, in April 1935 I received by registered letter a Redeverbot (ban on speaking) from the Gestapo, signed by the notorious Reinhard Heydrich. It stated 'that for the protection of the German people, I was forbidden to speak in public and at closed meetings until further notice.' As I was worried that this Redeverbot would stop me from arranging coaching courses, I went to the feared headquarters of the Gestapo to ask an official whether I could continue my work. To my astonishment, I was marched up the central staircase flanked by two SS men to meet Heydrich himself, whom I had seen some time before when he fenced with Germany's Olympic candidates. He was writing and, after not reacting to my entrance, I said 'Guten Morgen'. He looked up and seemed startled, presumably not being used to this form of greeting anymore. In reply to my questions concerning whether this would stop me teaching sport, I received just a 'No' and a sharp 'but I warn you' and I left as quickly as possible. Only many years later did I learn that the Redeverbot was also given to *Martin Buber, Rabbi Prinz* and a few others who had spoken frequently to Jewish audiences, offering moral support wherever possible.

At this time, persons whose ancestry would not stand up to the demands of the 1935 'Nuremberg' Laws for an Ahnennachweis, a certificate that declared the holder's classification as an 'Aryan' – a person of 'German blood', were called 'Mischlinge'.[9] There were a few others who would have been of the 'right blood' but somehow did not fit into the picture of the new regime and were trying to avoid an alignment with it.

Carl Diem

One who did not fit into the new regime was Carl Diem, an individual who had a special influence on the Berlin Olympics and was, without any doubt, the most creative sports organiser in Germany during the first part of the twentieth century.

A classical scholar steeped in the Hellenistic world of Olympia, Diem, quite simply, transformed Germany's engagement with physical education from the narrow ultra-patriotic age of

---

9   The Mischlinge classification could be given to anyone – that is, it was not exclusively applied to Jews, and any 'non-Aryans' or – for example – socialists and clergymen could be classified as such.

20. *Dr Theodor Lewald, president of the German National Olympic Committee.*

21. *Dr Arthur Liebrecht, appointed Olympic Commissar December 1936 (Germany).*

22. *Gretel Bergmann (Germany) equals German high jump record.*

23. *Captain Wolfgang Fürstner, commandant of the Olympic village (1936).*

'Turnvater Jahn' to a modern internationally accredited sports movement. After the First World War he approached universities with the challenging message that sport would benefit from a scientific approach and that there was a place in the academic world for sports scientists; he also challenged schools to provide a daily lesson in physical education. Diem then created the 'Das Deutsche Sportabzeichen' (German Sports Badge) for men, women and youth, and special awards for seniors and those who were keen to test their own performances from year-to-year. Additionally, Diem introduced indoor athletics competitions and road relays with a large number of participants in each competing team. He also drafted a law for the protection and creation of playing fields whilst he was still serving as an officer in the First World War.

These efforts had an impact on my life. When I entered secondary education a few years after the First World War my PE teachers were mainly ex-officers and a few former students of the Deutschland Hochschule fur Leibesübungen (DHFL – German High School for Physical Education) that Diem founded on his own initiative in 1920. We used the extra games afternoon to prepare for Diem's Reichsjugendwettkämpfe (National Youth Contest), which was based on a points system for combining achievements in athletics, gymnastics and swimming. Competitions took place in all parts of Germany for all secondary schools, whatever type they may have been. Because I was a member of a swimming club with its own pool at the River Rhine and an active athletics section I had an advantage over our best gymnasts and won the competitions for the upper age groups in my home town, Wiesbaden. Being Jewish and coming first in front of an SS man was a great joy to my headmaster, who was an ardent democrat.

When the IOC awarded Berlin with the staging of the 1916 Olympics, Diem joined Lewald and Schiff – who acted as the secretary general to Diem at the DHFL and on the National Olympic Committee as head of its finance committee – in preparing for the Games and planning a new stadium in Berlin.

Diem, who had Jewish ancestry, nonetheless had German nationalist tendencies.[10] However, in spite of his German

---

10 The apparent conflict between Diem's classicism and nationalism has become a major dispute today because of the numerous honours and naming of streets, halls, school and other places after his name when the war ended.

chauvinism, Diem was no anti-Semite; neither was he a party member, racist or believer in Hitler's aims. Indeed, because of support from German Jewish industry and his connections with a Jewish family in Berlin some Nazis called Diem a 'white Jew'. Shortly after Hitler came to power Diem lost his position as rector of the DHFL, not just because his wife *Lislott* was a 'non-Aryan' but also because of the number of Jewish lecturers, students and administrators in his college. Lislott also had to leave the DHFL and was no longer registered as a teacher. At this point, Diem did not join the National Socialist Party, nor the SS or SA, but became a member of one of the many professional organisations which had been taken over by the Party, the gleichgeschaltet (annexed as the Writer's Guild).

Theodor Lewald – An Obedient Servant

Dr Theodor Lewald, like Diem's wife, was half-Jewish. He had been a secretary of state loyally serving his Kaiser, Wilhelm II, until the emperor's abdication and flight to the Netherlands.[11] He had been baptised at the age of seventeen, and always emphasised – especially in public life – that his mother's father had been Bishop of Saxonia. His aunt was the well-known writer *Fanny Lewald*, in whose 'Salon' he made many valuable contacts.

When *Hugo Preuss* became minister for internal affairs and was involved in the wording of the new 'Weimar Constitution', Lewald served as one of his most influential assistants, becoming known as 'His Excellency' Dr Theodor Lewald, and was also attached to the foreign minister, *Walther Rathenau*.[12] Lewald became the president of Germany's centralising sports organisation, the Deutsche Reichsausschuss für Leibesübungen (DRFL), of which Diem was appointed general secretary. Both Lewald and Diem served together on the German National Olympic Committee. Ultimately, though, Lewald lost various positions because, as a 'non-Aryan', he didn't fit into the new regime.

---

11 When a former girlfriend of Lewald was to be sent to a concentration camp, he used the 'old boy network' such connections afforded him to get Himmler to cancel the order.
12 Rathenau, whose father Emil was the founder of the well-known industrial company AEG, was murdered by Nazi thugs shortly after he started working with Lewald.

Arthur Liebrecht

Only a short time ago, a friend of mine, *Heinz Liebrecht*, told me that his Uncle *Arthur* had been appointed in 1933 to be Olympic Kommissar by the president of the German Committee, Dr Theodor Lewald, and the Berlin Oberbürgermeister (Mayor), Sahm. The Berlin daily *B.Z.am Mittag* (Noon) published a picture of the three representatives involved. Additionally, it carried a specially decorated page in its New Year edition with the heading: 'New Year thoughts of the Olympia Kommissar'. But when all Jews were expelled from holding a public position, Liebrecht was also dismissed. Shortly after, he died in Switzerland, maybe – as his nephew feels – of a broken heart.

Alfred Schiff

Alfred Schiff, a young German archaeologist, had participated in excavations at Olympia in Greece under the German scientist Ernst Curtius and had greeted the German Olympic team at the first Games in 1896 in Athens. He stayed on in Greece, where he served as an ambulance driver in the Greek–Turkish war, for which he received a decoration. Years later, he studied at Rostock University, where he was awarded a Professorship in 1908. In support of Carl Diem and Theodor Lewald's preparation for the Games to take place in Berlin in the summer of 1916, Schiff was involved with the construction of the new stadium in the Grunewald with its 500-metre running track.[13] Furthermore, based on his excavations at Olympia and his special knowledge of the ancient Games, Schiff started to put together an exhibition about Olympia. He also received a lecturing post at the DHFL which was not far from the stadium, which was already under construction.

When the IOC finally confirmed the award of the 1936 Olympic Games to Berlin, Schiff remembered his preparation for an Olympic exhibition cancelled in 1916 and it appears that he recommended preparing for the exhibition – to be mounted in 1936 – as soon as it was known that Berlin would be able to present the Games. He gained the support from Lewald's foundation to obtain copies of statues and even to purchase three original sculptures: 'The Scraper', 'the Fist Fighter' and the highly sought 'Zeus throwing

---

13   I ran on this track as a student when enrolling in 1932 at the University of Berlin.

the Javelin'. With the preparatory work nearly complete, Schiff lost his positions at the DHFL – the same time that Diem lost his.

Whilst Diem – being 'Aryan' – could become the general secretary of the German National Olympic Committee, with Lewald as its president, the Jewish Schiff had no chance to fulfil his dream. The powers in charge decided to show Schiff's exhibition during the Olympic Games in 1936, but at the Archaeological Institute and under the name of its director, Carl Blümel, as a cover-up.[14] The King of Greece, aware of what had occurred, awarded the 'Greek Commander Cross' to Schiff, who tragically died destitute three years later; Carl Diem inherited his estate.

Gretel Bergmann

Gretel Bergmann had been the most outstanding athlete at the Ettlingen course. Her hometown, Laupheim (near Ulm), had a well-integrated Jewish community which constituted 10 per cent of the total population. Her father owned a factory, which manufactured hairnets and similar goods. She had three brothers and went to the local school, and afterwards to an all boys' school in Ulm as this was the only establishment suitable for her academic attainments. When she applied later for admission to the High School for Physical Education in Berlin, she failed to be admitted because she was a Jew. She then attended the private sports institution Kiedaisch in Stuttgart to gain a diploma in Physical Education. After this, she went to London to continue her studies, but could only find a language course at the Regent Street Polytechnic.

During her time in England she competed in the British Athletics Championships and was delighted when her father came over from Germany to see her become the British high jump champion. He then told her in confidence that he had actually come over to take her back to Germany and that he had received an instruction from the German authorities that Gretel, as a German, was expected to join the German Olympic team, not the British squad (which in any case was not possible). Failure to do so would have 'severe consequences', not only for her family but also for the Jewish sports organisations.

---

14 When I was invited by the German Olympic Institute to the shores of the 'Kleine Wannsee' between Berlin and Potsdam for a presentation of my book in its original German language version, I stayed overnight but still did not find enough time to do justice to Schiff's work, which is displayed there.

Gretel returned to Germany in 1934 and became a member of the Kernmannschaft (the core of the German team). When competing as a guest at the Württemberg championships, she equalled the German high jump record by clearing 1.60 metres, but complained later that the attitude of the German officials was pretty 'grim'; it was, she said, her rage at this treatment that drove her to jump better than ever before. Despite this excellent performance she was not selected for the German Olympic team. At the moment that the American team had left for Germany and was sailing across the Atlantic, the authorities informed Gretel – by way of a letter from the Reichssportführer – of her deselection and told the members of the German team that she was injured and so unable to compete, which was a complete fabrication. This all, moreover, happened too late for a replacement to be nominated. Hajo Bernett and I always failed to understand why the German authorities would have wished to create a situation which they would find difficult to solve, by forcing Bergmann to return to Germany and, then, not selecting her. The whole sorry affair was, unfortunately, just another German dishonesty that sullied the Games.

It was Burkhard Volkholz, a councillor from Laupheim, who long after the war approached Gretel and the German authorities to draw their attention to the scandalous treatment she had suffered in 1936; in so doing Volkholz indirectly encouraged Gretel to an exchange of letters with both Hajo Bernett and myself. In one of her letters she wrote:

> Your question 'If Gretel had been offered a place in the German team would she have accepted?' is easily answered. I suppose you mean I would have competed in the Olympics had I been given the opportunity. Let me say first that I was on the team. I signed the Olympic oath ... You might also remember that I was blackmailed in 1934 to return to Germany under threats to my family and the whole Jewish sports movement, thus ruining a hope of becoming a member of the British Olympic team. I had absolutely no choice but had to do what I was told to do and the same would have held true as far as competing in the Games was concerned. Those certainly were not the days when you could do as your conscience dictated; you did as ordered to do. One thing is sure, had I been allowed to compete I would have done my damnedest to win, which would certainly have shot holes into Hitler's theory of the inferiority of the Jews.[15]

---

15   Gretel Bergmann, Letter to the author, 25 March 1986.

From corresponding with Gretel, I also learned that she had withdrawn after her exclusion to Baden Baden, deeply hurt and wanting to be alone with her pain. Later, Gretel and her whole family emigrated to the USA via England, where she not only became the American high jump and shot-put champion but also married *Bruno Lambert*, whom she had met at the Ettlingen course (Bruno later served in the Second World War as a physician in the USA). They were living in New York when I visited her, but Gretel refused to speak German.[16]

While Gretel was cruelly denied the opportunity to win the ultimate prize her athletic talents deserved, she has received belated recognition and honours. In 1996, Gretel became the Guest of Honour of the German National Olympic Committee at the Atlanta Games. She also received the prestigious sports award the 'Opelpreiss' in Frankfurt and revisited Laupheim, where she was born, thanks to Volkholz's efforts to help her make a visit to her hometown again.

Helene Mayer – An Enigma

When the host country Germany selected its very large team, Helene Mayer received letters from the Reichssportführer, as well as from the president of the German Olympic Games Committee, inviting her to compete for Germany's team once again. As she had been repeatedly American fencing champion she was informed that there would be no need for her to attend pre-selection competitions. Helene replied that she was only willing to compete as a member of their fencing team if she was granted the status of 'Staatsbürger' as defined by the 1935 Nuremberg Law.[17]

---

16 While at the University of Stuttgart, Claudia Diederix wrote her thesis on Gretel Bergmann ('Die Judenfrage im Sport: Eine Untersuchung am Beispiel des lebensweges der jüdischen Sportlerin Gretel Bergmann' ('The Jewish Question in Sport: An investigation in particular into the life and career of the Jewish Sportswoman Gretel Bergmann') (Stuttgart: Magisterarbeit, 1993)). In 1993, Claudia visited me first before she left to meet Gretel in the States as part of her research for this thesis; Gretel still refused to speak German. In 2002, the International Society of Olympic Historians (ISOH), which I joined a short time ago, published a summary of Claudia's updated findings.

17 I knew from my own later experience that Jewish emigrants had been issued with passports marked with a large 'J' which would require a renewal only after a few months had elapsed. This happened to my wife Ilse's cousin and to various friends as an attempt to deprive them of their nationality. I do not know whether Helene needed an extension of her old passport or received a new one as a 'German Staatsbürger'.

Whatever the case was, Helene happily accepted the invitation to return. Naturally, she must have been homesick and looking forward to attending the final training session under the guidance of her old fencing master, Gazerra, and to meet again so many old fencing friends from previous competitions assembled together once again in Berlin. Of course, she also wanted to be reunited with her mother and brothers, who still resided in her hometown, Offenbach (near Frankfurt).

Her acceptance to compete in Germany, though, caused a furore among all those who had opposed American participation in the Games because of Hitler's racist policies. There were also others, however, who wanted to find out whether Jews were really to be admitted to the Games, using Helene in this way to 'call Hitler's bluff', and, finally, others who wanted the Games in Berlin to go on. Helene, for her part, appeared to be apolitical and took refuge in her real religion – her fencing.

Lured and pulled by the Germans on one side and deplored and even insulted by the Americans on the other, Helene left for Germany – after winning a silver medal in the Games – in the summer of 1936 with an assurance to Mills College that she would return there. Whilst at college in California she must have been aware of Hitler's racist policies and about the exclusion of Jews, the 'Mischlinge' and 'non-Aryans' as part of Nazi racism. She must, moreover, have read in the American newspapers and heard on the radio about the persecution of Jews and their expulsion from German sports. She must also have wondered what might have happened to her own family. Were their letters already censored? Did the family conceal unpleasant news? Finally, she must have been told that she had been excluded from German sport in 1933 in spite of her status as a winner of an Olympic gold medal in 1928 and former European and German fencing champion.

At the same time she must have learned of the exclusion of her older brother, *Eugen*, who had gained fencing honours, as had *Hans Halberstadt*, the German champion, and *Fritz Stark*, the best junior fencer in the country. All of them must have been deeply hurt by their unwarranted expulsion. As for Helene, she received information that her German stipend had been withdrawn but, with the help of 'Scripps College', she could complete her studies

---

18 Some years later, Helene became a professor at the University of California, Berkeley.

there and at Mills.[18] To all of us who had followed her career with admiration, we realised that she had become the enigma of the Berlin Games.[19]

Propaganda and American Pressure

Hitler ultimately became convinced of the unique propaganda value of the Games and agreed to an unlimited budget, including the building of a new Olympic stadium to replace the one that had already been built to stage the 1916 Games.

Neither the German nor the Jewish press reported the variation in treatment of Jews as Jewish newspapers in Germany were forbidden to report news items about the Olympic Games and the German media also operated under strict guidelines. Therefore, many participants and probably none of the spectators knew whether there were any Jewish competitors at all. There were some reports about the various meetings and debate in the USA – including an American campaign to stop the next Games being held in Berlin, but the Nazis declared these to be nothing more than Jewish anti-German propaganda.[20]

Whilst discussion about the Games was going on in America, there were talks taking place between the IOC and the host country's representatives. The years between the ascent of Hitler to power in 1933 and the opening of the XI Olympic Games in August

19 I am aware of the discussions about the victors in the ladies fencing competition, and regret now having used the attractive picture of them standing on the winner's podium with Helene Mayer raising her arm to give the so-called 'Deutsche Gruss'. I could not believe my eyes when I saw it, but there is still much we do not know about her. Dr Uri Simri one of the most knowledgeable Jewish sports historians in Israel, has rejected my choice of those fencing girls for publicity in connection with my exhibition about the Berlin Games and the use of this picture in support of some of my writings. I accept that, in spite of statements by others, Ellen Preis was not in anyway Jewish; a picture of Ilona Elek-Schacherer, though, appears in a catalogue in support of Hungarian Jewish competitors. Finally, the Jewish Museum in the former Rothschild Palais on the embankment of the Main in Frankfurt exhibits a large portrait of Helene Mayer, who had moved from her fencing club in Offenbach to Frankfurt, making her a local girl. Apart from the frequently published pictures of those three women, there are so many good photographs of other Jewish medal winners at hand that I regret having followed a majority of sports historians and presented this picture so prominently more than sixty years after it had been taken. Still, it is sports history in one way or the other.

20 Goebbels and his Reichs Presse Kammer (State Press Office) had an exclusive foreign news service and were collecting reports about Germany and the Olympic Games from papers such as *Los Angeles Times*, *The New York Herald Tribune*, *The Boston Sportsman* and many others, especially those periodicals published by various minority groups, such as the Jews, Catholics and Socialists.

1936 were marked by Hitler's so-often declared attitude towards minorities, of which *Mein Kampf* is an early example.[21] As this period of time went on, there was an increase in racially discriminatory statements in the various party publications and Hitler's speeches.

Shortly before the start of the Games, the leading party publication 'Der Völkische Beobachter' demanded the banning of black athletes from the Games. As this and many other demands were unacceptable to the IOC, the German National Olympic Committee was asked for a declaration from Hitler about his position towards the traditional Games as they had been celebrated in many other countries. It needed the persuasion of Goebbels and reliable assurances from Lewald to convince Hitler of the potentially great propagandistic value of these international Games.

The American National Olympic Committee, knowing about Hitler's hatred of the Jews and blacks, approached the IOC, suggesting that Hitler's attitude towards the Games should be investigated. Hitler, who was only interested in motor sport and boxing, gave a non-committal assurance that he was, 'indeed, interested in the Games'. Whilst there were further discussions between the IOC and the German authorities, an increasing number of voices in America demanded a boycott (nearly six million Jews lived in the USA at this time).

When the first refugees of Nazi oppression arrived, New York already had a Jewish population of 1.72 million, the largest minority group in the city. At that time, though, it was known that some of the members of the American National Olympic Games Committee had anti-Jewish tendencies. The German historian Joachim Rolfe states in a publication sponsored by the Friedrich Ebert Stiftung (a charity) that, when interviewing 56 senators (some of whom were members of the National Olympic Committee), he observed:

> [T]here are communities [in the USA] who do not want Jews
> ... that many Jews did not recognize that their situation is as

---

21 For example, in one passage from *Mein Kampf*, Hitler explicates his beliefs about the Jewish minority as follows: 'The Jew is the exact opposite of the Aryan ... He is guided by pure self-seeking ... he is ever a parasite on the bodies of other nations'. In another passage, Hitler compares Jewish athletic capability to that of 'negro tribes': 'Among the inferior races the Jews have done nothing in the athletic sphere. They are surpassed even by the lowest of the Negro tribes...' Adolf Hitler, *Mein Kampf*, first published in 1925.

precarious as the one of the blacks...that there is anti-Semitism in the upper ranks of the USA society...[making] remarks in associations and clubs...it is hidden in the commercial life, but exists. To give an example...Jews are not admitted to some Country Clubs.[22]

No doubt Avery Brundage, the president of the American Athletics Union (AAU), confirmed this attitude towards Jews when he later stated in Berlin that his golf club also refused Jewish members.

Furthermore, the anti-black attitudes in some of the southern states of the USA expressed itself not only through the despicable actions of the Ku Klux Klan but also in the anti-black tendencies of parts of the AAU. This part of the organisation made it clear that it was preferable for all selections for the next Olympic USA team to take place in more Northern States – remember the Jim Crow laws, segregating America across East/West lines.

I am much indebted at this point to Arnd Krüger, the sports historian of the University of Göttingen, Germany, who not only represented his country at the Olympic Games as a middle-distance runner but also studied in the USA and had special access to the papers of Avery Brundage, for allowing me to have sight of – and quote from – a manuscript published in 2002 by the University of Illinois. On the context of sport in 1930s America, Krüger writes:

> Most Americans cared little about sport outside North America, and there was not a single sports reporter in Europe in the 1930s on the staff of an American paper. Golf and tennis had some international appeal, but these were minority sports, while boxing was professional: it was really only with the Olympic Games that the US sporting public as a whole became interested in international competition. In 1936 there was the added ingredient of politics, keenly felt in a nation with an influential Jewish minority and whose major athletes included a small but significant number of blacks.[23]

In Krüger's words, Brundage, for his part, saw three possibilities for the 1936 Olympics:

---

22 Joachim Rolfes, *Juden in den Vereinigten Staaten (Jews in the United States)* (Friedrich-Ebert-Stiftung, 1950).
23 Krüger Manuscript.

...the Games could be transferred to a different country as Rome and Tokyo had interested themselves in staging the Games; they might be totally cancelled as in 1916, or the Games would take place in Berlin, but be boycotted by so many countries since Germany did not respect the Olympic spirit of racial, religious and political tolerance, that the Games would have no propaganda value for the organizer.[24]

Subsequently, Baillet-Latour, the president of the IOC, received a letter in which Brundage expressed the view of the AAU in the following terms:

> I am not personally fond of Jews and of the Jewish influence but will not have them molested in one way or another. In 1933...[the] AAU resolved that it would not certify any American Olympic athletes for the Games in Nazi Germany until and unless the position of the German Olympic Committee ... is so changed in fact as well as in theory as to permit and encourage German Athletes of Jewish faith or heritage to train, prepare for and participate in the Olympic Games of 1936.[25]

To this, Krüger adds:

> ...Avery Brundage assured all who wanted to know that he would not allow the Games to be held in a country that violated Olympic rules...The precise nature of the 'Olympic rules' was widely discussed in the American press, and while it was agreed that the Germans would be good hosts and would not interfere in the selection of the athletes in visiting teams, the issue of Jews in Germany could not so easily be dismissed.[26]

The resultant pressure from the IOC on the German authorities induced them to organise training courses such as those I attended in Ettlingen, which were ultimately deceitful examples of the inclusiveness that Germany was now compelled to demonstrate in order to keep the 1936 Games. We had already thought in 1934 that

24 Ibid.
25 Ibid.
26 Ibid.

this was the case, that the Ettlingen course was a make believe, a sham to appease those who did not want the Olympic Games to take place in Berlin.

Prior to the next meeting of the IOC, Avery Brundage, who had participated in the December meeting of the AAU, was approached by his committee as their president of very long-standing, to undertake a fact-finding tour of the new Germany, where he had a number of friends, including Karl Ritter von Halt – they met as competitors in the decathlon at the Stockholm Games in 1912. Brundage was a wealthy man who had made his fortune in the construction industry, but any suggestion that he combined his German tour with his business interests was never substantiated.

When the Reichsportführer received information that the president of the AAU was visiting Germany on a fact-finding mission, he arranged a meeting of the various representatives, including those from the Reichsauschuss der Jüdischen Sportverbände. *Robert Atlasz*, from Maccabi, reported in detail in his book *Bar Kochba* about this meeting, which was also attended by representatives of the Sportbund Schild.[27] Atlasz emphasised how difficult it had been to make a statement or to give a truthful answer to questions put to the Jewish participants at the meeting, which was arranged at the prestigious hotel by Kaiserhof von Tschammer. He did not attend personally but had instructed his deputy, Breitmeyer, to do so, who appeared in his SS uniform and high jackboots to stamp his authority on the meeting. The Jewish representatives were afraid of the consequences for the Jewish sports organisations had any statement from their contingent appeared to be unfavourable to securing the international support for the Olympic Games. Consequently, the attitude of the representatives was evasive and non-committal.

Brundage and Sigfried Edström, the Swedish vice-president of the IOC who was also in attendance (both later became presidents of the IOC – with Brundage succeeding Edström), were both anxious that in no way should the future of the Games become a problem. It was at this meeting that Brundage made the so-often quoted remark about 'no admission of Jews to the Chicago Golf Club'. Edström, who spoke German fluently, left early and avoided getting involved in any such pronouncements.

27 Robert Atlasz, *'Bar Kochba': Makkabi Deutschland 1898–1938* (Tel Aviv: 1977), p. 141.

I remember the discussion we had at our Sportbund Schild after this meeting, hoping that Brundage would have understood our position and report accordingly to the AAU and the American National Olympic Committee. He published a pamphlet entitled 'Fair play for American Athletes', which provoked the Olympic boycott movement to publish their pamphlet 'Preserve the Olympic Ideal'. The internal debate finally became a political issue between the Republicans (as was Brundage) and the Democrats, led by Roosevelt and his secretary of state Untermeyer, with other major politicians also becoming involved.

The American media had a heyday, especially after a Gallup poll recorded that 43 per cent were in favour of America refusing to participate in the Olympic Games. Even more astonishing was the result from the vote taken by the deciding committee. As late as December 1935, the boycott movement was defeated by 58 to 55 votes. The delayed decision of the Americans, though, did not seem to slow down German preparation for the Games, nor did it influence other countries.

Finally, it must be said that had Hitler refused to give in to the demands of Baillet-Latour and the IOC and threatened to go ahead with an international sports festival in Germany that didn't involve the Americans, French or maybe the British and the Commonwealth, the majority of countries nonetheless would not have withdrawn their teams, and athletes would have hoped that Brundage and Edström would have reversed any decision and later recognised the Berlin Games as an Olympic event as a result of their close connections with Hitler's Germany. I am, furthermore, in no doubt that the large majority of teams would have responded to the desire of their athletes to carry on with the Games. In spite of Coubertin's first objection to award retrospective recognition of the 'extra' Games back in 1906, he finally gave in; one expects that the same may have happened with Berlin should the IOC have cancelled the Games at short notice.

I frequently visit Germany to talk to University students or to attend special gatherings of sports historians. They are always interested in meeting with what they term a 'Zeitzeuge' – a witness from that time. Even now, National Socialism and Hitler become the topic of an exchange of opinion on the Fuhrer's political obsession with sport. His past relationship with sport was negligible and he had never shown an interest prior to the preparations for the Olympics. He was aware that his Games might not be recognised by the IOC, but he also had hopes that should they succumb, they would repeat the support for another holding of the Games in Germany, and he was profoundly disappointed when he realised that the next Games after 1936 were scheduled for Tokyo. He could not accept that in accord with IOC protocol, the next Games after Berlin had already been awarded years ahead.

He saw the Berlin Games as a major triumph in spite of the fact that his country's team had not won a single track event in Berlin, but this did not distract him from his visions for the future, and he asked his favourite architect Albert Speer to use one of his rather dilettante sketches as a basis for design for the 'next' Olympic Games which would take place in Nuremberg, the 'Hauptstadt' (Capital) of his Party in Germany. Architects in his service, we were always asked to produce over 6 metre models.

Speer, who contrary to Hitler, was a great follower of sport and the Olympic Movement questioned the feasibility of such a colossal stadium for 400,000 spectators especially as the dimensions of the 400m track and other facilities within the oval would not conform to Olympic standards and protocol. Speer arranged for a feasibility study using a high hill as a slope to ascertain whether the top back seats would offer an unrestricted view. With the old stadium, the Berlin Grunewald still serviceable, there was little support for an 'monster' edifice which would bear the hallmark of Hitler's megalomania.

The idea of Hitler usurping the protocol of the Olympic Games and the construction of a giant stadium never materialised as a result of the Second World War. Luckily for the world, though, Hitler's 1936 Games were organised in accordance with the rules for the staging of Olympic Games and under the supervision of the IOC.

Garmisch-Partenkirchen

Before the winter Games began, the President of the IOC, Count Baillet-Latour visited the sites prepared for the competitions. When he saw defamatory and anti-Semitic signs which would be offensive to participants in the Games and in any case violated their ethos he acted without further delay. Documents available to Lord Killanin, later the president of the IOC, and John Rodda, the sports journalist of the *Guardian*, describe the ensuing exchange as follows:

> At the foot of the Zugspitze the two villages of Garmisch and Partenkirchen were arranged with characteristic Bavarian Gemütlichkeit... [signs] 'Dogs and Jews are not allowed' had been placed outside the toilet facilities at Olympic sites. Baillet-Latour saw them and again requested an interview with Hitler. After the customary courtesies, he said, 'Mr Chancellor, the signs shown to visitors to the Games are not in conformity with Olympic principles.' Hitler replied, 'Mr President, when you are invited to a friend's house, you don't tell him how to run it, do you?' Baillet-Latour thought a minute and replied 'Excuse me, Mr Chancellor, when the five circled flag is raised over the Stadium, it is no longer Germany, it is Olympia and we are masters there.' The signs were removed.[28]

Final impediments removed, the Games at Garmisch-Partenkirchen were opened by Adolf Hitler in February 1936.[29] In total, 755 competitors from 28 countries assembled at the foot of the Bavarian Alps, among them Jewish sportsmen and women.

As Bavaria was the birthplace of Hitler's National Socialist Party (NSDAP), the German minister for propaganda – the notorious anti-Semite Joseph Goebbels – issued instructions that under no circumstances should the German press or public get involved in any racist encounters. He emphasised that all visitors to the Games had to be made most welcome and that there should be no discrimination. To support his statement, Goebbels made it known that the German national Olympic committee had included in their team two 'non Aryan' participants, meaning two 'half Jews' who had previously gained medals in earlier Olympic Games. One of the two was Olympic medal winner Rudi Ball, a favourite with Berlin's ice hockey fans. Rudi had already left Germany to play in Italy but was asked to return to Germany to be

---

28 Quoted by Monique Berlioux in Killanin and Rodda, *The Olympic Games*, p. 17. The chapter on the IOC in this book was written by Monique, who had been its head of press and public relations (and later became director). With this input, there is no doubt that the reports contained in the book should be treated as documentary evidence.

29 Hitler had been asked by Lewald to replace the late president von Hindenburg as patron of these Games.

a member of the national ice hockey team. To his surprise, he was received by a brass band on his arrival at Garmisch. After the Games Rudi played again for Germany before he travelled to South Africa via Italy to settle with his brother.

Apart from Rudi, there were also other Jewish ice hockey players in the Games. *Sándor Miklós* and the brothers *Andras* and *Lasló Gergely* all represented the Hungarian ice hockey team, which missed out on a podium position behind eventual winners Great Britain.

Berlin

When the Games in Berlin commenced, the minority problem had somehow lost its priority status. Even for me, a resident and a Jew, Berlin seemed little changed and stayed that way throughout the Games. Most signs stating 'Juden unerwünscht' had disappeared from the city and the only noticeable differences were the flags everywhere (by order) and the variety of military and party uniforms on display. I continued to live at the Kurfürstendamm in a flat which I shared with a few other non-Jewish tenants (in spite of various laws and regulations) until I married Ilse in 1938. As far as I was concerned, the Holocaust actually started with the November Pogrom a year before the mass murders of the Second World War.[30]

The Opening Ceremony

I managed to witness the opening ceremony and some of the athletic events as tickets became available when those earmarked for spectators from overseas were returned unsold, thus becoming available to me, my Jewish friends and many others.

Therefore, on the first of August we watched Adolf Hitler and his entourage descend the steps from the Langemark Chapel into

---

30 One of the few people in the Olympic movement to see through the ostensible reasons for the Games was Baillet-Latour. It is reported that, at a reception for the Games in 1936, he met the wife of Baldur von Schirach, the Reichsjugendführer (Reich's Youth Leader). According to sports writer Duff Hart-Davis, she stated 'how happy she was to see the great festival of youth, peace and reconciliation going so well'. Baillet-Latour retorted, 'Madam, may God preserve you from your illusions. If you ask me, we shall have war in three years.' As President of the IOC, he had seen what the Games disguised. Duff Hart-Davis, *Hitler's Games: The 1936 Olympics* (London: Century, 1986), p. 79.

the arena. By visiting this memorial to the young students who had given their lives in an attack whilst singing the 'Deutschlandlied' in the First World War, Hitler tried to bridge the gap between a heroic past and his new nationalism.

In contrast to all the VIPs following him into the stadium, Hitler was dressed in the NSDAP's stormtrooper uniform but wearing his personally designed military-style peak cap. As always, he displayed the golden party badge of the NSDAP. Was this a kind of political demonstration contrary to the ethos of the Olympic movement? In addition to his uniform and badge, on his brown shirt he proudly wore his Iron Cross, which had been presented to him by the Oberleutnant (first lieutenant) Hugo Guttmann of the Bavarian Infantry regiment for bravery. (Did Hitler remember this event? Did his closest comrades who strode behind him know?)

Beside Hitler walked the two presidents: Count Baillat-Latour, Coubertin's successor as president of the IOC, and Dr Theodor Lewald, the president of the German Olympic Committee.[31] Baillat-Latour wore the traditional black morning coat worn on official occasions, but many of the entourage preferred uniforms. Göring, as the Reich's Marshal, wore a white outfit, as did Tschammer-Osten, the Reichssportführer, but he could not compete with the many decorations displayed by Göring, which he gained as a squadron leader in the First World War. Even the otherwise non-militaristic Goebbels wore the brown party uniform alongside another member in the black uniform and steel helmet of the SS (Schutz Staffel – Nazi special security force).

Beethoven's Ninth Symphony was played and a choir sang 'Alle Menschen werden Brüder' (all people become brothers) and other messages of peace. Hitler had asked Richard Strauss to compose a special Olympic hymn, but the IOC preferred the later version by a Greek composer as played at the first – and all subsequent – Games. The 'Deutschland' anthem, which had not changed since the KaiserReich, was now followed by the 'Horst Wessel Lied', attributed by Goebbels to the young student who was killed in street fighting, who with his lyrics had 'stolen' an ensnaring piece of music, which German youth and also we

---

31 Former IOC president Baron Pierre de Coubertin was too ill to attend in person. Coubertin died in 1942 and was buried in Lausanne; his heart, as requested, was taken to his beloved Olympia.

Jewish groups had sung with another text.[32] For the next 16 days, the Horst Wessel song followed the 'Deutschlandlied' like an echo whenever a victory was achieved, and the new German black, white and red flag with the Swastika in its centre was raised.

It had been the idea of Carl Diem, the secretary of the National Olympic Committee, to arrange a long-distance torch relay from ancient Olympia in Greece via the Balkans and Western Europe. He wanted to bring a (sunlit) fire to kindle a holy flame and to keep it burning at the stadium in Berlin during the Games. Shortly before, a huge bell of over 16 tons was installed in a special clock tower, inscribed with the words 'Ich rufe die Jugend der Welt' ('I Call the Youth of the World').

We watched Hitler and the various dignitaries take their places amongst members of the IOC which, from now on, was in charge of the Games. Finally, the teams of the 49 nations, represented by 4,066 competitors – of whom 328 were women – and many officials, marched into the stadium behind their country's flag. Greece led the parade of nations, being first by tradition, and the host country Germany brought up the rear with the largest team (over 400 competitors). In the parade were, of course, the black American competitors – whom Goebbels attacked in his daily newspaper *Der Angriff* as the 'black auxiliaries of the American team' – who marched into the stadium behind the Stars and Stripes to take their place in an arena which was ringed by the flags of all the participating nations.

We could hear from afar the welcoming cheers for the torchbearer, which were taken up by the 100,000 spectators already in the stadium when the last runner of the relay from Olympia started to ascend the steps with the torch raised, greeting competitors and spectators, before lighting the Olympic flame. To my surprise, he was the student champion Fritz Schilgen, whom I knew from the youth championships in Hessen, where I had competed a few years earlier. With his fair hair and blue eyes he was the image of an 'Aryan youth'.

---

32 Originally, the tune was from 'Josef and his brothers', an opera by the Frenchman Etienne Nicholas Mehúl, and an old Jewish story from the Bible composed in 1807 and adapted as a marching song by Napoleon's soldiers. My mentor, the late sports historian Hajo Bernett from the University of Bonn, wrote often about the many old symbols and ceremonies and usages copied and used by the Nazis. See Hajo Bernett, *Der Jüdische Sport im National sozialistischen Deutschland, 1933–1938* (Schorndorf: 1978)

After Schilgen had lit the flame, hundreds of doves were released to convey a message of peace. Now, the flag-bearers moved forward to form a semicircle behind a German athlete who recited the Olympic Oath, followed by a representative of all the judges for these Games. Now Hitler stepped forward on his balcony and declared the XI Olympic Games of the modern era open. It was then left to presidents Baillat-Latour and Lewald to address the assembly. This was followed by the roar of the engines of the zeppelin 'Hindenburg' circling overhead, representing Germany's technical achievements.[33]

Jewish Refusals

The majority of athletes worldwide wanted to participate in spite of Hitler's doctrines, but others refused to compete in Nazi Germany. Among these were such former medal winners as the American discus thrower Lilian Copeland, who had previously won a gold, and the Dane Ivan Osiier, who won a fencing medal in 1912 and was to win another in his sixtieth year. *Harry Cohen*, an Australian boxer, made certain he registered as a professional to avoid being nominated to fight in Berlin as an amateur. The Czech water polo player *Frank Fisher* refused to play as part of his country's team, in spite of other Jews who were willing to do so.

There were not only those who refused to participate because they were Jewish or belonged to another minority discredited by Hitler and his followers. The entire Dutch wrestling team and weightlifting team and some leading American basketball players declined to take part. Other players were instructed not to compete by the organisations they belonged to. *Professor Brodetsky*, the president of the Maccabi World Union, instructed all Maccabim to stay away from the Berlin Games. The majority of Jews, though, who wanted to demonstrate by their achievements the invalidity of Hitler's pronouncements, took part – and some won medals.

Other would-be participants missed out because of the anti-Semitism of those running their national teams. The Austrians, of

---

33 The development of an air-filled balloon into a rigid but dirigible airship had been made possible by two engineers, Karl Arnstein and David Schwartz, and caused serious damage in England during the First World War. Some months later, this zeppelin exploded at Lakehurst in the USA after being struck by lightning; the crew and passengers were lost. Among the dead was Baron Ernst Günther von Hühnefeld, who had a Jewish mother; another member of the von Huhnefeld family had served on the German Olympic Committee.

whom it was said that they were even more anti-Semitic as a nation than the Germans, banned three of their swimming champions – *Judith Deutsch, Lucie Goldner* and *Ruth Langer* – for two years. All three girls left Vienna, with Deutsch going to Israel and Ruth Langer, later *Lewis*, to Britain, where she became one of the country's best long-distance swimmers; but what happened to Goldner is unknown to me.

Of course, other Jewish sports people of the time would have excelled in events which were not yet part of the Olympics. The ju-jitsu team of the RJF, who were German champions, had received the Adlerplakette – a highly prestigious decoration from the Reich's president, von Hindenburg – years previously.[34] The same misfortune of Olympic non-representation of his sport befell the glider pilot *Robert Kronfeld*, the world record holder, who left Germany as a refugee when Hitler came to power.[35]

The Olympic Village

A few thousand athletes stayed in a well-designed Olympic village, which was the best provided so far as it made it possible for all male competitors to live together in comradeship and harmony, irrespective of faith, race, class and nationality. Women, though, stayed at the former High School for Physical Education in the vicinity of the stadium. Among those staying at the village were quite a number of Jews. However, as only medal winners are listed, we can only guess at the number of the Jewish contingent.

On this subject, it is rather difficult to establish the difference between being a medal winner and an 'also ran' at the Games: the ratio was probably about one in ten. The chances of being a winner are, of course, higher for those who have to overcome challenging qualifying competitions for a place in the team of a large country with extensive organised sports, rather than those who were just chosen because their country was entitled to field at least one

---

34 Helene Mayer had already received this additional honour after having won a gold medal at the Amsterdam Games in 1928.

35 Norman Bentwich reported in his book *I Understand the Risk* that Kronfeld was the first glider pilot to cross the English Channel. During the Second World War Kronfeld trained the British forces as a high-ranking officer but was killed preparing for the Allied invasion when the tail-less glider design he had been experimenting with crashed. The title of Bentwich's book is taken from the declaration of a small group, including myself, which was signed before joining Britain's Special Operation Executive (SOE). Norman Bentwich, *I Understand the Risk* (London: Gollancz, 1950).

24. *Károly Kárpáti, wrestling gold medallist (Hungary).*

25. *Ibola Czák won a gold medal for Hungary in the ladies high jump, in the absence of Gretal Bergmann.*

27. *Robert Fein, Austrian silver medallist in weightlifting.*

26. *Fencer Endré Kábos won two gold medals for Hungary.*

took gold, wrestler Károly Kárpáti, who won gold in the lightweight freestyle competition to go with his silver medal from 1932, and the fencer *Endre Kabos*, who won top individual and team honours with his sabre – adding to his gold medal collection.

Kárpáti met the German champion Wolfgang Ehrl in the final. Whenever a German victory could be expected, Hitler was informed and frequently attended the contests to show his support. I do not know whether Hitler saw Kárpáty defeating his German champion but I am sure that nobody would have dared to tell him that Kárpáti was a Hungarian Jew from the Carpathian Mountains.[37]

Of Kabos, an Olympic gold medallist in Los Angeles in 1932, *David Wallechinski* reported in his quite unique history of the Olympic Games that, as a boy, Kabos had not shown any interest in sport and was teased by his friends so often that the family decided to present him with a fencing outfit in order for him to learn how to fence. He then joined a fencing club in Budapest and, many years later as his final reply to the teasing of his friends, he won two Olympic gold medals, first in the single and then in the team event.[38]

Other Hungarian Jews that should be mentioned include *Endre Salgo*, the handballer, *Lászlo Hódi*, the high-board diver, *Imri Mandi*, the boxer, and *Istva Angral* and *Madolna Lenke*, both swimmers.[39] Perhaps unsurprisingly, Hungary managed to come in a hugely creditable third place (especially taking its relatively small size into account) in a kind of unofficial points system with 16 medals, with many of these won by Jewish athletes – a fact largely unknown at the time by us Jews and everybody else.

37 I also learned from Subert that Béla's tombstone had been designed by Alfréd Guttmann, the swimming star at the first Games who had also gained a silver medal in the Olympic art contest with his plans for a stadium in 1924. Guttmann's ideas for a national swimming stadium were later used for the National Pool in Budapest.

38 The late Rabbi Hugo Gryn was one of the boys who were rescued from the concentration camps and brought to England. Hugo later studied in the USA and after having been the Rabbi to a congregation in India, he returned to London. He had been a member of the Primrose Youth Club, of which I was appointed the full-time leader. We had formed the club for the benefit of those kids rescued from the camps. Later Hugo became the Senior Rabbi of the West London Synagogue of British Jews, with a great following in the inter-faith movement. His participation in the weekly BBC Radio Four programme 'The Moral Maze' is much remembered. Finally he was honoured by the Queen with a CBE. He came from a small town in the Carpathian Mountains named Beregovo and went to school where, so he told me, Kárpáti had been his PE teacher at the Jewish gymnasium in Debrecen.

39 David Wallechinski, *The Complete Book of the Olympics* (London: 1996), p. 419. When in doubt I consult this most reliable and outstanding reference book: Wallechinski mentions the first eight finishers in every event and gives the names of all the playing teams who reached the quarter finals. Wallechinski is the son of the crime writer Edgar Wallace and is still one of the driving forces in the ISOH.

Samuel Balter won the only gold medal won by a Jew from a country other than Hungary at the Games as part of the American basketball team; it was the first time basketball was played at the Olympics. The final was staged outdoors and suffered from rain and a soft playing surface. As other basketball players, mainly students, had refused to participate in Hitler's Games, the American boycott movement deplored the fact that Balter had represented the States in the final against the Canadians, who had been coached by *Julian Goldmann* and fielded *Irving Meretzky*. The score was low but, from then on, basketball became the favourite Olympic team game.[40]

In the lightweight division of the weightlifting the Austrian *Robert Fein* set a new Olympic record in the press with 105 kg, which stood for many years. But the Egyptian Amar Mohammed Mesbah set two new records in the snatch and jerk and had the same total of 342.5 kg as Fein – a new Olympic and world record. According to the referee's return, Fein did not win as he was the heavier competitor, he had to be satisfied with a silver medal. One of the rare mistakes made by David Wallechinski was when he insisted that Fein had, in fact, won the gold.

Jadwiga Wajsowna from Poland managed to win a silver medal in the women's discus behind Gisela Mauermeyer, one of the few German Olympic medal winners who remained loyal to her Führer, even after the war.[41] Finally, Gérard Blitz, after so many years, again played water polo for the Belgian team, gaining a bronze for his efforts, the same position he and his team achieved in 1924 when his older brother was also a member of the team.

---

39 Subert gave me a number of names of the Hungarians who travelled to Berlin, but did not bring medals home. Sadly, quite a number of the largest countries can only be bothered to mention the names of medal winners. For them, winning is still so much more than taking part.

40 Thanks to Nat Holmann, known as 'Mr Basketball', the game grew into something of enormous importance in the USA as a professional sport. *Abe Saperstein* became the coach and promoter of the legendary Harlem Globetrotters, who I watched with great delight many years later. It was here that Jews and blacks worked together and claimed for basketball recognition as the third American ball game next to baseball and American football, both of which were professional sports. The all conquering American team – and especially the all-professional 'Dream Team' (from 1992 onwards) – has often been the main attraction at the Games.

41 The women's discus was an event that Jewish women were often to excel at in future years.

A Cause Célèbre

For me, the ladies' high jump – which the Hungarian *Ibolya Czák* won, as we have already mentioned – was an event in which I had a special interest because an old comrade of mine, *Gretel Bergmann*, was due to take part. We already knew about the infamous letter she had received from the authorities stating that the Reichssportführer had not been in a position to include her in Germany's athletics team. As a result only two women, instead of the maximum of three, represented Germany: Elfrieda Kaun and Dora Ratjen. These two – along with all the other competitors – knew the real reason for this breach of the spirit of the Games: anti-semitism.

Gretel had enjoyed the residential training courses for the core team and the camaraderie with the other girls. She had even overcome her misgivings when being told to share a room with Dora Ratjen. Gretel knew that something was wrong, but how accurate her suspicions had been was only revealed after the Games when Dora became Hermann and later declared his hermaphroditism. The honours he had gained in earlier competitions were therefore declared void. Ratjen insisted that he had been told to pose as a woman in order to take part in the Games, whilst the German authorities declared that they did not know Bergmann had already suspected that Dora was a man.

We watched the competition itself with baited breath. When we saw the Hungarian Ibolya Czák raising her arms in a victory salute, we knew that Gretel had been cheated out of a great opportunity. She had cleared, in what she called 'grim' conditions, 1.60 metres in Stuttgart a short time before the Games. Now, under ideal conditions in a close contest, the gold medal had been secured with the same height. Taking these two factors into account, I believe that Gretel would have won gold with a new record.[42] The story of this 'betrayal' became known soon afterwards, and her fate became the cause célèbre of the Games.

---

42 My memories of Gretel's earlier performances in throwing, running and other jumping events convinced me that she would have been an Olympic pentathlon champion, as a number of other Jewish women became in the years after, had this been an Olympic event during her peak years.

28. *Luz Long (left) took silver for Germany in the long jump, behind Jesse Owens (right).*

29. *Marty Glickman (left) and Sam Stoller.*

30. *American Jesse Owens (USA), the star of the Games who won four gold medals.*

31. *A controversial victory ceremony owing to the winner's Jewish background: (from left to right) Ellen Preis (Austria – bronze), Ilona Elek-Schacherer (Hungary – gold) and Helene Mayer (Germany – silver).*

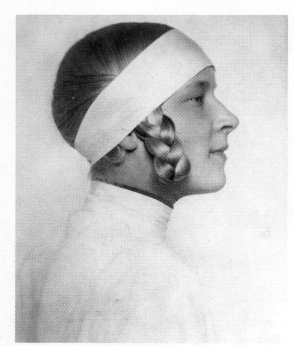

32. Helene Mayer.

33. P. Yogi Mayer, Olympia course, Ettlingan, 1935, high jump.

The Black Minority

In the village, the most admired and successful inhabitants were the black athletes, especially Jesse Owens. My friends and I had made sure that we had seats near the long jump to watch the expected duel between Luz Long, the German champion, and Owens, the world record holder. I was fascinated by the intensity of the combat between Owens and Long, with both trying to assist the other when measuring their run-ups before the competition began. When Owens finally won with an Olympic record-breaking last jump of 8.06 metres, it was only the second time in athletics history that 8 metres had been exceeded.[43] Then, in front of 100,000 thrilled spectators and other competitors, he and Long sat down on the grass verge next to the long jump pit and talked for quite some time. Hitler must have realised at that moment that his theory of Aryan superiority had now been brought into serious question as thousands of his jubilant 'Volksgenossen' (fellow citizens) cheered the long jump contest.

One of the first events to be concluded was the men's high jump. Peter Wilson, in his contribution to *The Olympic Games*, a book edited by John Rodda and Lord Killanin, recalls events in the following way:

> There was the amusing sight of Cornelius Johnson and Dave Albritton, two lanky American blacks who only bothered to remove their track suits after a number of other competitors had been eliminated from the high jump, apparently killing time between their leaps by shooting craps against each other. In the end both did strip for action and Johnson cleared 2.03m (6 ft 7^1/$_2$ in), 3 cm (1^1/$_4$ in) higher than Albritton but 4 cm (1^1/$_2$ in) lower than the world record which they had jointly established a month earlier in New York.[44]

As entertaining foreign guests was an important part of the Olympic programme, Hitler intended to receive his VIPs and guests from abroad in the lobby behind his balcony, as well as German medal winners.[45] When Hitler became aware that there

---

43 Owens had also been the first to exceed the magical 8-metre barrier, setting a world record of 8.13 metres in 1935 which stood for 25 years.
44 Killanin and Rodda, *The Olympic Games*, p. 58.
45 Many years later, the architect now in charge of the former Olympic stadium took me and two of my friends, Hajo Bernett and Hans Joachim Teichler, on a tour. He showed us the tunnel that led underneath the main stand to a lift from where Hitler reached this lobby, which was behind his balcony overlooking the arena.

would be no German athletes among the medal winners from the men's high jump competition, he did not invite Johnson or Albritton to the lobby, nor the third American, Thurber, who was white and had won a bronze, and, instead, left the stadium. When the IOC noticed that Hitler only intended to invite German medal winners to meet him in the lobby, he was told that he had to receive all victors or none – not just the Germans.

For many years these events became connected with the name of Jesse Owens who, after all, won four gold medals in these Games and became the darling of most of the spectators, not only because of his athletic prowess but because of his pleasant and modest demeanour. The vestige of modesty in a man who equalled or broke six world records in 45 minutes at an American college event in 1935 is most impressive! The writer Duff Hart-Davis spoke about his book *Hitler's Games*, which was published at the same time as my exhibition 'Hitler's Olympia' 50 years after the Berlin Games at The Institute for Contemporary History and Wiener Library. On this occasion, Hart-Davis told us that the story about Hitler and Owens was a legend, and quoted from his book a passage that von Schirach, the Reichsjugendführer, had recorded:

> [A]fter Owens's victory, the Führer said 'The Americans should be ashamed of themselves, letting negroes win their medals for them. I shall not shake hands with this negro'. Tschammer von Osten, who was also present, pleaded with him to meet the hero of the hour 'in the interests of sport', and later von Schirach claims that he himself sought to keep up the pressure in Hitler's Chancellery; 'America will see the treatment of Jesse Owens as unfair', I said. 'He is an American citizen and it's not for us to decide whom the Americans let compete. Besides, he's a friendly and educated man, a college student.' Hitler's response was violent. For only the second time in the 11 years that Schirach had known him, he shouted 'do you really think', he yelled, 'that I will allow myself to be photographed with a Negro?'[46]

There is no doubt that the jubilant shouts of 'Jesse! Jesse!' must have been extremely aggravating to Hitler and his challenging statements about black athletes, especially as his own athletes did not win a single track event.

---

46 Duff Hart-Cooper, *Hitler's Games*, p. 177.

The American Relay Selection

For many years after the Berlin Games, the discussion about the composition of the American sprint relay team still lingered on. Originally, the USA selected their team before departure and included two Jews, both of whom were sprinters: *Marty Glickman* and the 19-year-old *Sam Stoller*. But, to our surprise, we learned that the American team selectors, who included Avery Brundage, decided that because of expected competition from Italy and Germany two of the four relay squad members would now be replaced.[47] The places of the two Jewish runners – Glickman and Stoller – would be taken by the winner and runner-up of the 100 metre race: Jesse Owens and Ralph Metcalf. Brundage gave the additional reason that fielding another two potentially victorious black runners might hurt Hitler again. Of course, the general public would not have noticed that Glickman and Stoller were circumcised Jews! However, the Americans must have been of the opinion that for Hitler, from his balcony, it would have been even more offensive to face two Jewish sprinters on the podium than two blacks, in which case their actual reasons were to minimise the potential humiliation felt by Hitler. So blacks before Jews, even though Brundage, for his part, had no love for Owens, making sure that he was banned at the first opportunity on his return to America. Ultimately, the American squad won the relay by 15 metres from the Italians, a performance I watched with much admiration.

When the Games were over, the American team competed in three European cities: Hamburg, London and Paris. Only recently have I learned that an exhibition in San Diego brought back memories for Marty Glickman that both Jewish sprinters proved through their performances during the European tour just how badly they had been treated at the Games. They were, after all, the only American runners who were selected for the Berlin Games but, thanks to Brundage and his fellow selectors, deprived of participation.[48]

Glickman – now given the chance to run – demonstrated just how fast he was. In Hamburg he ran in the 100 metre race against

---

47 It is worth noting here that it only became possible to field a different team in heats and the final of the relay events years after the Berlin Games.

48 Glickman and Stoller therefore shared to some extent the hurt experienced by Gretel Bergmann, who was also robbed of her chance to win a medal.

the German Eric Borchmeyer, who was placed fifth at the Olympics in that event. But, as he recalled, 'I beat him by a yard'. Glickman told of the preceding two European meetings in the following words:

> After that I ran in a track meet in London. It was a Great Britain–USA duel meet, where I ran with Jesse Owens, Frank Wyckoff and Ralph Metcalf and we set a world's record for the 4 x 100-metre relay... And then after that, we stopped in Paris, and I ran in a triangular meet – USA, Japan and France – and I won, beating Frank Wyckoff, who had been the anchor man on the (gold medal-winning) relay team in Berlin.

The following year, he was winning glory as an offensive and defensive player on Syracuse University football team – and starting his career as a broadcaster.

After the Games

Once the Games had ended with a closing ceremony that was in faithful accordance with the IOC protocol for the occasion, the eyes of athletes and organisers turned towards Japan and Tokyo. Germany, for its part, had used the Games to shield its preparation for a war aimed to extend its boundaries predominantly eastwards but which eventually started in the west.

In this foreboding situation, the opportunities for Jews and their sports organisations diminished rapidly and momentum for emigration to wherever possible increased markedly. More and more Jews were now losing their employment and, therefore, less financial support could be given to clubs in order for them to continue with their activities. Soon, the cinder track at the Grunewald venue in Berlin, which was created by the Jewish community, became the one and only location left for Jews in Germany to hold track events; other clubs had to adapt fields for football and handball matches. Synagogue halls were utilised to conduct indoor activities and school playgrounds were also adapted for sport by clubs. There were, then, fewer and fewer opportunities for sport and recreation, apart from individual involvement in hiking, swimming in open lakes and rivers, and – for a few – some winter skiing abroad.

competitor as long as he or she reached the Olympic standard required. So, with over 4,000 competitors participating in these games in Berlin, taking into consideration the number of medals won by Jewish athletes, this is indicative that there may have been between 30 to 40 Jewish competitors. An even greater ratio of medal winners to those who 'also ran' was achieved by those whom the Nazis called 'blacks' and, perhaps, by other minorities, as well.

Most of the competitors staying at the Olympic village, though, will not have been aware of the tragic story of Staff Captain *Wolfgang Fürstner*, who was to have command of the village for the duration of the Games. When it became known that Fürstner had a Jewish forebear, a fact of which he himself may not have been aware, he was dismissed from his post and, broken hearted, he took his service pistol and shot himself. The German Army insisted on a funeral with the full military honours that were due to a German officer, to – as one can imagine – the annoyance of the Nazis. I am certain that the competitors in the village were not aware of the reasons for the change in command of the village as it was not the responsibility of the IOC but a separate provision of the host country.

Jewish Participants and Medal Winners

The majority of Jewish medal winners in Berlin were Hungarian. As in previous Games, their water polo players won gold, with György Brody playing in goal as before and *Miklós Sárkány* acting as captain. Béla Komjádi, the creator of this amazingly successful team and who was referred to as 'Béla Basci' ('Uncle Béla') by the players, tragically collapsed and died at the side of the pool in Budapest in 1933. A journalist from Budapest, Zoltan Subert, wrote to me in an exchange of letters that one of the small oak saplings, which were presented to all medal winners instead of a bunch of flowers, was taken by the team to the Jewish cemetery and planted on Komjádi's grave whose bronze bust stands today in the entrance hall of the National Pool in Budapest.[36]

I received various names of Jewish participants in the Berlin Games to support my statement about the large number of Hungarian Jews who represented their country and travelled to Berlin. Altogether, 16 Jewish competitors won a medal, 9 of which want to Hungary. These included high jumper *Ibolya Csák*, who

'Propaganda' and Leni Riefenstahl

The German government made the best of the propaganda value arising from the Olympic Games. An Olympia book published by the Zigarretten Bilder Dienst (picture service) offered excellent photo material as collectors' items. The text of the book, though, was equal, if not worse, than the pompous, bombastic, pretentious and overbearing language of the official reports of the 'Völkische Beobachter', which even today I find untranslatable into standard language. Reading the local and national press from those times did, however, enable me to gather more information about competitions at the Games that I had missed to some degree.

In addition to these reports, some time later I was able to widen my first-hand knowledge of the Games by watching Leni Riefenstahl's film 'Olympia', which documents the Berlin Olympics and covers many events I did not have the opportunity to witness.

I had first seen this beautiful, dark southern European actress in the mountain films of the producer Franck and the actor Louis Trenker, who both eventually emigrated to the USA. Their films *Das Blaue Licht (The Blue Light)* and *Die Weisse Holle vom Piz Palü (The White Hell of the Piz Palu)*, and the performances of Riefenstahl must have impressed Hitler enough to commission her to produce a film about his 'Parteitag' ('Day of the party rally'). She called her film *Triumph des Willens (Triumph of the Will)*, which depicted the fascinating power of Hitler with his hoarse yelling voice whipping and intoxicating his followers into a kind of mass hypnosis – a frightening picture when seen in the light of what was to come. The film also conveyed the nearly automated movements of the marching SA and SS as well as the Hitler Youth and their corresponding Bund Deutscher Mädchen (BDM – an association for German girls).

Following this, Riefenstahl was exclusively given the potentially enormous task of documenting the Berlin Olympics, which was met by a fitting effort from Riefenstahl and her film crew: it took Riefenstahl over a year to edit the many thousands of metres of negatives taken at the various venues of all Olympic events. The film, though, was ready for Hitler's birthday on 20 April 1937 and was greeted in Germany and internationally as the most brilliant film ever made about sport: in 1938 it gained first prize at the Venice Film Festival and also garnered a special award from the IOC.

Undoubtedly, the film conveyed a picture of happiness in the peaceful combat of those thousands of participating athletes. It was more than a documentary – it told the story of the beauty of the human body in motion. Often, Riefenstahl pictured just one competitor in action, but not necessarily the victor, and in so doing disregarded the notion of whether the athlete was Asiatic, European or of African origin. I cannot recall whether she dared to include Jews, but at no time were there any scenes depicting racial propaganda for the blond and blue-eyed Nordic ideal of the Nazi race doctrine. When I saw the film many years after its release I admired again and again not only the brilliance of the photography but also the avoidance of the pathos of various written reports of the Games. Initially, however, many countries banned 'Olympia' as it showed that the Germans had gained 89 medals in comparison to the 56 won by the Americans, thereby apparently portraying German superiority.

Hitler hoped that he could also use Riefenstahl's genius as a film photographer at the Eastern Front at the beginning of the war, but she preferred to shoot neutral films far away from any front. Twice after the war she was 'de-nazified' as she was never a party member, in spite of her admiration for Hitler. Later, whilst in her nineties, Riefenstahl retreated to East Africa and filmed the graceful Masai as well as capturing on celluloid the underwater world with all of its amazing colours.

Badges and Prizes

When the Games were over and 'Olympia' was being edited, Hitler became intoxicated with the success of his Olympics and decided to award special medals. In February 1937, Hitler created the German Olympic Honour Badge, which was awarded many thousands of times: 767 First Class, 3,364 Second Class and 54,915 Third Class. A reward was also given to foreign teams by decorating their flags with a special Olympic ribbon as a souvenir of 'Hitler's Games'. Furthermore, awards were presented to German medal winners, including Helene Mayer, who was proud to be able to shake hands with Hitler at his chancellery. Medals also went to Lewald and Diem, who had conveniently forgotten that they had been dismissed by Hitler and were only reinstated to the head of the German National Olympic Committee at the insistence of Baillet-Latour (had the Baron forgotten as well?). In order to avoid breaking the amateur principle which still governed participation in the Games, it was left to others – that is, not the IOC – to reward those who had won gold for Germany with 'cash in kind'. The town of Hamburg presented the hammer thrower Karl Hein with a house; Frankfurt gave javelin thrower Tilli Fleischer a car; and others such as Gisela Mauermeyer and the shot-putter Hans Woellke received professional promotions. Tangible unofficial and private presents had, of course, already been given to the victors of the very first modern Olympic Games in Athens, but not by the IOC.

Dreams and Harsh Realities

With the Games over, sport in Germany shifted into another gear in order to generate new impetus in preparing the nation for war. The emphasis was on encouraging a gradual shift from sport to warfare – 'Wehrsport' – with weapons like hand grenades replacing sports equipment and implements for throwing events, uniforms replacing tracksuits, and stonewalls and barbed wire coils becoming the obstacles to be tackled in heavy army boots. This momentum replaced the ideal of 'sport for sport's sake'.

In his book *Internationale Sportpolitik im Dritten Reich*, Hans Joachim Teichler gives details of the militarisation of sport in Nazi Germany. German Jews barred from army service by law, were of course, not involved in Wehrsport. In their decline they had first hoped that the international character of the Olympic Games and the government guidelines to refrain from showing any racist or anti-Semitic tendencies would prevail after the Games. But that proved to be wishful thinking – a foolish dream of many Jews and others.

I had never given up hope for a change through international pressure, but soon learned that the persecution of Jews and other minorities had actually increased. A small example was the so called 'Judennummer' introduced in Berlin. In 1938, I had to take my old 'Adler' car for the equivalent of today's MOT test. When I finally obtained a pass and the 'Judennummer' which was a number plate starting with 380 thousand I drove through Berlin with the 'Jew car'. Some policemen at crossings gave me a twinkle of the eye and waved me on. Other policemen loved to catch out a Jew and stopped me. Because I was a Jew, my fine was increased tenfold. Finally I had to sell my car and relinquished an essential aid to carry my bulky equipment for sports courses.

The increase in military service (Wehrpflicht) from one year to two years and the increased pressure from employers to join a party organisation brought a heavy decline in membership in mere sports organisations.[49]

> Still intoxicated by the success of the Olympic Games as an international festival of sport, many young people believed that there would be another Olympic Games in Tokyo in 1940. So the Olympic dream had not yet died, even for Jewish sportsmen and women abroad, and even foolishly among us who still hoped that Hitler's rule would soon come to an end.

Jesse Owens

Jesse Owens' accomplishments are synonymous with the memory of the 1936 Olympics. By his achievements and demeanour, Owens defeated Hitler's theory of the 'Master Race'.[50] However, he, too, returned to harsh realities immediately after the Games. When he returned to his home country, Jesse found that there were no rewards waiting for him, not even a secure means to survive. Among a number of performances, Jesse ran at a circus, against horses and cars and during a ball game interval. Latterly, Jesse became a youth and community leader, but remained a rather poor man.[51] Years later he was invited to revisit Berlin to appear in a film by *Bud Greenspan* entitled *Jesse Owens returns to Berlin*. At that time he recalled:

> 'I was a Negro. So it was something of a struggle just to compete for the sake of doing one's best, and to enjoy the full Olympic purpose of international friendship through, as the founder of the modern Games put it 'not conquering, but fighting well'. But Luz made it possible for me to win that struggle. He looked past skin colour and political heritage to

---

49 Hans Joachim Teichler, *Internationale Sportpolitik im Dritten Reich (International Sportpolitics in the Third Reich)* (Schorndorf: Verlag Karl Hoffmann, 1991). Similar themes are also covered in an essay by Teichler entitled 'Sporthistorische Betrachtung der Olympischen Spiele – 1936 im Berlin' ('Sport-historical Reflection of the Olympic Games – 1936 in Berlin').

50 Of course, we must also remember the successes of other black athletes at the Berlin Games who by their achievements, also disproved Hitler's theory. Owens, though, was by far the most successful and, consequently, became the most iconic.

51 He certainly retained his speed, though. As the mark of a truly natural athlete, Owens could still cover 100 yards in 9.8 seconds at the age of 43!

what you were as a man, and he asked nothing more in return. We grew to be fast friends through the Games. Hitler or no Hitler, Nazi Germany or no Nazi Germany, competition to win or no competition to win...'

Jesse, it seems, never forgot his friends. One report states that he and Marty Glickman stayed friends throughout life, despite the fact that Owens had unwillingly replaced Glickman in the relay race.[52] Jesse also never forgot that Hitler had avoided meeting him and his fellow black gold medal winners or that he had pronounced: 'people, whose antecedents came from the jungle were primitive...their physiques were stronger than those of civilised whites...they represented an unfair competition and hence must be excluded from future games.'[53]

The Aftermath

Fifty million people lost their lives because of Hitler's megalomania, but the Führer, Goebbels and Göring preferred suicide to taking responsibility for their criminal actions. We do not know, however, which of Hitler's millions of victims, directly or indirectly, perished in the fighting forces or as civilians in their homes or in the camps. The list will always be connected with the message on the Grave of the Unknown Soldier in Westminster Abbey and memorials all over the world in honoured memory of the dead.

When the war was over, the Jews who had survived found themselves in another extremely difficult situation. Robert Atlasz, with whom I had many arguments about politics in the 1930s, wrote a book about Bar Kochba which ends with a unique and very

---

52 The same report quotes Glickman recalling Owens' funeral as follows: 'As a matter of fact, and this is touchy, but it is true, absolutely so; a lot of guys will vouch for it because they were there: At Jesse Owens' funeral, which was in a magnificent Cathedral in Chicago, I got there late and stood in the rear of the church and could see where the 1936 Olympic athletes had gathered. One of them saw me – Mack Robinson, Jackie Robinson's brother, who was also a sprinter (he won the silver medal in the 200 metres). He waved for me to come and join them. I went to where the other Olympic athletes were, and as I stood with these guys, I noted that I was the only white man amongst the athletes who were there for Jesse's funeral.' It seems that, despite black/white relations in the USA and the potential animosity that could have arisen between Owens and Glickman over the 1936 Olympic relay squad selections, both men transcended such concerns – even if the latter was, once again, reminded of his minority status.
53 Hitler, *Mein Kampf*, first published in 1925, and from 'Der Angriff'.

34. Lilli Henoch (Germany)
(1889–1942). Murdered
near Riga

35. Ilja Szrajbman.
Poland's 200m freestyle
swimmer in 1936.

36. Attila Petschauer
(Hungary) (1904–1943).
Fencing medallist in the
1928 Amsterdam Games.

37. Roman Kantor
(1912–1943). Poland's top
fencer in the 1936 Games
died in Majdanek
concentration camp.

38. Johann Trollmann
(1907–1943). A Sinti boxer
who died in Neuengamme
concentration camp.

39. Werner Seelenbinder
(1904–1944). A German
wrestler who finished fourth
in the Berlin Games,
Seelenbinder opposed the
Nazis and was beheaded for
treason.

40. János Garai
(1889–1944).
Hungarian Jewish
fencer who won a gold
medal at the 1928
Games.

41. Dr. Otto
Herschmann
(1877–194?). The
Austrian 100m
freestyle swimmer
finished second in the
1896 Athens Games.
He died in Izbica
concentration camp.

informative section about Jewish sport and the transit camps for displaced persons.[54] Post-war Europe must have been like an anthill. Millions moved to and fro across countries in search of old homes. When Jews found their former homes destroyed and often their return met with some local hostility, they landed up in these camps, where some waited for their affidavit from the USA to materialise. Others were able to reach Palestine (State of Israel since 1948) legally or, more often, illegally. Survivors joined others who had spent their war in different countries and united in an effort to rebuild a worldwide network for Jewish sports organisations like the Maccabi World Union. Many also tried to use sport as a springboard for recognition in their newly acquired domicile.

Generally, though, there was great disappointment and disillusionment for those in transit camps when the world did not open its many borders.[55] The USA admitted all those whose affidavits had expired during the last years of the war and who had not been able to immigrate before the end of the conflict. They now had to wait their turn until after American soldiers had returned home in 1945. Britain, for its part, decided that it could not open the borders of its protectorate Palestine for increased legal immigration nor would it tolerate many illegal attempts to enter the country by force.

Whilst the Jews were fighting for an existence within the camps and elsewhere, amazingly, the first attempts at normalisation were being made in the form of the revival of sports and games. Ten thousand DPs (Displaced Persons) watched a boxing championship at the tented Circus Krone in Munich.

However, among those six million Jews who had perished during the war there were, of course, many who had keenly participated in sport, along with quite a number who had previously distinguished themselves at the Olympic Games or had at least taken part. Only some time after the war did it become known that among those many Olympians and German champions who had died since the Games there were also Jews who had not been able to leave Germany or the occupied territories in time.

---

54 Atlasz, *Bar Kochba*, p.147.
55 Ten thousand children had entered Britain with the 'kindertransport' before 1939. Many had lost contact with their parents and had given up hoping for a reunion in Britain or elsewhere; thousands never met their parents again. Their story is unique.

It took me many years to discover most of the names of those Jewish athletes who participated in the various Olympic Games and details of those who perished as a result of the Holocaust. It was, above all, difficult to elicit information from the big players such as Russia and America, especially when it came to naming Jewish members and their Olympic participation; some countries, quite simply, would not involve themselves in an effort to research the past and remember its victims. By contrast, Holland, Denmark, Hungary and Poland were the most helpful – as is Germany today. Of course, their committees quite rightly declined to keep team records of faith, race and ethnic background, but many were keen to assist me on a private basis in my endeavour to highlight issues of minority.

What follows is an account of what became of many of these distinguished sportsmen and women during the war, grouped under their country of origin.[56]

Germany

As already reported, there were two Jewish footballers of the Karlsruhe FC who had represented Germany against Russia at the Stockholm Olympics in 1912. 'Juller' Hirsch did not manage to emigrate, as his comrade Gottfried Fuchs did – to Canada in 1942. Shortly after, Juller Hirsch, the 72-year-old international player, was arrested and sent to an extermination camp. His grandson, with whom I exchanged letters, recently found facts that confirmed his grandfather's fate following his own return to Karlsruhe after the war.

Hermann Baruch was Europe's best weightlifter and a German wrestling champion, as was his brother, Julius. They were badly injured by a Nazi mob during the pogroms in 1938 before being sent to camps in the east. I wrote many letters to my town of birth, Bad Kreuznach, until it agreed to my proposal: a new road be named the '*"Gebrüder" Baruch* Strasse' and be given an additional small sign which explained that both men had been sent to the notorious camps Buchenwald and Auschwitz and died in Theresienstadt.

---

56 As a further note, it was mainly the West European countries who supplied names of those Jews who participated in the Olympics but did not win medals, individuals who therefore may not be mentioned in my lists of winners.

Some German Jewish Olympians and champions had been able to escape from what was termed 'the Final Solution' through emigration, maybe because of their reputation abroad. Sadly, not Lilli Henoch. The world record holder and ten times German champion was shot near Riga together with her mother and maybe with some of her beloved school children; all were buried in a mass grave.

In 1936, Germany published a list of former gold medal winners who were to be invited to be guests of honour by the National Olympic Committee. Amongst those invited were Alfred and Gustav-Felix Flatow, who both competed at the first Games in Athens. Sadly, one will also find both their names on quite another list published by the Nazis in 1943 – the list of the names of all of those to be transported to the east. Both Flatows died of starvation in Theresienstadt.[57] The grave of Gustav-Felix Flatow was found by the German sports historian Volker Kluge. *Rabbi Leo Baeck*, the official head of Germany's Jewry and also a camp inmate, recited memorial prayers and the Kaddish at Flatow's grave.

Regretfully, we do not have detailed information about all Jewish participants in the Berlin Games. However, there is additional information from Germany, some of which was collected as part of the 1986 exhibition '1936, Die Olympischen Spiele und der Nationalsozialismus', which I became involved in when two researchers, from a preparation team sent by Reinhard Rürup, visited me in London.[58] In addition to the exhibition a catalogue was published with many details that the exhibition could not show. Printed in German and English, it not only tells the story of the Jews but also of other minorities. It is estimated that approximately 500,000 Sintis and Romanies may have lost their lives during the Holocaust, including *Johann Trollman* – one of Germany's leading boxers.[59] Expelled from the German Boxers' Association in 1933, he was arrested ten years later and lost his life in Neuengamme. Another non-conformer mentioned in later reports was the wrestler Werner Seelenbinder – who remained a

---

57 Remarkably, all of the Flatow's trophies were subsequently handed over to the German Olympic Committee by the son of Gustav-Felix.
58 The exhibition, shown for many months in the west end of Berlin, was a special effort of the Stiftung Topograhie des Terrors (a trust), with Hajo Bernett and Hans Joachim Teichler as advisors.
59 The catalogue also mentions that 14 days before the opening of the Games 600 so called 'Gypsies' were arrested and transported to a special camp at Marzahn, where they were later joined by other minorities.

convinced member of the Workers Sports' movement. He was beheaded in 1942 after two years in prison.

It is also interesting to mention here Max Schmeling and Otto Peltzer. Both were non-Jewish but somehow came into conflict with the powers who ruled the so-called 'Third Reich'. Schmeling, who at the time of writing is about 100 years old, lives in Hamburg. After Schmeling became the heavyweight champion of the world, he was beaten by the American *Max Baer* of German Jewish origin but regained his title in a return fight. Hitler demanded that Schmeling separate himself from the American Jew *Joe Jacobs* who was his manager. Goebbels, moreover, disliked the fact that Schmeling did not make himself available for a propaganda role for the new Germany. Schmeling was called up early in the war and then dropped by parachute into Crete in May 1941. He was wounded but survived, and Goebbels missed his chance to use him as a hero and martyr, one of his devilish ideas, which was only made known after the war. Only recently it became known that Schmeling had hidden two Jewish boys named *Levene* during the November pogrom, who then emigrated to the USA.

Dr Otto Pelzer, who also had Jewish friends, taught at a rather progressive residential school at Wickerdorf. My friends and I admired him for beating the 'Flying Finn' Paavo Nurmi and for setting a number of world records as a middle-distance runner. Pelzer was charged under Paragraph 175 of the German Criminal Code with the offence of bathing in the nude with young boys and sent to prison. But because of the coming Olympic Games and his international reputation as a runner he was released and then permitted to live in Sweden. When his passport and visa expired he had to return to Germany, where, on arrival, he was arrested by the Gestapo and, without trial, sent to the KZ (concentration camp) Mauthausen to work in its notorious quarries. At the end of the war and finally liberated by the Soviets, the severely disabled Pelzer accepted a post to teach athletes in India, something he did with great success. Only years later we learned that, because of his conviction as a homosexual, he had also been unacceptable to Germany, even after Hitler.

The Soviet Union

When writing about the sufferings of minorities, especially Jews, during the last war, we must not forget those who died in Stalin's

Gulags and army or the many thousands who served in the Allied forces or had joined the underground and resistance movements in the many occupied countries, even in Germany.

It was not easy to get names and lists from the Soviet Union and difficult to find out about those who had distinguished themselves in the Games in which the USSR later participated. This, perhaps ironically, became even more difficult after glasnost – a policy which putatively promotes wider dissemination of information – and the establishment of a number of individual states that now compete under their own independent flag. Another factor was that Russian Jews also tended to avoid being listed as being Jewish.

The IOC, moreover, never issued an official ranking list of countries' achievements in a league table format. They even changed the Competitors' Oath by replacing the word 'country' with 'team'. But the media and a number of sports historians continue to produce listed information after all the Games, which I have used to mention the achievements of the various Jewish Olympians in order of the countries they represented.[60]

Poland

Of the three million Jewish Poles, the biggest communities were the 350,000 that lived in Warsaw and the 156,000 in Lodz. Altogether, 10 per cent of the pre-war population were Jewish, of which the majority lived in small Shtetls (little towns). Most of them were Orthodox and therefore did not compete in sports on the Sabbath, but a significant number were also convinced Socialists belonging to the 'Bund' and the sports association Morgenshtern, and also to the Zionist Maccabi or to the orthodox Esra or Kadimah. Altogether, there may have been as many as 250 Jewish clubs in Poland before the war.

Furthermore, a number of Polish Jews represented their country at the Olympic Games, including *Irena Kirszenstein*, who was born just after the war, and the discus thrower *Jadwiga Wajs*, who gained a silver in Berlin and again with a much weaker performance in the first Games after the war in 1948 (how she survived the war is not known).

---

60 Many names of those Olympians who were victims of persecution and lost their lives in the Holocaust can be found in the Appendix but others remain unknown.

There may have also been an additional number of Polish Jews who competed in the Olympics and lost their lives during the Holocaust. Of the various lists that have been produced, one of them names four athletes – but without reliable detail: *Bronislaw Czech*, whose name I could not find in the list of skiers in 1936, nor *Lesnek Lubiez*, who was supposed to have won a bronze in 1932; *Wlasyslaw Karas*, a shooter in 1936, and *Jozef Klukowski* complete the list of four.

For historical reasons, the westernisation of the mainly Yiddish-speaking Jews took much longer than in other East European countries. Of only fifty thousand Jews who survived the Holocaust in Poland, perhaps no more than a tenth remained in the country.

France

When approached, the French mentioned their swimming champion *Alfred Nakache*, a finalist in Berlin in the 4 x 100-metre relay, and mentioned three professional world-champion boxers who did not take part in the Olympics: *Robert Cohn*, *Alphonse Halami* and *Young Perez* (the 20-year-old flyweight world champion), all of whom died in the Holocaust.

The Netherlands

In addition to the lists of Jewish athletes who gained medals in the Berlin Olympics, Ruud Paauw from Leiden sent me a copy of a letter I had seen in the aforementioned exhibition, which exacerbates one's pain when reading about Anne Frank. In addition to this letter, Anthony T. Bijerk, the General Secretary of the ISOH has sent me another letter that Paauw sent to him:[61]

> ... As to your request: we have no specific records of Dutch Jewish sportsmen or women. As a matter of fact we had/have no interest to know whether a sportsman is Roman Catholic, Protestant or Jewish. What counts is whether they are good sportsmen and show good sportsmanship. But I can see your point and I have respect for your work. So I shall try and help you.

61 Ruud Paauw and Anthony Bijerk of the ISOC have spent many years in finding out what happened to a number of medal winners, about whom no records are available. These two researchers from the Netherlands were in a unique position as their country was overrun by the Germans and many refugees were taken back to Germany.

Some years ago we did some research to know which Dutch Olympians died in German concentration camps and then, in that Connection [sic], we found among others the list of Dutch Jewish sportsmen/women who once represented their country. You have already the names of the Gold winning [sic] Jewish women gymnasts of 1928 who died in the Gas chambers. The others we found are:

Abraham Mok (1888–1944, Auschwitz) gymnast, participated in the Olympic Games of 1908; *I Goudeket* (date unknown but died in the camps), gymnast 1908; *Abraham de Olivereira* (1880–1943, Sobibor), gymnast 1908. *Jonas Slier* (1886–1942, Auschwitz), gymnast 1908; *Mozes Jacobs* (1905–1943, Sobibor) gymnast 1928; *Elias Melkman* (1903–1942 Auschwitz) gymnast 1928. *Israel Wijnschenk* (1895–1943 Auschwitz) gymnast 1928; Note: all these gymnasts were born and lived in Amsterdam. Before the war we had an amazing number of excellent Jewish gymnasts. *Heinz Levy* (1904–1944 Auschwitz) boxer 1924; *Simon Okker* (1944 Auschwitz) fencer 1908; *Jacob van Moppes* (1876–1943 Sobibor) wrestler 1908. One who survived was boxer *Ben Bril* (he is still alive). He participated in the Games of 1928 (16 years old!). In 1936 he was one of our best amateur boxers and chosen to go to the Games in Berlin, but refused. The reason was that in 1934 he had been in Germany on the invitation of Maccabi-Berlin to box there and had seen what was going on. He therefore decided not to go to the Games. After the war he became [sic] an international boxing referee of reputation and participated as such in three Olympic Games (1964, 1968 1976) He refused to go to Munich in 1972. 'I am glad to stay in Holland' he said on that occasion.

Then there was the tragic story of *Hans Hollander* once a first-class soccer player but his immense popularity came later as a radio sports reporter. He reported all the international football matches of the Dutch national team in the period 1930–1940 and really was adored by all. No reporter could equal him. You have no idea how popular he was. In radio reporting 'Hans Hollander' is still a household name here after all these years. As a Jew he was in danger after the occupation of Holland and friends urged him to go underground. But he refused to do so. He said he had a diploma signed by Hitler for his work as a radio reporter during the 1936 Games and that would give him protection. Of course it did not and he was sent to the Gas chambers.[62]

One of the most heartbreaking stories of Jewish sports people from the Netherlands, though, is that of the five girls who won gold as part of the gymnastics team in the Amsterdam Olympics in 1928. Of the five – Estrella Agsteribbe, Helena Nordheim, Annie Polak, Elke de Levie and Judikje Simons (a substitute who did not compete), only de Levie survived the war. The others, tragically, were murdered at Auschwitz or Sobibor in 1943–44, as was team coach *Gerrit Kleerekoper*.

Denmark

In 1998 I received a letter from Peter Bistrup of the Danish Olympic Committee after I had enquired about the Jews and the Danish king during the German Occupation 1940–45. It reads:

> [I]n your letter of August 14th you asked about the Danish king would wear the yellow star. If this sign should be forced on the Danish Jews. I often have remarked about this rumour – especially when I have talked with peoples in Israel, and many years later I read about it in *Leon Uris' Exodus*. But it is not correct, To be sure I wrote to the Royal Danish Court and I received the following letter. You will find the letter translated in English.
>
> It is correct that the Jews in Denmark were warned before the German troops tried to arrest them in October 1943. A German officer Kannstein told two young Danish Social democratic politicians, Hans Hedtoft and H. Hansen, (who both later became prime ministers) about the arresting plans. The rumour of what was going to happen, spread fast to the Jews, and in a few days most of them were evacuated by boats of all kinds to Sweden where they stayed to the end of the war. The men – among them the best Jewish sportsmen – joined the Danish Brigade, a Swedish educated army of Danish soldiers who helped the British Army in Denmark, and in Northern Germany in the first months after the war had ended in 1945.

---

62 Ruud Paauw, Letter to Anthony T. Bijerk, (see Appendices, p. 239)

The letter from the Royal Danish Court disputes the popular story of the Danish King Christian X and the Jewish Star during the War.

In reply to your above inquiry I enclose a copy of an Illustration in Hans-Sode Madsen's book *Foreren har Befalet (The Fuhrer has ordered)* where the historian Hans Kirchhoff probably has found the root to the myth you are referring to. However it cannot be excluded that Ragnald Blix's drawing is inspired by the British propaganda organisation Political Warfare Executive (PWE) which organisation found it extremely important to emphasize the Kings German-hostile attitude at the expense of the Government of Collaboration. Furthermore Her Majesty the Queen has by several occasions done her utmost to invalidate the myth.[63]

Research into the fate of those lost six million Jews in Europe will never be completed, but enough proof has been obtained to highlight the large number who had represented their country in the Olympic Games and then lost their lives somehow, somewhere, just because they were Jews or from other minority groups. I hope that the material I have produced has described the final conclusion of the first epoch of the era of the modern Games, which ended with the beginning of the Second World War. When the Games were revived in 1948, there were still some former participants ready to enter a new Olympic competition in their desire to compete again and, if possible, to win honour for their teams and themselves.

Renewed Hope

A few years ago, when I was invited to participate in a debate entitled 'Berlin 2000 – a suitable venue for the Millennium Games?' in anticipation I revisited the former Olympia stadium in the Grunewald. I remembered that I had read that the British Royal Engineers had dismantled the bell tower, which had already been damaged during the last weeks of the Second World War. The cracked bell with its inscription 'Ich rufe die Jugend der Welt' now stood on a socket with the final message 'Im Gedenken an die

---

63 Peter Bistrup, Letter to Paul Yogi Mayer, 1998. See Appendices.

Olympia kämpfer der Welt, die durch Krieg and Gewalt ihr Leben verloren haben', which translates as 'In memory of the Olympic combatants who through war and terror have lost their lives'.[64]

During this anticipatory visit, I also noticed how badly the stadium was now in need of repair and further modernisation. For me, someone who sat there 60 years ago and later learned about the tragic death of those many young people at the end of the last war, I felt that the stadium was haunted and no place for another Olympic Games. But when, in 1948, I took care of those boys who were survivors of concentration camps, I was amazed at their enthusiasm for any kind of sport. Among them was a Polish boy called *Ben Helfgott*, who to me stood out not only in integrity and determination but also physically and intellectually; he became their leader right from the beginning in London. Finally, when a young adult, Ben became a weightlifter and was crowned British national champion, and later was to represent Britain at the Commonwealth Games and at two Olympics. He was a boy from Auschwitz: how could I ask for more?

---

64 These words reminded me of Ernest Hemingway's book, *For Whom the Bell Tolls*. The title is taken from John Donne's seventeenth-century poem that begins with 'no man is an island' and ends with the words 'send not to know for whom the bell tolls – it tolls for thee'.

Part IV

The Games after the Second World War

1948: London – Germans Not Welcome (Deutsche Unerwünscht)

Whilst the Second World War was still raging and the Soviets had involved Finland in the conflict, the IOC decided on a postal ballot to determine the location for the next Olympic Games after the war: London was chosen to be the next venue.

The Jewish community in Britain had increased before the war to approximately 500,000 through the influx of 70,000 or so refugees from Nazi oppression, of whom 10,000 had been rescued through the 'Kindertransport'. Adults were also admitted if they had an affidavit to emigrate to the USA or a Capitalist certificate for Palestine – if only to get them out of the concentration camps via Britain. Women were allowed to work as housemaids, young people to complete their education and various artists, musicians and – especially – scientists were welcome on merit: amongst those granted residence were a number of Nobel Prize winners.

All of these individuals were termed 'victims of Nazi oppression' and, then later legally became part of the British nation – as my family and I did. It was Churchill who coined the phrase 'Hitler's loss is our gain', and this proved especially true when the war started. During the war, all holders of German passports became 'enemy aliens', an identity which did not stop more than 1,000 joining His Majesty's Forces, whilst others were interned and even sent overseas without any obvious reason. Whether there were any future Olympians amongst the refugees was impossible to ascertain, but the future of the Olympics was of little concern at that time. However, the fate of all those Jews we had left behind in Germany, Austria, Czechoslovakia and Hungary deeply worried us, but there was nothing we could do to help. We never saw most of them again.

New, Absent and Banned Nations

The map of Europe and the world had been redrawn since the Berlin Games and some of the new states were not yet recognised by the IOC. Others had disappeared completely and, understandably, many more had been so affected by the traumas of war that they could not think of training and equipping a team to send to the Games. The Soviets, for one, stayed away, maybe for political reasons as well. Germany and Italy, having been found guilty of starting the war, were banned from participating. (Austria was admitted, having been 'illegally' annexed by Germany.) It is clear, moreover, that some three years after the war potential German participants were themselves not welcome (unerwünscht).

Nineteen forty eight was also the year that the state of Israel was proclaimed; Palestine had been invited to participate but the invitation was withdrawn. On this subject, *Ernst Simon* exchanged a number of letters from Israel with me with regard to Carl Diem. Particularly interesting was his information that on 15 May 1948 a cable was received stating that 'as the State of Palestine does not exist anymore, therefore we cannot accept your registration', so neither Palestine nor the newly proclaimed state of Israel could participate in the London Games.[1] Another letter from Simon, though, illustrates the speed of Israel's acceptance into the 'international community' of the Olympics:

> I met Diem again in 1948 at the Olympic Games in London, from which Germany was excluded. Diem had a personal invitation. The State of Israel had just been proclaimed. Palestine received an invitation prior to this event, but this had been withdrawn. I was not invited by the Olympic Committee, but by the Board of Education to a lecture at Congress prior to the Games, this in spite of the absence of diplomatic relations between Great Britain and Israel . . . I took an Israeli flag along and it was hoisted together with the flags of all participating nations.[2]

Acceptance, then, obviously came too late for Israel to participate in the London Olympics, but helped to clear significant hurdles to its participation four years later.

---

1   Ernst Simon, letters to the author.
2   Ibid.

When the war finally ended many British families were homeless as a result of the Luftwaffe's extensive bombing campaign. The planned building of 500,000 homes a year was therefore a priority for all governments. Many were happy to be able to live in prefabricated huts, universally called 'Prefabs'. My family and I managed quite well post-war with our allocation of coupons for food, clothing and furniture – we were even able to purchase a pram for our daughters, Monica and Carol, both of whom were born here in England.

Under these 'utility' circumstances the housing of over 4,000 Olympic competitors and officials, press and spectators was a significant problem. The solution was to house men in refurbished military camps and women in the various halls of residence belonging to universities; some, though, were offered bed and breakfast in private houses.

For the coverage of the Games, the BBC invited applications from persons with a good general knowledge of sport and the Olympics who would be able to broadcast in their native tongue, that is, not English. Having previously participated in a few discussions on the radio, the BBC – based on the recommendations of friends – invited me to participate in tests in connection with the athletic championships as part of this effort to find suitable broadcasters in foreign languages for the coming Games. My mind must have been distracted by something else as all running events were already allocated and all that was left for me was to report about the hammer throw. When at this audition the green light came on – a sign for me to start to speak – I had difficulty with my first sentences, something that improved with the distance the throwers achieved, but once the hammer had reached its zenith I had difficulties 'talking it down' again. Furthermore, when it came to the final throws I dried up completely. Furious with myself, I did not notice that somebody with a well-known face stood next to me: it was none other than Harold Abrahams, the gold medal winner in 1924 and the best-known athletics reporter of the time. He asked me: 'Why did you not use a flower piece?' 'I never heard of it,' I replied. 'Watch me.' He then produced a wooden tray hanging from his neck like a balcony, which was covered with various coloured sheets of paper. 'Didn't you have any prepared descriptions of the scene, details about the competitors, something about the rules of this not so well-known event, a review of the competition at the previous Games, the standing of the thrower among other competitors?' Suffice to say, I didn't!

The Staging of the Games

Despite the war damage and a life marked with utility restrictions, Britain – in its staging of the postponed Olympics – provided some first-class facilities, many of which were long-established international venues for the various competitions. Bisley was used for target shooting, Henley for rowing, Torbay for yachting and Wembley Stadium for football and athletics – with the greyhound track covered with a temporary surface for the latter events. No wonder so many athletes ran like greyhounds to establish new Olympic records, especially over the middle distances. Additionally, Wembley also staged hockey and show jumping. Facilities in the close-by Exhibition Halls, which had been used for the Empire Exhibition years ago, were used for boxing, with swimming events staged in the Empire Pool. Indoor facilities, moreover, were of special value in our English climate. At Earls Court, various competitions, including gymnastics, wrestling and weightlifting, took place; and basketball was staged at Haringey Arena.

The Games

King George VI opened the Games with the traditional declaration: 'I proclaim open the Games of London to celebrate the XIV Olympic Games of the Modern era.' However, the Games opened with a delay. Lord Burghley, the chairman of the British Olympic Association, former Governor of Burma and the gold medal winner in the 400-metre hurdles competition in 1932, must have been rather embarrassed that the markings for the 400-metre hurdles were so incorrect that the start of the athletics competition had to be delayed!

As expected, sadly the number of Jewish competitors was very much reduced: after all, six million European Jews lost their lives in the Holocaust. Still, five American and only a few European Jews managed to gain medals in London. *Ágnes Kéleti* was one of only two Jewish Hungarian competitors and won a silver medal – the first of many Olympic medals – in the team gymnastics. The other, Ilona Elek-Schacherer, repeated her victory of 1936 in the foils. An even longer time between medal-winning performances had passed for the Danish fencer Dr Ivan Osiier, who had

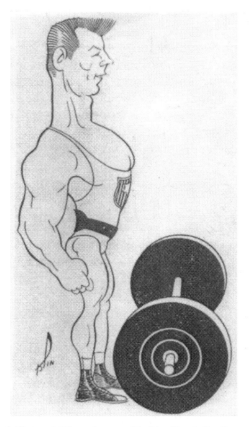

42. Gold medallist and Olympic record holder Frank Spellman (USA).

competed in the 1908 and 1912 Games. Now, at 60 years of age, Osiier won a silver in the épée fencing, a full 36 years after his first Olympic medal. *Karel Lachmann*, another Dane, also won a silver medal, finishing runner-up in the women's foil. *Fritze Wulff-Nathansen*, also a Dane, won a silver medal in the 4 × 100-metre freestyle swimming relay.[3] This Danish success can only be explained by the amazing evacuation during the war of 6,000 Jews by sea to nearby Sweden.[4] (See Appendices.)

---

3   Fritze, who also won a European swimming title, had the married name of Fritze Carstensen. Her family was 'old Danish' and one of her forefathers was Ludwig Nathansen, a well-known Danish author. Her daughter Nina became a Danish javelin champion.

4   See the letter from Peter Bistrup mentioned in the previous chapter for an explanation of why there were no young Jewish athletes and why the Holocaust affected the Danes less than many other Jewish communities in Europe.

The American Jews were understandably emotionally affected by what had happened during the Holocaust and therefore participated in far smaller numbers than at previous Games, but not without success. *Frank Spellman* won a gold medal in the middleweight weightlifting and the wrestler and police officer *Henry Wittenberg* had the same success in the light-heavyweight division. Three other Jewish members of their team also gained medals, all of them bronze: *James Fuchs* in the shot-put, *Steve Seymour* in the javelin and *Norman Armitage* as part of the foil fencing team.

Finally, a number of prominent Jews – including Abrahams – contributed day-by-day reports to the official coverage of the 1948 London Games. *Willy Meisl*, for example, wrote an article about football, and *Oscar State*, the honourable secretary of the British Weightlifting Association, wrote one about weightlifting; State was also the organiser and a judge for the weightlifting competitions at the London Games.

Friendship Renewed

At the time of the London Games one of the survivors of the concentration camps became acquainted and later married a girl from Hungary. Both were keen swimmers. The girl, *Susi Nador* (later married to *Norman Halter*, a friend of Ben Helfgott), told me that she and *Éva Székely* had been close friends in Budapest, had worked compulsorily in the same factory and lived in the same room in the Judenhaus (House for Jews). Young as they were, they just had to get out and about and so discarded their yellow Jewish star from time to time to go swimming and continue with their training. Later, Éva – as did many others – gained the protection of Swedish diplomats and Susi managed to reach England when the war ended. Éva became a multiple Olympic medal winner, including gold, and Susi is now one of the world's best swimmers in the masters class for the over seventies and competes all over the world. Both are still friends and in close contact with each other. They met again here in London in 1948 where Susi was a stand-by for the Hungarian Olympic relay team, but, sadly for her, she was not needed.

1952: Oslo and Helsinki

Oslo

The winter Games had been awarded to Oslo, rather than Helsinki with its great tradition in winter sports, in order to avoid overburdening the Finns with Olympic preparations. Twenty-two countries sent teams with a total of 732 competitors, of whom 109 were women. No names of Jewish participants are known, either as competitors or medal winners.

Helsinki – The Soviets Compete Again

With the return of the Soviets and the acceptance of the young State of Israel in lieu of Palestine, the IOC entered a period of steady progression in member nations. The admission of Taiwan as an autonomous state, though, caused mainland China to withdraw. Nonetheless, the number of participating countries and competitors increased from 59 to 69 nations, together bringing a total of 5,000 competitors – of whom 518 were women. Clearly, the Games were still dominated by males.

The Helsinki Olympics was the last time that the IOC agreed to the provision of two separate villages for competitors, although the reasons behind this segregation were different to previous Games. Those who belonged to teams of countries who had an allegiance to the Soviet bloc stayed at Otaneimi, whilst all others lived together at nearby Kapyla.

From a Jewish perspective, the Helsinki Games gave many positive signs. When the Games were celebrated in Sweden in 1912, the Jewish population had been nearly 2,000, but had been reduced to slightly more than 1,000 after the war, of whom the majority lived in Helsinki. Whilst Jews in Finland were largely unaffected by the war, Jewish communities in other Scandinavian

43. Olympic 200m breaststroke
champion Éva Székely, 1952 gold
medalist for Hungary.

44. Ágnes Kéleti, Hungary's
many times champion
gymnast at the Helsinki
Games.

countries suffered very much under the German occupation. Most of Denmark's Jewry was, ultimately, saved but Norway suffered greatly, and out of 1,500 Jews less than half returned from concentration camps. Sweden, though, was entirely different: it took in children and refugees before the war, together with thousands of Danish Jews during the war. Additionally, Sweden rescued others, including future Hungarian gold medallist Éva Székely, and took many survivors into their country during and after the war. Today, Sweden has a Jewish population ten times larger than Finland.

In spite of the deaths of six million European Jews and of hundreds of thousands who had been forced to emigrate from their homelands, it was astonishing that the number of Jewish athletes in these first 'normal' games after 1912 was greater than in any previous Olympics. This was probably due to Soviet participation and also – incredibly – from the Hungarian Jewish community, which had lost 85 per cent of its members in the worst possible circumstances. It was a demonstration of the will to survive.

The most successful competitor was the Soviet (formerly Hungarian) gymnast *Maria Gorokhovskaya*, who started her Olympic career in Helsinki.[1] With six medals, she became the female competitor who had won most medals in any one Games, a feat which is all-but impossible in any other competition.[2] Her medal haul was as follows: silver on the beam, the horse vault, the asymmetrical bars and the floor exercises, and gold in the combined exercises – both individually and as a member of the winning Soviet team. At first – as with so many others – it was difficult to ascertain whether Maria was Jewish, but some years later she joined Ágnes Kéleti in Israel as a sports teacher at the Wingate Institute, conclusively indicating that she was Jewish.

Also successful was *Mikhail Perelman*, who won his gold medal as a member of the Soviet men's gymnastic team. Other gold medal winners were the Hungarian water polo team, in which

---

1   The spelling of Maria's surname differs from one sports historian to another, as is the case with other Soviet and Hungarian competitors.
2   Gymnasts have a potential medal-winning advantage over participants in all other Olympic events as their various individual events also count towards the team event – where the whole team can win medals. This parallel competition structure – with its opportunity to win two medals with one performance – does not exist in other events. Nonetheless, winning six medals at one Games is an extraordinary achievement. Only Mark Spitz, with seven swimming golds, has done better.

Róbert Antal and *Kálman Markowitz* continued the tradition of their late coach Béla Komjádi. Éva Székely, who competed but did not win a medal in the London Games, won her first gold medal in the 200-metre breaststroke. Her unique style persuaded FINA, the international swimming association (whose president was the Hungarian *Donath*), to accept the proposal to separate breaststroke from butterfly, which are different in style and efficiency. There was no query about style in the 400-metre event, which was won by *Valéria Gyenge*, reportedly a Hungarian Jewess.

The Soviet *Grigor Nowak* came second in the weightlifting competition and the American Henry Wittenberg added a silver to his previous gold medal in the light-heavyweight freestyle wrestling event. Bronze medals were won in gymnastics by the Hungarian Ágnes Kéleti on the asymmetrical bars and in the team competition and in the fencing by Dane Karen Lachman. Doubts increased as to whether Ilona Elek-Schacherer, who won a silver medal in the fencing, was Jewish – doubts which still remain today.

Other Jewish medallists were the Soviet *Lev Vainschtein*, who came third in the three-position rifle shooting, the American *James Fuchs*, who came third in the shot-put, *Leonid Gissen*, who rowed in the Soviet eight, and *Aleksandr Moiseyev*, who played for the winning team in the frequently interrupted basketball match between the Americans and Soviets, which – surprisingly – was won by the latter.

Finally, the Helsinki Olympics saw a change at the head of the IOC. The Swede Sigfried Edström, who had taken over the presidency of the IOC a relatively short time before, retired after the 1952 Olympics; his friend, the American Avery Brundage, succeeded him.

1956: Cortina d'Ampezzo and Melbourne

Cortina d'Ampezzo

It was at this beautiful winter sports resort in the Dolomites that the VII Winter Olympics – where females constituted 132 of a total of 819 competitors – were opened by a woman taking the Olympic Oath. Despite a strong contingent of Soviets, only one name of a Jewish participant in their team has been made known – *Rafael Gratsch*, who won a silver medal in the 500-metre speed skating.

Melbourne – The First Games South of the Equator

The Games had been awarded to Melbourne in spite of worries about the distance from the majority of participating countries coming from Europe and North America.[1] The number of participating teams, however, was only two less than the previous Games, but the 67 countries taking part had to cut the expenditure involved in sending teams and officials by a quarter in order to successfully fund their teams. Regardless of these cuts, the number of Jewish athletes competing remained roughly the same as in previous Games.

In addition to the geographical difficulties, there were several political problems: the Suez Canal invasion, which involved Great Britain, North America, Israel and Egypt; the invasion of Hungary by the Soviet Union, to which Switzerland, the Netherlands and Spain reacted by ignoring these Games as an expression of their revulsion about this 'act of aggression'; and China would not send

---

1   Equestrian events were actually held in Stockholm, no doubt as a result of these concerns.

a team as they would have to compete with Taiwan, which Mao Tse Tung believed was still a rightful part of China and should not, therefore, be recognised by the IOC as an autonomous state. For the competing countries, though, the Games were declared open by the Duke of Edinburgh.

Far away from all but one large Jewish community (the approximately 50,000-strong community in Sydney), the Melbourne Jews provided an enthusiastic reception and support for Jewish participants from all over the globe. It is often quoted that, amid the transportation of London criminals to Australia two hundred years ago, there were some Jewish offenders whose descendants finally gained recognition in Australia – and to a remarkable extent, at that. Some, such as *Sir Isaac Isaacs* and later *Sir Zelman Cowan*, achieved fame and became Governor Generals. It was, furthermore, in a Melbourne park where I saw the first and only Horse and Rider memorial in honour of a Jewish soldier – *General Sir John Monash* – erected. Monash commanded the Australian Army in the First World War, including Gallipoli – where very heavy losses were recorded – and, later, on the Western Front.

We know that Jewish athletes participated in the Australian team (amongst these were there descendants of the transported Jewish criminals? We will probably never know) but did not gain any medals. In Europe, only a few of the nations to the west had a larger Jewish population than Hungary before the Holocaust. Among the survivors was Maria Gorokhovskaya, the winner – as we have already noted – of six medals in 1952 for her adopted home country of Russia.[2] Her phenomenal performances were followed in the 1956 Games by another brilliant gymnast of Hungarian origin, Ágnes Kéleti, who competed for the home country and had already won four medals in the previous Games and a silver medal in 1948. Kéleti, now 35 years old and the mother of two children, excelled by winning gold on three and silver on two occasions in individual and team events – one of these team golds also being shared by *Aleze Kértesz*.

Éva Székely once again enjoyed the limelight in the 200-metre breaststroke, but this time had to be satisfied with a silver medal. Éva married fellow Olympian Deszö Gyarmati, ultimately a winner of medals at five Olympics but whose water polo team

---

2   Gorokhovskaya had a Swedish diplomat to thank for providing the false papers which enabled her to flee Hungary and so survive the Holocaust.

45. *Israeli-born Isaac Berger won gold for the United States in 1956 as a featherweight weightlifter. He was the son of a rabbi.*

failed to rise to the height of previous Hungarian teams on this occasion. Despite this unusually poor showing by the Hungarian team, Jews did not go unrepresented on the water polo podium, with *Boris Goikhman* receiving a bronze medal as a member of the Soviet team.

Besides established medal-winning individuals and nations, a Jewish Romanian featured on the podium: *Leon Rotman* won both the 1,000-metre kayaking and the 10,000-metre Canadian canoeing event. Finally, as so often the case in the past, a number of Jewish athletes were successful in the fencing competitions. This time, *Claude Netter* took silver with the French foils team and *Yves Dreyfus* and *Armand Mouyal* won bronze medals as part of the French épée team. Two sabre fencers from Russia, *Yakov Rylsky* and *David Tyschler*, also won bronze medals.

1960: Squaw Valley and Rome

Squaw Valley

Unlike 1932, when it staged both the summer and winter Games, the United States hosted only the latter in 1960 – at Squaw Valley, California. The Soviet speed skater *Rafael Gratsch*, who had already won a medal in the previous Games, gained another medal over 500 metres by finishing in third place. His countryman *Alfred Kuchowsky* played in the Soviet ice hockey team which lost in the semi-final to the Canadian team, and so had to be satisfied with a bronze medal.

Rome – Games in the Ancient City

To provide for the opening and closing ceremonies and to stage an attractive athletics programme, a new stadium had to be built in Rome with a capacity of nearly 100,000 spectators. The old stadium, with its surrounding rows of copies of original statues, was used as a warm-up track and for some minor competitions. In addition, some of the restored ancient buildings were used for various events. As a result, these Roman Games had a special character quite different to earlier Olympics. The gymnasts, for example, competed in the former Baths of Caracalla, the wrestlers at the Basilica di Massenzio and the marathon runners used the Via Appia from Capitol Hill, completing their run under the triumphal Arch of Constantine.

The Italian president, Giovanni Gronchi, opened the Games in the traditional manner and 5,000 competitors from 83 countries watched the lighting of the Olympic Flame.[1] Once again, though, only approximately 10 per cent of all competitors, officials and judges were women, and an even smaller percentage was represented on the policy-making committee of the IOC. Doves, messengers of peace, were released when the flag-bearers formed a semicircle around the Italian athlete who recited the Olympic Oath.

The Jewish community in Rome had shrunk from 50,000 to 34,000 during the war years through Hitler's pressure on Mussolini. Many Jews had gone into hiding or joined the Resistance. *Primo Levi*, the Italian Nobel Prize winner for Literature, not only wrote about life in a concentration camp and its brutalities, but also about the part which Jews played as resistance fighters amongst Soviet and Polish partisans. Whether there were any Jewish athletes in the Italian team is not known. Still, the number of Jewish competitors at the Games increased further, especially through Soviet participation, but, again, it is only possible to identify some of the Jewish athletes who took part.

Alan Jay, a fencer, won two silver medals in the Rome Games. Jay was captain of the British épée team and had just missed a medal in the previous Games. *David Segal*, another Briton, won a bronze in the sprint relay. *Robert Halperin* sailed to a bronze for the USA in the star class yachting and compatriot *Isaac Berger* took silver in the featherweight weightlifting, just one podium place lower than he had reached four years earlier.

Albert Axelrod, an American, won a bronze in the foils competition, *Leonid Kolumbet* cycled to bronze in the 4,000-metre team pursuit for the Soviet Union and *Moyses Blas* played in the bronze-medal-winning Brazilian basketball team. *Guy Nosbaum* rowed for France in the fours, taking silver, and Leon Rotman secured a bronze with a partner in the 500-metre canoeing – his third Olympic medal; other Jewish canoeists were *Klara Fried-Banvalfi* and *Imri Fárkas*, both Hungarians, the latter winning a bronze in the 1,000-metre Canadian pairs event. Other Hungarian Jewish interest included *Íldiko Ujláky-Réjtö* winning silver as a member of the Hungarian ladies foil fencing team and the men's water polo team – of which *Kátmáro Markovitz* and *Mihály Mayer* were team members – losing in the semi-final to the Soviets.

1   I watched the Rome Games on television and met some of the medal winners later at the Maccabiah in Israel, an event I enjoyed as coach and deputy leader of the British team – in which we had a number of Olympic athletes.

46. *Ben Helfgott, a concentration camp survivor, competed for Great Britain in weightlifting at the Rome Olympics and won a bronze medal in the Commonwealth Games.*

47. *Russian Tamara Press won gold in the discus in 1960 and again in the shot-put in 1964. Her sister Iryna won the Olympic pentathlon in 1964.*

The Soviet Union, for its part, also boasted Jewish medal winners: *Vira Krepina* won the ladies' long jump, *Leonid Geishtor* shared gold in the canoe pairs over 1,000 metres, *Mark Midler* struck gold with the men's foil fencing team, Boris Goikhman took silver with the water polo team – one place better than 1956 – and *Vladimir Portnoi* also took silver as a member of the men's gymnastic squad.

However, two of the most successful – and later the most disputed – Soviet competitors were the two *Press* sisters, *Irina* and *Tamara*. The slightly built Irina won a gold medal in the 80-metre hurdles,[2] while the more powerfully built Tamara added a silver in the discus to her gold in the shot-put; the year after she set a new discus world best and went on to set further records. Although these records were allowed to stand, the IOC ultimately annulled the Olympic results of both sisters, as we shall see in the next chapter.

---

2   The women's sprint hurdles were run over 80 metres between 1932 and 1968, and over 100 metres from 1972 onwards.

1964: Innsbruck and Tokyo

Innsbruck

As the winter sports facilities in Japan were still in their infancy in comparison to Europe and North America, rather than try and stage both winter and summer Games in Japan the IOC decided to award the XII Winter Olympics to the old university city of Innsbruck, which is situated between high mountains in the Inn Valley. Thousands of spectators watched over 1,000 competitors in action in close proximity to the city and the high mountain Patschenkofel on one side and nearby Seefeld above the town.

Jewish participants were quite successful, with *Vitaly Davidov* winning a gold medal as a member of the Soviet ice hockey team and Frenchman *Alain Calmat* winning a silver medal in the figure skating – an event in which the American pair *Ronald* and *Vivian Joseph* ultimately secured third position after the original third-placed pair was disqualified.

Tokyo – The First Games in Asia

The IOC agreed that the Games would be declared open by Emperor Hirohito, who – notoriously – was the Japanese warlord at a time when gross atrocities took place. However, Korea – one of the countries most affected by Japanese militarism under Hirohito – did not participate. Indonesia also stayed away, protesting at the participation of Israel. Another country lacking Olympic Games representation in 1964 was South Africa – still excluded because of its Apartheid policies.

Judging by the reports in the media and supported by an excellent film record, the Tokyo Games do appear to have been one of the best Olympics ever with 93 countries sending 5,140 representatives, of whom 683 were women. It was remarkable that, in spite of geographical distances from Europe, the representation of Jewish competitors was one of the highest ever.[1] Furthermore, it is quite astonishing that the European Jewish community did so well in Tokyo, with only 19 years having passed since the Second World War and the Holocaust in which so many Jews lost their lives, including potential Olympians – scarcely enough time for a new generation of sportsmen and women to mature.[2]

Irena Kirszenstein (later known under her married name of *Szewinska*) was born in Poland at the beginning of the war but grew up in Stalingrad, eventually returning to Poland to study economics in Warsaw. Irena became one of the most successful athletes in the 1960s, beginning with the Tokyo Games. In spite of being only 18 years old at the time, Irena won a medal in the 200 metres, taking silver just 1/10th of a second behind the winner and, largely thanks to Irena, the Polish girls beat the Americans to take gold in the sprint relay; Irena had to settle for another silver medal in the long jump.

Tokyo was the last time that the Press sisters represented the Soviet Union, adding more medals to their tally. Again, Tamara won the shot-put and Irina set a new world record in the pentathlon and big sister Tamara went on to add the discus title to her other successes in the throwing events.[3]

However, there was a problem with both the Press girls when, following tests shortly after Tokyo, they were belatedly disqualified and their Olympic results declared null and void – but not their many world and Olympic records. The reasons for the disqualifications are still disputed. Some sports historians claim that both were disqualified because tests showed the presence of male hormones in their blood, while others contend that they failed chromosome tests introduced in 1967. It was their level of success, moreover, which convinced the IOC that a sex

---

1   As a caveat to this statement, many of the Jewish athletes at the Tokyo Games were representing the Soviet Union: not only were the major Soviet cities the closest European conurbations to Japan in geographic terms, but its eastern coastline is literally only a few miles from Japan. The journey is, nonetheless, a long one.

2   The Tokyo Games would also have been especially difficult for the British, Australian and – in particular – the American team, who all had to overcome their memories of the pain inflicted on their men, women and children by the Japanese during the war.

3   This event is one in which Jewish girls had excelled in the past, with Lillian Copeland, Jadwiga Wajs and later Faina Melnik all doing extremely well. It is also remarkable that Inge Mello (Pfuller), my old acquaintance from Ettlingen, qualified twice in London and Helsinki for the ladies discus final for Argentina in spite of her expulsion – due to her Jewishness – from German sports some years before.

determination test was much needed – just as the current stringent rules on drug taking are today.

Whatever the precise nature of the tests and the exact reason for their disqualification, both sisters were declared to be hermaphrodites soon after the Games. Still, many sports historians choose to ignore tests that were taken years after the Olympics and continue to list both athletes as, collectively, the winners of five gold medals and holders of world records.[4]

Fortunately, the Tokyo Games witnessed many other outstanding Jewish performances that were not to be annulled at a later date. Surprisingly, the Hungarians won the football tournament, with *Árpád Orbán* and *János Fárkas* active team members. Besides this, there were many more gold medals for Jewish competitors. *Mihály Mayer* won gold playing in the unbeaten Hungarian water polo team, *Lawrence Brown* played in the American basketball team and *Yuri Venherovsky* was part of the Soviet men's volleyball squad. Another Soviet, *Boris Dubrovski*, won gold rowing in the double sculls event, *Gerald Ashworth* was a member of the victorious American sprint relay team, and *Marilyn Ramenofsky*, another American, was narrowly beaten into silver position by a compatriot in the 400-metre freestyle.

As so often in the past, Hungarian fencers were particularly successful, with *Támás Gábor* and *Grigori Kriss* members of the gold-medal-winning épée team; Soviet *Mark Rakita* also struck gold in the team sabre event. Íldiko Ujláky-Réjtö surpassed her achievements of four years before, winning gold individually and as part of the Hungarian women's foils team.

The American Isaac Berger was disappointed not to be able to repeat his victory in the weightlifting four years earlier and had to be satisfied with a silver medal, and *Maria Itkina* had to settle for even less when the relay team she was running in missed out on a top-three place altogether. Other Jewish silver medallists were the Hungarian *Mihály Hesz* in the 1,000-metre canoeing and Soviet *Nelly Abramova* from the women's volleyball team. Finally, the American *James Bergmann* participated in the new judo event and won a bronze. Altogether, Jewish athletes gained 29 medals at the Tokyo Games – of which 18 were gold – a best-ever performance.

---

4   Another 'controversy' from the Tokyo Games surrounded the home nation. As the Japanese had won a total of 16 swimming medals between 1928 and 1936 – including five golds – a group of sports scientists put forward the proposition that the Japanese had an advantage because their body shape of broad shoulders and narrow hips could give them an unfair advantage in the water!

1968: Grenoble and Mexico City

Grenoble

In spite of Mexico's high altitude it was not climatically suitable for winter sports and so the search for a location for these events shifted from one extreme to another – from Asia to Central America, and finally back again to the reliable Alps. Ultimately, the IOC arranged that the Games would take place at Grenoble in the French Alps. President Charles de Gaulle opened the Games in an especially constructed ice sports stadium with space for 12,000 spectators.

At the time of these Games, France had a Jewish population of 600,000, equal to the Ukraine. The French had lost nearly 200,000 Jews through the Holocaust, but immigration from North Africa boosted the Jewish population. None of them, however, was able to reach the standard to participate in these winter Games. Once again, the strongest Jewish participation came from the Soviet Union. As in the previous Games, the ice hockey team did not disappoint – winning the gold medal with a team that included Vitaly Davidov, *Victor Zinger* and *Yuri Moiseyev*.

Mexico City

The altitude of Mexico City was always going to be a factor at these Olympics. France and the United States established high-altitude training camps in advance of the Games, which they kindly offered to other teams to use. The 40,000-strong Jewish population of Mexico had a well-equipped luxurious country club, which was also used by many teams for training prior to and during the Games. When competition started, world-class athletic performances did not vanish into thin air; rather, participants in endurance events found the conditions particularly difficult, but those in the so-called 'explosive events' were helped considerably by the thin air and set various world records. Any illicit performance-enhancing factors that could have contributed to such records were, for the first time, covered by the sex and doping tests compulsory for all competitors – the result of the scandal surrounding the Press sisters.

Whilst South Africa was still excluded because of their Apartheid policies, there were also acute political problems due to the occupation by the Soviet Union of Czechoslovakia. The occupation led to demonstrations in various cities around the world, especially in Paris and Mexico, where, shortly before the start of the Games, hundreds of students were shot at when protesting that 'The games should be stopped'.

There were also demonstrations in the USA, mainly confined to the south, about a still-prevailing attitude towards the black minority. These particular disturbances also found expression within the Games. When the Stars and Stripes were raised to the tune of the American national anthem during the victory ceremony for the 200 metres, Tommy Smith and John Carlos – two black sprinters – raised their black-gloved, clenched fists and bowed their heads in sorrow.[1] It is reported that Tommy Smith had also said: 'If I win, I am an American, but if I do something bad, they would say I am a Negro.' How often would other minorities share similar experiences? Having made their protest, Smith and Carlos were expelled from the Olympic village and suspended from the Games. The IOC, however, retained their names on the official winners' list.

Another black athlete, long jumper Bob Beamon, became the talk of track and field when he leapt 8.90 metres. This was a huge 55cm beyond the previous record and so close to 9 metres – a distance that many believed was impossible for a long jumper to get close to, let alone reach.

---

1   This quite unique protest by a minority was watched by many millions on television, including me. The Mexico City Olympics were also the first Games where the 100-metre sprint was contested entirely by black athletes, with Bob Hayes racing to victory. Therefore, not only were these Games used as a platform for the expression of minority opinion but they also demonstrated how powerful the Games could be as a springboard for minorities to demonstrate their talents to a global audience. It is interesting to note, though, as a counterpoint to the reaction to the protest of Smith and Carlos, that the 'Deutsche Gruss' salute (where the right arm is raised straight up beyond the level of the shoulders) provoked no reaction from the IOC whatsoever. Still, it was a lawful gesture in 1936.

Signs of protest

Black Power raised its angry fist more than once in Mexico City, where the 1968 Olympics were preceded by threats of boycotts and

48. *Black Power raises its fist in Mexico.*

A Jewish athlete was also making a name for himself, but the 18-year-old American *Mark Spitz* appeared at first to be rather arrogant when he expressed his disappointment 'only' to have won four swimming medals, two of which were gold and gained as a member of two relay teams (Spitz, after all, had predicted that he'd win six golds). Spitz's medal haul also included a silver in the 100-metre butterfly and a bronze in the 100-metre freestyle. Four years later, he would live up to his boast of being the best swimmer in the world.

Once again, Jewish fencers thrust and parried to a number of medals. The only gold was won when the Russian *Edward Vinokurov* shared in the team award with his sabre. His countryman Grigori Kriss gained two silvers in the individual and team épée, and another countryman, Mark Rakita, was equally successful with the sabre in the individual event, while *Yosif Vitebsky* also won a silver medal in the team épée contest. Íldiko Ujláky-Réjtö, the only Hungarian to gain fencing medals during these Games, won a silver as part of the team foils and a bronze in the individual foil competition.

Jewish water sportsmen and women were also highly competitive. The Soviet *Naum Prokupets* paddled to gold in the pairs kayak and bronze in the pairs 500-metre canoeing, *Valentin Mankin* – also a Soviet – sailed his finn class yacht to gold and the Hungarian *Anna Pfeffer* took silver with her partner in the 500-metre kayak event.

Finally, *Yevhen Lapinski* and *Valentina Vinogradova* respectively played in the Soviet Union's victorious men's and women's volleyball teams and the highly successful Irena Szewinska-Kirszenstein won gold in the 200 metres – setting a world record of 22.58 seconds – and bronze in the shorter sprint, her fourth and fifth Olympic medals overall.

1972: Sapporo and Munich

Sapporo

After 32 years, the Winter Olympics finally came to Sapporo in Japan. They had originally been awarded to a Japanese venue after the Berlin Games, and the XI winter Games were now – finally – declared open by Emperor Hirohito.

The Games began after the disqualification of Austria's best skier, who was declared to be a professional after receiving payments for promotions. A different view was taken of the state-promoted team of Soviet ice hockey players, but Coubertin's principle of amateur status was already showing signs of deterioration.

The ice skating pairs competition was won by the Russian *Irena Rodnina* in partnership with Alexie Ulanov. The latter fell in love with one of the runners-up in the competition, Ludmila Smirnova, and married her soon after the Games. Left on her own, Rodnina searched for a new partner in time for the next Games. She received her medal from the Emperor himself.

Munich – Eleven Israelis Murdered

The XX Olympic Games were awarded to Munich by the IOC. They were of a special importance, not only for the Olympic Movement in general, but especially for the post-war German republic and the independent state of Israel. Both countries were proud of their cooperation and their joint desire to overcome a horrendous past that had brought so much suffering to Germany, Jews and many other people all over the world, far beyond the Holocaust.

Perhaps in recognition of the achievements of West German democracy 122 countries sent 7,156 competitors, of whom over one

Yosef Gotfreund (40)

Yakov Springer (52)

Andrej Spitzer (27)

Mark Slavin (18)

Eliezer Halfin (24)

Shorr Kehat (55)

Joseph Romano (32)

Zeev Friedmann (28)

Amitzer Shapira (32)

David Berger (28)

Moshe Weinberg (33)

Anton Fliegenbauer (32)

49. *The 11 Israelis murdered in Munich: (left to right) Yosef Gotfreund (wrestling judge), Yakov Springer (weightlifting judge), Andrej Spitzer (fencing coach), Mark Slavin (wrestler), Eliezer Halfin (wrestler), Shorr Kehat (shooting coach), Joseph Romano (weightlifter), Zeev Friedmann (weightlifter), Amitzur Shapira (athletics coach), David Berger (weightlifter), Moshe Weinberg (wrestling coach).*

thousand were women – a record number. For the second consecutive Games there were two German teams: the Federal German Republic (FDR) – also known as West Germany – and East Germany (GDR). As a result, Germany once again had a total of six places in all competitions. This state of affairs remained until reunification in 1990. The president of Federal Germany, Gustav Heinemann, declared the Games open on 26 August in the

Bavarian capital in a beautiful stadium that I had had the opportunity to see shortly before its completion.

As in nearly all the Games of the modern era, there were political demonstrations. Another two Afro-Americans followed the example of Smith and Carlos, raising their black-gloved fists as a sign of protest. They were banned by the Americans from any further participation.

Murder

Half way through the well-organised and peaceful Games – through which Germany hoped to erase the memory of the Berlin Games – another kind of protest happened. This event was to prove unprecedented in the history of the Games and shocked deeply not only Walther Tröger,[1] the man in charge of the Olympic village – where these events took place, but the whole of Germany, and sent shockwaves to many parts of the world. I vividly recall these events and my own feelings of horror as I watched the events unfold on television.

There are many written and visual accounts about what happened during the night beginning on 5 September 1972, when the perimeter fence which surrounded the Olympic village was scaled by Palestinian terrorists, who carried out a well-prepared attack on the temporary residence of the Israeli representatives at 31 Connelly Strasse. It was established later that the attack was orchestrated by 'Black September', a known violent wing of the Palestinian Liberation Organisation (PLO).

Those in charge of the Olympic camp and security were unprepared for any acts of violence. Two Israelis were killed whilst resisting the eight Palestinians, but others in different areas of the building managed to escape. Among those was the team's leader, *Dr Shaul Ladany*, a university lecturer and also the world record holder for the 100km walk. Others escaped when awakened by a German cleaning woman.

After numerous negotiations some of the surviving Israelis were flown by helicopter to Munich airport to be transferred to a waiting plane. Overall, 11 Israelis died – 2 at the village and 9 in a helicopter explosion, the latter also claiming the lives of 5

---

1 Tröger later became the president of the German National Olympic Committee, a position he still holds.

Palestinian terrorists. A German policeman was also murdered. The killings did not stop as Israelis hunted down the terrorists and got their revenge whenever in a 'Wrath of God mission' they killed surviving members of the Palestinian Black September group. Legal arguments are ongoing and have not as yet led to a financial settlement with those who lost their loved ones.

The story of the massacre was told in the Oscar-winning film documentary *One Day in September* directed by Kevin Macdonald, produced by John Bassek and *Arthur Cohen*, and narrated by *Michael Douglas*. I saw Macdonald at a cinema here in Hampstead, where he lives and where he spoke about the film which took him two-and-a-half years to complete. The film was based on the research of the *Times* investigative journalist Simon Reeve, who described the events in an outstanding book, from which the film took its title.[2] Reeve writes not only about the massacre as it happens, but pursues the political issues concerning the aggressors and the reactions of countries, including Israel and the Arab world. According to him, the attack may have been planned over a number of years and the terrorist groups of Black September had been in close contact with other organisations with similar aims – like the so-called 'Red Army', the 'Baader-Meinhof' gang and even groups in East Germany. Their freedom was included in demands for an exchange of 236 prisoners mainly held in Israel, plus 40 of the Israeli athletes and officials at the Olympic Games.

Eye Witnesses

Friends of mine who were eye witnesses confirmed the official account of later years and the facts recorded by Simon Reeve. *Henry Kuttner*, working as a BBC studio manager and interpreter in Munich, recalls his memories as follows:

> The first I knew of it was at 07.30, coming down for breakfast and seeing a BBC colleague from the News department who had just flown in. He explained why he was here. These Games had suddenly become not just a sports event, but headline news for all the world's media. From then on, the only news we had access to was gleaned from German TV and radio broadcasts...

---

2   Simon Reeve, *One Day in September: The Story of the 1972 Munich Olympic Disaster* (Faber and Faber, 2000). Reeve dedicated his book in the following words: 'For all families who had suffered as a result of the events of the 5th September 1972'.

Unfortunately this news and most of what followed was heavily censored, inaccurate and grossly misleading. After the airport shoot out when the German police must have known the full extent of the massacres, but neither German TV nor radio was being allowed to tell its audience the full story. And all the time, I was relaying these untruths in good faith. When at last the dreadful truth emerged, I felt guilty of a crime, having translated all those lies.[3]

Stan Greenberg, a leading sports statistician, worked for many years for the *Guinness Book of Records* and was involved in many projects involving books about the Olympics. He was in Munich also working for the BBC as a statistician and recalls that 5 September was a rest day for the athletes and, therefore, him too:

I was awoken by commentator Ron Pickering who told me to get dressed quickly as there was serious trouble... The BBC office was overlooking the street where it was all happening, and going outside, I had a front row seat... At one point I could see the four balaclava-wearing terrorists on the balcony – a picture that went round the world – while all about me were hundreds of armed German police and soldiers. I found that it all got to me quite badly, and I eventually had to go back to my room... The following day there was a very moving memorial service in the stadium to which David Coleman, the senior BBC commentator gave perhaps his greatest ever commentary... There were some great sporting achievements in the following days, but I must admit that my heart really wasn't in it any more, and I was very pleased when I got home.[4]

Ben Helfgott, who competed in the 1956 and 1960 Games as well as the Commonwealth Games in 1958 and four Maccabiah Games, remembers Munich in an article he had written for the *Jewish Quarterly*:

How well I remember this twenty-hour drama. Ten days earlier I had been at the opening ceremony and had watched with pride and deep emotion as the Israel team received a

---

3   Personal report to the author.
4   Personal report to the author.

tumultuous welcoming applause by the 80,000 spectators. During the next few days, I spent a lot of time with them at different venues and receptions and shared in the excitement and euphoria of the Games. The last time I saw five of them was early in the morning of Tuesday 5 September after the completion of the weightlifting competition. I was awakened a few hours later by a friend informing me that the Israeli team was being held hostage.

Ben goes on to describe the aftermath and discussions on continuing the Games:

This unanticipated event overshadowed everything that took place before and after it. The Olympic Village was considered to be hallowed ground and its violation was repugnant and unacceptable to all civilized people. For the first time in history the Olympic Games were suspended so that a memorial service could be held for the murdered Israelis. The mourning ceremony took place in the Olympic Stadium with most of the teams participating. The Soviet and East German teams did not appear... The Games resumed but the soul had gone out of them. Some Dutch and Norwegian competitors went home in protest.[5]

'The Games must go on'

Avery Brundage, the president of the IOC, and Walther Tröger, who was in charge of the Olympic village, a number of German politicians and others including the Israel officials – who were in constant contact with their prime minister, *Golda Meir* – eventually came to the conclusion that 'The Games must go on', reasoning that, if the Games had been abandoned, the murderers would have scored a deplorable victory.

Some dozen years later, *Shmuel Lalkin*, the leader of the Israeli Olympic team, reflected on the terrible events in words that echoed the above reasoning:

The main question was whether the Games should go on or not. It caused quite a dispute also in this country, whether we

5   Ben Helfgott, *Jewish Quarterly*, 39, 146 (Summer 1992).

should go on or not. We pulled our team out. We couldn't go on without them [the murdered team members]. But for the Games to go on...I think the decision was right to keep the Games going, because if not, the terrorists would have gained in their purpose to stop the Games.[6]

In addition to Israel, the Netherlands, the Philippines and Norway – as well as the contingent from the GDR – would not accept the continuation of the Games, with the latter feeling that this would be seen as a kind of victory for the West. Other individuals left and a general feeling of depression and devastation remained until the end of the Games.

The Winners

Nearly 30 medals were won by Jewish competitors – 13 of them gold. Although this sounds like a major success for many athletes, it was dominated by the realisation of the dream of Mark Spitz, the Jewish American swimmer. Spitz achieved the outstanding distinction of winning more medals than anyone before or since at one Olympic Games. He gained seven of the thirteen-gold total, adding to the two he had won four years earlier. His gold-medal individual performances were in the 100- and 200-metre freestyle and the 100- and 200-metre butterfly; as a relay team-member he helped the Americans win the 4 x 100-metre medley and the 4 x 100 and 4 x 200-metre freestyle. Moreover, all four of his individual performances and two of the three relay performances set world records, a unique achievement.

However, under the prevailing circumstances arising from the massacre of the Israelis, Spitz had to leave the Games in a hurry under police protection as it was not as yet apparent whether the attack was a result of anti-Semitism or an exclusively anti-Israeli campaign. After the Games, probably because of his outstanding success, Spitz was reported to be rather flamboyant in his attitude and reminiscent in attitude to another champion – *Bobby Fischer*, the world chess champion. This was a great departure from his early career as a dentist – but his good looks and sporting fame eventually made modelling a much more lucrative career prospect than dentistry.

---

6   Personal report to the author.

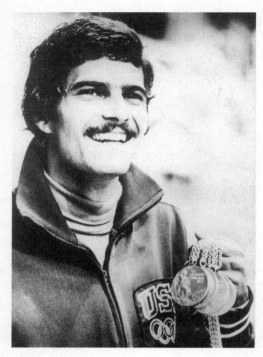

50. Mark Spitz (USA) won seven gold medals in 1972 in addition to two in 1968, making him the most successful Olympic swimming champion.

51. Sir Arthur Gold CBE was chairman of the British team for the Munich Games and many other events.

Another outstanding Jewish sportsperson, Irena Szewinska-Kirszenstein, couldn't repeat her golden performances of the previous two Games and only managed to gain a bronze medal over 200 metres but thought that after the birth of her son she had lost her natural speed as she had *only* finished third. She was honoured not only by her native Poland but also by the Soviet Union and the United States as the 'sportswoman of the year'.

Once again, Jewish fencers compiled their typically impressive medal haul. *Sandor Erdös* gained his gold as a member of the Hungarian épée team. The Soviets Eduard Vinokurov and Mark Rakita collected silver medals, Rakita's second in successive Games. Another Soviet, Grigori Kriss, had to be satisfied with third place for the team épée, one place lower than in Mexico City. Hungarian multi-Olympian Íldiko Ujláky-Réitjö also had to be content with standing lower on the podium, winning a bronze as part of the foils team to follow his silver four years earlier, two golds in 1964 and silver in 1960; this time around she was one of the few Hungarian medal winners.

Three Jewish participants in the water polo competition won medals, with *Nikolai Melnikov* faring best as part of the winning Soviet team and *Peter Asch* and *Barry Weitzenberg* taking bronze along with the rest of the American team. Two further bronze medals were won by volleyball players: the Soviets Yevhen Lapinski and *Vladimir Patkin*. Another Soviet, *Fanîa Melnik*, took gold in the discus – as so many female Jewish discus throwers had before.[7] Other golden Soviets were Valentin Mankin, who sailed with a partner in the tempest class yachting to take his second medal in two Games (two more Games and two more medals were to follow), and *Yakiv Zhelesnyak*, who set a new Olympic record with his rifle shooting.

For the first time, Jewish American horsemen distinguished themselves in an equestrian event. *Bruce Davidson* won a silver medal in the three-day eventing with his horse 'Plain Sailing' and *Neal Shapiro* came third on 'Sloopy' in the show jumping event.[8] Finally, *Andrea Gyarmati*, the daughter of the famous Éva Székely,

---

7   Stan Greenberg told me an interesting anecdote about Fan a Melnik: 'Apparently, a Jewish journalist tried to confirm whether she was Jewish or not, but she avoided the direct question – no doubt because of the "minders" hanging around. So he had an idea, and instead asked her if she would tell him the names of her father and mother. She replied that they were "Shmuel and Sarah". "Thank you, Miss Melnik", said the press man. "You're welcome," replied Melnik with a smile.'

8   Years later in England, I saw both riders competing in various horse trials.

won two medals – a silver in the backstroke and a bronze in the butterfly.

The carefully and enthusiastically prepared Games finally ended with some disqualifications and disputes. Maybe it was impossible to overcome a kind of deep disappointment after the shattering actions of those Black September terrorists.[9] It was hoped, though, that the Olympic spirit would overcome this understandable depression when the next Games were held in Montreal.

9 Despite the terrible events that had taken place there, the Olympic village was regrettably sold, as pre-arranged, as soon as the Games ended.

1976: Innsbruck and Montreal

Innsbruck Saves the Winter Olympics

The intention of the IOC was to hold the 1976 winter and summer Games on the same continent. Canada seemed to be having great financial problems with their preparations for both events, and so the decision was finally taken to switch the winter Games to Innsbruck. The excellent facilities previously used for the 1964 Games in Innsbruck were still in good condition, so hosting the event required far less financial support than Denver, another candidate city.

When the sporting endeavours finally began in earnest, *Yuri Lapkin* won a gold medal as part of the Soviet ice hockey squad.

Montreal – A Financial Fiasco

The Montreal Games were only secured at the last moment by foregoing the provision of the planned suspended roof and a 60-metre-high tower. The Canadian tax payers were burdened with the huge wage bill required to pay all those involved with the preparation of the Games – with construction workers taking a significant share. Beyond this, large additional payments needed to be made in order to make sure that the stadium was ready for Queen Elizabeth II, as head of the Commonwealth, to declare the Games open. The fact that Montreal was taking an enormous financial risk and that potential future host nations might be reluctant to take such a gamble led the IOC to rethink the financial arrangements for future Games.

Besides the monetary issues involved, there were also the by-now not unexpected political issues in the form of another boycott,

52. Irena Kirszenstein gained seven medals in five different events between 1964 and 1976. She won the women's 400m in 1976.

this time by 20 nations who wanted New Zealand to be banned for playing South Africa at rugby. Taiwan also protested because they wanted to be called 'The Republic of China'. The various withdrawals and the uncertainty about the readiness of the Games provoked last-minute efforts to rescue various competitions and cancel some others. When the Olympic flame was finally lit at the customary opening ceremony, romantics may wish to know that a French-speaking boy and an English-speaking girl walked hand-in-hand when carrying the Olympic torch and, a few years later, got married.

Twenty medals were won by Jewish competitors, mainly from the Soviet Union, but once again there is no information as to how many Jewish competitors took part in total. The Canadian team, for its part, had comparatively few Jews representing it, something that had been the case in many previous Games.[1]

It was at these Games that the 30-year-old Irena Szewinska-Kirszenstein set a new world record in the 400 metres, which was significant in terms of barriers being broken because a woman had run one lap in under 50 seconds for the first time. With that performance Irena established herself as one of the most successful and distinguished female athletes ever, having won seven track medals in four Games.

Two Soviets won gold in weightlifting, with *David Rigert* setting new Olympic records in the middleweight class and *Valery Shary* setting a new Olympic best in the light-heavyweight division. Other Soviets also took Gold: *Alexsandr Vinogradov* in the canoe pairs over 500 and 1,000 metres, and Eduard Vinokurov as a member of the winning sabre fencing team – his third medal in three Games (one more medal was to follow).

A Jewish American, *Ernest Grunfeld*, claimed gold as part of the winning basketball team and another, *Nancy Lieberman*, coached and played in the silver-medal-winning women's basketball team. When Lieberman saw that the Soviets fielded a player who was said to be 2.10m tall she searched for players to strengthen – or rather, heighten – her team but failed to match a height which, according to Stan Greenberg, was actually 2.18m.[2] The Soviets did not play their giant regularly so as to keep the tournament going as a competitive spectacle – as long as they were certain to become champions! As a result of this lofty Soviet the question of height became a topic during the Games and proposals were put forward to limit the height or to create special limits for certain competitions such as volleyball. Other sports, such as boxing, already had some weight stipulations and classifications.

---

1   As part of a tercentenary scholarship I was awarded in celebration of the anniversary of the return of Jews to England three hundred years previously, I was required to visit a number of Jewish community centres in America and Canada. Whilst undertaking this requirement, I spoke to the person in charge of a swimming pool situated in one of the centres. He was a former English champion who had represented his country in the Olympic Games and was now the Jewish centre's swimming coach. When I asked him whether he had succeeded in getting swimmers up to an Olympic standard he did not respond at first but finally said: 'I am not permitted to encourage competitions, they are supposed to spoil the character of the youngsters here.' Maybe this was an explanation as to why only a few Jews have represented Canada at the Olympic Games.
2   As a statistician, Stan takes a special interest in listing the Olympic competitors whose age, height, weight etc can only be described with recourse to superlatives.

While some Soviets sauntered their way to victory, others were suffering surprise defeats. *Larisa Bergen* and *Natalia Kushnir* were both members of the Soviet women's volleyball team that lost to Japan in the final. Other Jewish silver medallists were *Valentin Mankin*, another Soviet, who sailed his tempest class yacht into the runner-up position (Mankin took gold in the finn class four years earlier), and Hungarian *Anna Pfeffer*, who – along with her team-mate – paddled her way to second in the 500-metre kayak pairs.

Jewish bronze medallists included Soviet footballer *Leonid Buryak*, Romanian welterweight boxer *Victor Zilberman*, horse rider *Edith Master* – part of the American dressage team, and American 800-metre freestyle swimmer *Wendy Weinberg*.

The 1976 Games marked the last time that *Sir Arthur Gold CBE* was the leader of the British Olympic Games representation under the presidency of Princess Anne. He had been elected as life president of the European Athletics Association. He himself had cleared 1.92 cm in the high jump to qualify for Hitler's Berlin Games. He had told me that he regretted missing the occasion due to illness and would have loved to oppose the Fuhrer's racial prejudices by being there as a Jew, representing Great Britain.

1980: Lake Placid and Moscow

Lake Placid

The winter Games in Lake Placid had no financial problems like those that bedevilled Montreal. The Games had been moved from the west of North America to Lake Placid, which is on the east side, not far from the city of New York, as a precaution against a low turn-out of spectators – as at the last time the winter Games had been held in America. The close proximity of a populous metropolitan city guaranteed an income from large numbers of spectators which would secure the Games against any losses. The Games which had been staged at the same venue in 1932 had been very successful; fully modernised, the facilities once again created – as expected – a worthy venue.

There was special American interest in the ice hockey, where the home team hoped to avenge the very narrow defeat inflicted on them by the Russians in Innsbruck four years earlier. They succeeded – so *Vladimir Nyschkin* had to be happy with a silver medal as a member of the Soviet team. Another ice hockey medal also went to a Jewish player at these Games – Sweden's *Ulf Weinstock*, who won bronze as part of the losing semi-final team; Weinstock, moreover, was the only Jew from a country other than the Soviet Union to win a medal at either the winter or summer Games in 1980.

Moscow – More Boycotts

This time it was the turn of the Americans to boycott the Games, with only Coca-Cola, the National Broadcasting Corporation (NBC) and a few other American companies representing the US in

Moscow. The reason for this boycott sounds more than a little ironic 22 years after the event: the Russian invasion of Afghanistan. Issues surrounding this invasion aside, the American response made it clear that things had changed in the Olympic Movement. Once again the Olympics were being misused for political purposes, but this time by a country like the United States which, in the past, had been such a strong supporter of Coubertin's dream of a festival of peace and friendship between all nations.

Apart from the boycott by the United States, Japan, Australia and other nations declined to participate including the Federal Republic of Germany and a number of smaller states, who for political reasons (they were anti-communist) or economic ties with America, also stayed away. As a close ally of the American President, the British Prime Minister, Margaret Thatcher, intended a similar shoulder-to-shoulder attitude, but had to face a revolt in her own country. The British Olympic Association decided to leave it to the various sports organisations to decide whether to send any competitors to Moscow, and the majority decided to ignore the prime minister and the political issues, and so a strong team was ultimately sent. However, the British team did not march into the arena during the opening ceremony, and it was left to their flag-bearer to proceed alone.

Political cards were also played within the IOC itself. Juan Antonio Samaranch was not only the chief of protocol of the IOC but formally General Franco's Spanish ambassador to Moscow. By disregarding the American boycott, he hoped that his position in Spain and his support of the Games being held in a Communist country would secure him the votes he would need to succeed Lord Killanin as president of the IOC. The ambassador even wrote a book in English, which was published in New York, about Moscow as a city now awaiting the world to celebrate the XXII Games.

The Games themselves were well organised and enthusiastically supported by large crowds and various mass displays. This strong attendance by spectators was in spite of entrance fees for foreigners and hotel charges being exceptionally high: the hosts were in great need of foreign currency. With the Games opened by President Leonid Brezhnev and finally underway, the main events, including the opening and closing ceremonies, were staged at the Lenin Stadium with its space for over 100,000 spectators. Whilst the total number of participating countries shrank, female participation stayed roughly the same due to the provision of additional contests for women in athletics. Altogether there were 5,217 competitors, of which 1,125 were women.

The Soviets and the German Democratic Republic (GDR) won more than all the other medals gained by other countries. This big performance by such a small country as the GDR certainly raised a few questions, and for the swimmers of one country to win 26 out of the 35 medals awarded does, of course, raise suspicions about drug use. When the GDR repeated the feat of coming second in 1988, investigations and proof of doping were to follow.

There is no record of Jewish involvement in the GDR team. This, perhaps, is no surprise as the number of Jews in the East German region was only a few hundred after the war, and the previously large Jewish communities in east Berlin had fallen dramatically in number to just a handful of members. Today, Wroclaw (previously Breslau), and Upper Silesia are Polish again having previously been German for four hundred years.

The Jewish population of the Soviet Union had also declined significantly during the war, but its reduced membership of about 1.5 million after the war still meant it was the third largest Jewish community in the world after the USA and Israel. However, some things had not changed. Passports were still marked 'Jewish' and it seems that there had been a directive to Jewish team members not to talk about being Jewish – in line with the anti-religion attitude of the Soviet Union, although there had been some degree of increased freedom of expression over the years. It had been difficult ever since the First World War to ascertain to what extent Russian competitors and medal winners could be declared Jewish as they were officially discouraged from disclosing their religion.[1] And, over the years, many Jews emigrated – when it became possible, mainly to Israel and, surprisingly to Germany.

All but one Jewish medal winners in these Games were Russian. Three won gold: Valentin Mankin sailed his boat into first position for the third time in four Games, Eduard Vinokurov and the sabre team matched this three-out-of-four feat in the fencing and *Nikolai Chernetzky* took gold as a member of the victorious 4 x 400-metre relay team.

---

1   Ben Helfgott once told me a story that illustrated this situation. A few years ago one of the Russian champions had pointed to the 'Magen David' (Star of David) on a chain around Ben's neck and asked him whether he could have it for his father.

There were four silver medallists: *Svetlana Krachevskaja* in the shot-put, *Nikolai Polyakov* in the team yachting, Vladimir Novitzky in handball and Vladimir Nyschkin in ice hockey. Finally, three bronze medallists were *Yuri Gavrilov* in the football tournament, *Boris Lukemsky* in the épée team event and Swede Ulf Weinstock in the ice hockey.

At the closing ceremony the Mayor of Moscow handed over the Olympic flag to the Mayor of Los Angeles. The Games were deemed a success by the Russians, but officials must have been concerned as to what would happen at the next summer Games in America. Would the Russians retaliate with a boycott or shame the hosts by putting sport before politics?

1984: Sarajevo and Los Angeles

Sarajevo

All conflicts between the Soviet bloc and the Americans and their allies seem to have been forgotten when the Winter Olympics were opened by the President of the Socialist Republic of Yugoslavia in Sarajevo. I remember being told at school that the former capital of Bosnia had played a special part in history when the shooting of the heir to the Habsburg throne, Franz Ferdinand, and his wife precipitated the start of the First World War (arising from the political desire to be freed from the rule of the Habsburg Austrian monarchy). This is reminiscent of another 'starting shot' – the shooting of the German diplomat which brought on the start of the Holocaust and, indirectly, the Second World War.

Again, as at some previous winter Games, there was no Jewish participation.

Los Angeles – The Soviet Union Plays 'Tit for Tat'

In the period between the 1980 and 1984 Olympic Games the 'strategy' of the cold war never changed, in spite of the traditional exchange of flags which had taken place at the last games between Moscow and Los Angeles. With only a very short period of four weeks to go until the Los Angeles Games were due to begin, the Soviet Union declared that it could not risk sending a team because of a lack of security. As expected, Soviet satellite countries from behind the iron curtain also did not take part along with some Third World countries, in spite of a generous offer from the host nation to assist with fares and the transport of men and women participants and to accommodate them in hotels rather than in the

53. The gymnast Mitch Gaylord
won gold for the United States in
1984.

54. Flagbearer Carina Benninga
celebrates as captain of the
victorious Netherlands hockey team.

Olympic village. It is interesting to note that this offer of financial help from the USA was only made possible by direct commercial sponsorship, which was an alternative approach by Samaranch to the state-funded Games of the past.

Financial assistance aside, Los Angeles was a very distant place for Europeans and, as a result, the total number of participants was smaller that at some of the previous Games. The official figure given for the participation from 140 countries was 6,797 competitors, including 1,567 female contestants. The still-recovering European Jewish community and the withdrawal of the Soviet Union – which many of the Jewish medal winners at every Games since 1952 have represented – threatened to keep Jewish participants in the Los Angeles Games to a minimum. This situation, though, was softened by the contribution of the increased Jewish populations from non-European nations.

The opening ceremony of the XXIII Summer Olympics was attended by President Ronald Reagan, who declared the Games open at the refurbished Coliseum stadium – just one of many excellent venues – with its capacity of nearly one hundred thousand spectators. The ceremony took place with a mass display by gymnasts and dancers; *George Gershwin's* 'Rhapsody in Blue' was played on 85 grand pianos.

Surprisingly, considering past history, the Americans had now become very much aware of the past involvement of its minorities in its sporting endeavours, individuals who used sport as a springboard into equality – especially the Olympic Games. The torch relay, starting as always at Olympia, a permanent feature of all Olympic Games since being introduced by Carl Diem in Berlin, symbolised this increased historical awareness. The granddaughter of Jesse Owens ran together with Jim Thorpe's nephew on the first leg of its journey from Moscow to the American continent. Later in the relay, the American athlete Rafern Johnson handed the torch over to Ed Moses, the 400-metre hurdles world champion and record holder. The American Olympic Committee had finally recognised the great contribution of the descendants of black slaves – as well as Native Americans – who were now playing an important role as members of the American Olympic team.

It was Jewish Americans who also won most of the medals collected by Jews at these Games. *Tiffany Cohen* won gold medals in freestyle swimming over 400 and 800 metres, and *Dara Torres* helped the 4 x 100-metre freestyle relay team to gold in what was the first of her many successful Olympic performances. *Mitch Gaylord* took gold with the gymnastic team (coached by former Olympian *Abie Grossfeld*), with his individual performances on the horse, the rings and the parallel bars adding a silver and two bronze medals. Another Jewish American silver medallist was *Bob Berland* in the middleweight judo competition, while *Jay Glaser* took silver in the tornado-class yachting; Canadian *Mark Berger* managed a bronze, grappling his way to third place in the heavyweight judo event.

For the first time in Olympic history there were Jewish medal winners from South America. Brazilian *Daniel Adler* sailed to silver in the soling-class yachting and *Bernard Rajzman* did equally well as a member of the Brazilian volleyball team.

Astonishingly, even accounting for the absence of the Soviets and others, only one European Jew gained a gold medal – *Carina Benninga*, who captained the Dutch women's hockey team to gold. When I first read about Carina's exploits in the well-informed sports column of the British weekly publication *Jewish Chronicle* I thought that she might be a descendant of Spanish emigrants, driven out of the Iberian peninsula by the Inquisition. On wanting to clarify this I attempted to get in touch with her, but it was difficult to locate her. Finally, as so often in the past, my friends from the ISOH assisted and I received a very kind letter from Carina in answer to my enquiry, along with a wonderful picture showing her carrying the Netherlands flag at the Barcelona Games in 1992. The letter read as follows:

Dear Mr Mayer,
Hopefully, I can give you some more information. Let me start with one of the most important people in my life. And 'of course' that is my mother. Yes my mother is a Dutch citizen born and raised in Amsterdam. Her father left for England in 1940 to help Holland from there. He was in the Underground. Due to his flight to England, his family, his wife and three children were picked up by the Germans in 1940 or 1941. One of the children was my mother. She was taken to Bergen Belsen where they stayed and survived for four years. Of course this still has a major impact on her life today. A lot of my family died but my mother, her brother, and sister all came back as well as their mother and my grandmother. But she [my Grandmother] was very ill and died some years later.

Way too soon as she was a fantastic woman. My father who was a bit younger than my mother was hidden in a farm behind a closet. It was not as bad as my mother but he also suffers still from hiding, being so young and it was not all that easy at the places where he was. Now though, they are both healthy and we love them very much. No I don't think we are from Portugal I think we are really Dutch.

My Honours:

1983: Kuala Lumpur – World Champion; 1984: Los Angeles – Gold; 1984, 1986 and 1987: European Champion; 1988: Bronze – Seoul; 1992: Barcelona – I carried the Dutch flag at the opening ceremony; 1990: Sydney – World Champion (I was captain of the team and named as captain of the world team); In 1994 I was honoured by the Queen of Holland for my performances in women's hockey for Holland; In 2001 I was named in the Jewish Hall of Fame in Israel.

Yours sincerely,
Carina Benninga[1]

As a final and somewhat perplexing comment on the 1984 Olympics, although the total tally of 12 medals won by Jewish sportsmen and women at the Los Angeles Olympics was less than the tally won at all of the Games in the 1950s, 60s and 70s, it is in fact higher than the tally for three of the four Olympic years since 1984.

---

1   Carina Benninga, Letter to the author 2002.

1988: Calgary and Seoul

Calgary

As there were no Jewish medal winners listed for the winter Games, I am working on the assumption that there may not have been Jewish participation either. The 'star' of the Games was 'Eddie the Eagle Edwards', seen as a typical 'Mad Englishman'. Edwards, for the fun of it and to attract the limelight, participated in the challenging ski-jump without much chance of doing better than coming last!

Seoul

IOC president Juan Antonio Samaranch demonstrated by the controversial choice of this venue how things had changed by the extension of commercial enterprise. The South Korean government had offered the staging of certain competitions in Communist North Korea. The North, for its part, wanted to share half of the Games, but this was refused by the IOC as it preferred the status quo of one country hosting one winter or summer Games and confirmed that Seoul would be the single host of the Olympics.

By 1988 and contrary to Communist North Korea, South Korea now had close connections with and support from its former enemy, the United States of America. The US, though, would not alone guarantee the funding and a secure, well-prepared venue; nor the sale of tickets or souvenirs. However, American television companies offered substantial sums of money – providing that key events could be timed to be shown at 'prime-time viewing' in America. This deal was accepted, securing a considerable profit for the IOC and enabling Seoul to provide the standard of facilities required by the Olympic Movement.

The old Olympic flag designed by Coubertin was worn out and

had to be replaced, and the new flag was flown out to Seoul in time for the opening ceremony. It wasn't just the flag that had changed, though. The spirit of the Games was also beginning to change and so was its amateur principle. As far as the competitors were concerned, a new concept of professionalism allowed teachers of physical education – whether in schools, universities or sports clubs – to participate, but no direct payment of any prize money was permitted. It was the media, however, that began to dominate: the presentation of the Games in terms of the number of personnel working at the Games was nearly double the number of competitors!

This, the XXIV Olympic Games, attracted 8,465 competitors – over one quarter of them female – to South Korea in the autumn of 1988. One-hundred-and-fifty-nine countries were represented, including the Soviet Union, but some of the hard-line Communist states refused to take part.

Judging by the number of medals won by Jewish sportsmen and women, Jewish participation had declined even further than before. I find the reasons for this decline in Jewish participation difficult to assess, but the fact that there were no Jewish communities in East Asia and that those in distant Europe were further in decline may have played a large part. However, in stark contrast, the number of gold medals won by representatives of various other minority groups increased, and not only by black Americans.

Despite this strong showing by an American minority, the Soviets and the comparatively tiny GDR each gained more medals individually than the United States, who were placed third in the unofficial league table. Once again, after the Games had ended there were rumours of East German 'foul play'. Soon after the 'Wende' ('Reunification') it was confirmed by the GDR finance politician and sports historian Volker Kluge that East Germany had allocated a greater proportion of funds to sport than any other item in its annual budget, and compared with any other country's expenditure on sport. Today, not only are we aware of their use of drugs but also their much-advanced intensive training methods and the state financial support used to produce an elite. Gifted children were sent to special sports schools. There they were given a daily portion of what the pupils believed to be a kind of cod liver oil but was actually an illegal substance to enhance their future performance.

Years after unification, the former East German university of Potsdam targeted the approach the GDR took to prestige sports. The university collected documentary evidence to substantiate their claims, including an allegation that one of East Germany's most successful swimmers, six-times gold-medallist Kirstin Otto, was alleged to have been using performance-enhancing substances.[1]

Ultimately, there were nine direct disqualifications related to drug offences in Seoul, including that of the infamous Canadian sprinter Ben Johnson. It is clear that, under new initiatives by the IOC, all kinds of tests were introduced to effect a clean-up of competitive sports. No return of medals was demanded by the IOC as a result of these doping allegations but some track and field athletes were banned because they tested positive for illegal drugs.

As for Jewish participation, there was only one gold medal winner – American *David Berkoff* in the 200-metre medley relay. Carina Benninga followed up her gold of four years earlier with a bronze as captain of the Dutch women's hockey team; the same award went to her brother *Mark Benninga* in the men's hockey. Silver medals went to the *Josephson* sisters of America in the ladies' synchronised swimming event and *Attila Abraham* of Hungary, who was one of the four team-members in the 1,000-metre kayaking.

The impact of the creeping professionalism was – from a positive Jewish perspective – witnessed in the tennis. Now, for the first time since the Frenchmen Lacoste, Cochet and Borotra dominated team tennis at the 1924 Games, professional players were readmitted, with the American *Brad Gilbert* managing to win a bronze. Another American, rower *Seth Bauer*, took bronze as part of the ladies' rowing eights, and Dara Torres represented America in the 4 x 100-metre freestyle swimming relay once again, also winning a bronze medal.

---

1 The son of a former school comrade of mine in East Germany has told me about his work as a psychiatrist, which involved trying to repair the damage that state-sponsored drug taking had done to those former champions.

1992: Albertville and Barcelona

The traditional composition of nationalities participating in the Olympic Games changed considerably during the last decade of the twentieth century, largely due to the dissolution of the Soviet Union in 1991. It was as if an earthquake had struck, from the Berlin Wall to the countries bordering what had been – and was once again – Russia, breaking up some countries and pulling others back together.

Albertville

At Albertville in the French Alps, the new members of the Olympic Movement 'created' by upheavals in the former Soviet Union were not yet permitted to compete under their own colours but had to combine in a 'united team' called the Commonwealth of Independent States, which was seen as a compromise on the way to their full autonomy. Whichever flag Jewish participants competed under, we do not know of any of them winning medals – just as in the last winter Games.

Barcelona – South Africa returns

Further international political changes were reflected in the national teams competing at these Olympics. One of the most significant changes was on the southerly tip of the African continent, where Nelson Mandela had at last been liberated and became president of South Africa, formally ending the divisive and brutal Apartheid regime through democratic enfranchisement of its entire people, both the black majority and the white minority. With the barriers to its international acceptance removed, South Africa once again became an active part of the world sporting community.

The fall of the Berlin Wall in 1989 removed another barrier, this time one stretching through Germany. For the first time since Berlin in 1936, a united German team competed at the Olympics – with the team wearing their pre-Nazi national colours of black, red and gold.

Other political bridges had to be built by the host nation. Declarations of independence may have incited the Catalan population in the areas around Barcelona to increase its pressure for self-determination, but a compromise was reached with the Basque separatist movement ETA, who were determined to support the spirit of the Games. With this compromise agreed, the gold and red colours of the Spanish flag fluttered in the wind alongside the flag of Barcelona for the duration of the Games.

Generally speaking, demonstrations, withdrawals and protests appeared to be a thing of the past, and even the Yugoslavia 'reconstructed' in 1991, which was not able to take part, permitted its top athletes to compete as individuals in these XXV Games. Altogether, the number of participating countries rose to 169, bringing a total of 9,364 competitors, of whom 2,707 were female – a second great step forwards for female participation at the Games.

From watching the Games on television, reading reports in the media or hearing reports afterwards from participants and friends, it was clear we all felt that Barcelona must have come closest to fulfilling Coubertin's dreams. I will never forget the opening of the Games with the voices of José Carreras and Monserrat Caballé, and a 12-year-old boy's rendition of an 'Ode to Joy' from Beethoven's Ninth Symphony, the latter so badly misused in the Berlin Games.

Jews in Spain

There are no reports of any invitations from the Jewish community to visitors – invitations which had been a feature of many previous Games. At the time of these Games, though, there were only 25,000 Jews in Spain. Five hundred years previously, thousands of Jews had lost their lives when the Church under the 'Grand Inquisitor' Torquemada had burned the 'unbelievers' on pyres or had driven them out of the country. Many managed to be accepted as 'conversos' or had lived in disguise as Christians, later called 'Marranos' (from the Spanish for pigs!).

Simon Wiesenthal, the self-styled 'Nazi hunter', took great trouble to equate the greedy rule of Ferdinand and Isabella of Castile and Aragon in the late fifteenth and early sixteenth centuries with Hitler's persecution of the Jews in twentieth-century Germany. Was the notorious yellow star which German Jews had to display the same as the 'Limpieza de sangre' or a certificate of ancestry; and was the 'Ahnennachweis' also an idea Hitler copied with his 'Reichsfluchtsver' (a tax on those who had to leave the country)?

A statue of Columbus stands close to the entrance of the Olympic Stadium. Jewish American competitors may have been enthralled by a story that his family name was 'Colon' (Cohen) and that he had been born in Genoa but had changed his name to Christoforus Columbus when he planned his search for land across the Atlantic. Wiesenthal also suggests that he shifted his departure by one day to allow Jews to join him. Others have mentioned that Columbus took a Hebrew-speaking person with him. In his book *Sails of Hope* Weisenthal puts forward the theory that Columbus had expected to find one of the lost tribes of Israel. This title made a fitting slogan for anyone participating in the Games in beautiful Barcelona.

Jewish Winners

All of this was far away from the thinking of those who had their thoughts focused on producing their best performances at the Games. Two who did were the Jewish American twins Karen and Sarah Josephson, who went one better than their result in Seoul and picked up gold for their synchronised swimming. Dara Torres swam once again in the American 4 x 100-metre freestyle relay and gained a second gold medal to go with the one she had won eight years earlier; still this is not the last time we shall hear about Dara's performances. Completing the list of Jewish gold medal winners is another American, *Joe Jacobi*, who won gold with his partner after they successfully guided their canoe through the Canadian slalom.

There were also other medal winners: *Avital Seliger* of the Netherlands volleyball team won a silver medal and little *Kerri Strug* won a bronze in the team gymnastics event to add to America's medal tally. Furthermore, for the first time, two Israelis climbed the podium: *Shay Oren Smadga* won a bronze in the 78kg judo competition, and compatriot *Yael Arad* just missed out on a gold when judges faced with a tie in the 61kg judo competition deferred to the referees, who decided to award the gold to Catherin Fleuris of France. According to author David Wallechinski, there might also have been two more Israeli medals:

> Sela and Amir almost became Israel's first Olympic medallists. Unfortunately for them, the second race fell on the Jewish high holiday of Yom Kippur. Israeli Olympic officials made it clear that any of their athletes who competed on Yom Kippur would be withdrawn from the competition and sent home, a punishment which they did in fact mete out to the Israeli men's 470 crew. Sela and Amir would have won medals [in the flying Dutchman event] had they taken part in the second race and placed higher than eleventh, a result which they bettered in five of their six races.[1]

The 'Dream Team'

The undoubted stars of the Barcelona show were the players making up the basketball 'Dream Team'. Barcelona was the first Games where the basketball tournament was open to professionals. America, with the best league in the world, fielded a team that read like a who's who of basketball legends from the 1980s and 90s, with Michael Jordan, Magic Johnson and Larry Bird all playing in a team that no other nation could truly compete with. The Dream Team proved to be so popular that, rather than any protests about the further erosion of the Olympics amateur status, enthusiastic crowds of over 12,000 spectators turned up to watch most matches; in Spain, only football attracts larger crowds.

The successful presentation of these Barcelona Games, with its attractive position by the shores of the Mediterranean and unique Gaudi architecture, made the Games a real 'Fiesta Catalana'. For quite some time afterwards, the strands of the official tune of the Games – 'Barcelona' – would remind me of the searching sounds of Casal's Cello, his Catalan lament, but the Olympic Movement, for its part, had nothing to lament about Barcelona.

---

1   Wallechinski, *The Olympics*, p. 829.

1994/1996: Lillehammer and Atlanta

Lillehammer

For the first time, the winter Games were to be staged in the middle of the intermediate four years between summer Games. The XVII Winter Olympics had been awarded to the little town of Lillehammer in Norway as it was expected to provide ideal snow and ice conditions and was well equipped with the facilities required for a successful event. King Harald V opened the Games, which were partially financed by the American Broadcasting Corporation (ABC) and had excellent support from spectators. Again, we have no names of any Jewish winter sports competitors who won medals and one can assume that there were also no Jewish competitors.

Atlanta

The awarding of the XXVI summer Games to Atlanta had been a puzzle for many as to why for the first time an industrial town had been chosen as a host city. It was, moreover, the centenary of the modern Olympics and, quite rightly, Athens was deeply disappointed not to have been selected. One wonders whether it was due to a guarantee of support from a number of industrial giants such as Kodak, IBM and Coca-Cola which, together with ticket sales and television rights, would realise a profit.

Apart from the issue of corporate sponsorship there were other doubts about the integrity of the selection of this Games destination, especially as there were political considerations as to why this particular venue had been selected. Atlanta, in America's Deep South, still had anti-black prejudices, although one third of its population is black. This aside, one wonders at the sense of pride that the city must have felt when the much-loved and admired sportsman and Olympian Muhammed Ali was asked to take a prominent part in the opening ceremony.

Unfortunately, questions about the city did not stop with its selection. Atlanta is very compact and has limited public transport, so quite often the teams could not meet the arranged timetable, a difficulty not entirely offset by the high degree of goodwill and support by the local inhabitants who were providing the transport. During the Olympics – and particularly when difficulties like these arose, it became very apparent that Atlanta could not compete with the standards set by Seoul and, of course, Barcelona. On the positive side of the equation, a large new stadium housing nearly 100,000 spectators had been built.

For the first time ever the Games achieved a 'full house' as all 197 IOC-affiliated countries participated. The restructuring of Russia created opportunities for 11 new countries after the Ukraine, Belarus and the Baltic states had completed their transition to independent, post-Russian Federation countries. With over ten thousand participants representing 197 countries, there was the potential of 33 competitors and more in each event. With this many participants, housing could have been a problem, but the Olympic village was capacious enough. However, there were more media personnel in attendance than competitors and, in addition, there was an increase in the supporting crews of doctors, sports psychologists, and even chefs, some of whom provided Halal and Kosher food for minorities. This is why, when considering the Atlanta Games, it is difficult not to think that the whole Olympic event was getting far too big to retain its original essence.

In spite of the Games taking part in America there were only a few Jewish medal winners – and none from Russia or, geographically speaking, Europe. Israel, which within the world of sport is considered a European country, sent competitors, but many Arab nations would not compete against Israelis.[1] Israel, though, did have one medal success, with *Gail Friedman* sailing her boat into bronze position in the mistral yachting class. Another Jewish competitor also picked up a bronze: *Miryam Fox-Jerushalmi*, although she was married to the English canoeist Fox, continued to represent France and paddled to third place in the slalom kayaking event.

---

1   This even extends to international sporting events other than the Olympic Games.

55. *Champion gymnast Kerri Strug (USA) won a gold medal despite an injury – here carried by her coach Bela Karolyi.*

All other medals won by Jewish competitors were gold – and all of them were won by Americans. Swimmers *Lenny Krayzelburg* and *Brad Schumacher* won gold in the same 4 x 100-metre freestyle relay team, although Lenny's actual specialist stroke was backstroke! *Kirsty Thatcher* also swam to gold, this time in the women's 4 x 100-metre freestyle relay team.

This leaves Kerri Strug, a member of the American gymnastic team which had toured the country as a professional show. It was in Atlanta that Kerri, having represented America in the previous Games and won a bronze, now became the idol of the crowds watching the gymnastics, where – for the first time – America was able to outpoint the previously dominant East European teams. In fact, Kerri had made such an impression that she even received a special mention in the official report of the British Olympic Association:

For the United States and the wider world, however, Atlanta '96 will always be synonymous with Kerri Strug completing the vault that assured the home nation of the team gold in women's gymnastics.

Arms thrust back, face sharpened with pain, she hopped on one leg like a little bird before sinking to all fours and being carried from the mat. Strug – 18 years old and 4ft 9in – had injured her ankle ligaments on landing the first of her two scheduled jumps, but had carried on after urgent consultation with her coach Bela Karolyi. 'We got to go one more time', Karolyi said, knowing that the Russians, with two final competitors still to go in the floor exercise, could conceivably overhaul the home team. 'Can you?' 'I don't know yet...' Strug said. Then: 'I will do it, I will, I will.' She did, and her score of 9,712, improving on her first mark of 9,162, insured the United States their first team gold gymnastic medal. The response from the 30,000 spectators in the Georgia Dome was as enormous as anything else that happened in the entire Games. Many observers of the sport felt that the crowds who witnessed the gymnastics in Atlanta were embarrassingly, even insultingly partisan. But the tension and exultation of the night was unforgettable.[2]

The official British report, though, had far less complimentary things to say about Atlanta as an Olympic venue:

The Games of 96, sad to record, are destined primarily to be recalled for the woeful inadequacies of the venue. Atlanta was a provincial town standing on tiptoes and pretending to be an international city; selected for commercial convenience rather than the ability to stage an historic Olympics. In short, it was the wrong choice, made entirely for the wrong reasons.[3]

France Soir added:

Africa has been deprived of the Games since it began on the pretext that African countries don't have the necessary

2   British Olympic Association, official report, 1996.
3   Ibid.

infrastructure. After Atlanta, any country in the world can apply to host the Games.[4]

Despite what can only be considered a set-back after the triumph of Barcelona, there was great expectation as to what Sydney could stage, where the preparation for the next Games had already commenced.

4   *France Soir*, 1996.

1998/2000: Nagano and Sydney

Nagano

As far as I could ascertain, at the XVIII Winter Olympics in Nagano there were once again no Jewish medal winners. Emperor Akihito opened the Games and welcomed 2,302 representatives from 72 countries to Japan. The events were much affected by bad weather, often requiring last-minute changes and the reorganisation of the timetable.

Germany gained more medals than any other country but I have no further information about any participation of Jewish winter sportsmen and women.

Sydney – A Midsummer Night's Dream – The Millennium Games

After a certain disappointment in Atlanta's presentation of the Games four years earlier, the most appropriate description for these unique games derives from Shakespeare's magical vision and a dream that came true. Sydney had learned lessons from both Barcelona and Atlanta and had improved not only its communication network, but also gave priority to its infrastructure.

Bidding for the Games

As the bidding process for the 2000 Games entered its final stages, Sydney and Beijing were left as the most suitable applicants to host the Games. Would it be a choice between Games under the rule of a Communist state or sponsored by private enterprise? Would the sad boycotting experiences of Moscow and Los Angeles in the 1980s now be repeated? Finally, would the questions about how and why Atlanta won the right to stage the 1996 Games be addressed again?

While the questions asked of Atlanta's suitability could, ultimately, not be levelled at Sydney, other questions certainly could. My grandson Stefan had given me a book when I was in Australia called *The Bid: How Australia Won the 2000 Games* by Glenda Korporal and Rod McGeoch.[1] The book reads like a thriller and I have my reservations about the manner in which a large team of well-connected people secured the games for Sydney. A suspicious attitude to the way that modern Games bids are carried out is not always unjustified: 2000 also witnessed the bribery scandal surrounding the bid to take the winter Games to Salt Lake City in 2002.

A special assembly of the representatives of nearly two hundred countries belonging to the IOC was brought together in 1993 to announce the venue for the 2000 Games, which took place at a luxurious hotel in Monte Carlo. Their number was swollen by a news-hungry media. *The Bid* describes the amazing atmosphere and how the IOC set out to make a major impression. In a dramatic finale, the president of the IOC, Juan Antonio Samaranch, announced that Sydney had won the 2000 Games by just one vote.

The book then goes on to detail the far more acceptable face of Olympic preparation – how hundreds of people worked voluntarily for seven years to prepare Sydney for the Games. Hundreds of the names of those involved in these preparations are listed, from suppliers of facilities and equipment for the teams to catering and venues.

One person who played a significant role was *Samuel Pisar*, a concentration camp survivor who was brought to Australia by two of his uncles who survived the war. Pisar was only 12-years-old when he was incarcerated in a camp, where his mother and sister died; his father was killed when opposing the German army. Pisar went on to study law at Melbourne University, having gained his degree at Harvard prior to the Sorbonne. He joined the staff of Samaranch – General Franco's ambassador to Moscow.

---

1   Glenda Korporal and Rod McGeoch, *The Bid: How Australia Won the 2000 Games* (Sydney: William Heinemann, 1994).

Eventually, Pisar became the general consul to the IOC and the Australians and therefore established a valuable connection to the president of the IOC.[2]

Reading Korporal and McGeoch's book, there is no doubt in my mind that many attempts to gain the majority vote to promote the Olympics had been what one may call 'exercising an undue influence'. Of course, some members of national Olympic committees, even members of the IOC, may have been offered small gifts. For example, the authors mention the presentation of a wristwatch for the daughter of an IOC member.

However, it was only when the bidding for the winter Games in Salt Lake City was assessed that some members of the IOC were asked to retire and others were forced to do so. In any case, a review of the 'bidding process' was long overdue and the IOC will have to take significant steps to achieve the monumental task of keeping the Games clean.[3]

Time, Tickets and Transport

Apart from the political decisions, Sydney offered a backdrop to the Games which enthralled all those who watched events in the city, outside the main stadium and in other competition venues. The international dateline, however, proved a problem for television coverage in countries on both sides of the Atlantic. My wife and I had travelled 'down under' on several occasions as part of our family had emigrated to Australia some years ago. My wife and I were last in Australia a year before the event and were able to observe how much Sydney had prepared itself for these millennium Games. It was very impressive: the airport had been

---

2　Other Jewish individuals playing behind-the-scenes roles were John Wolfesson, a merchant banker who had fenced for Australia in the 1956 Games, and his friend David Gonski. Wolfesson and Gonski gained the support of the multi-millionaires Rupert Murdoch and Kerry Packer in order to establish links between the Olympics and the media.

3　In November 2002 IOC members voted 120 votes to 6 in favour of maintaining the suspension of visits to cities bidding for the Games. These visits were banned after the Salt Lake City scandal, when several IOC members made repeated trips to the city and received additional 'gifts' at every visit. Current IOC President Jacques Rogge, who has never visited a city making a bid to host the Olympics, introduced the motion at an IOC session in Mexico as a vote of confidence. Thankfully, the tactic paid off and the IOC does now appear to be engaged in a process of reorganisation in order to restore public confidence and prove that the organisation itself is not tarnishing the Games. For further details see Duncan Mackay, 'Rogge's gamble pays off as IOC back ban on site visits', *Guardian*, 30 Nov. 2002.

improved and extended and a large tunnel close to the Harbour Bridge relieved north-to-south congestion; the building of special venues for competitions had commenced way back in 1994. I recall reflecting on these positive signs and the general mood of expectation in Sydney and wondering if the best was yet to come for the Olympics.

I had been told that it was difficult for locals to obtain tickets, but easier for those who booked inclusive package holidays through agencies abroad. Tickets were bought by Australians from returns and additional ticket allocations. This enabled my sport-loving great grandchildren to see their first Olympic Games, a prospect which delighted me.

Never before was there so much enthusiastic involvement from the local inhabitants of a conurbation in a festival of sports as for these Games, which marked the beginning of a new century. How different this was from the 'command performance' in 1936 in Hitler's Berlin. It was as if Sydney wanted to prove to the rest of the world how much they were part of the Olympic community.

Jews in Australia

In the chapter about the 1956 Melbourne Games I mentioned the Jewish community. Recently, I had a letter from the Senior Rabbi, *Raymond Apple* from Sydney, who had previously worked in Britain with Jewish Youth organisations and knew me well. He had published an article about the first consignment of deported criminals from England to Australia. Later, an article was published in the *Sunday Times* by Sian Rees, concerning a special and urgent shipment of women criminals to Australia to meet the requirements of men transported some years earlier. It took nearly two years to transport them via South Africa and the Cape of Good Hope, and Rees reports that during this time a group of Jewish deportees among the passengers became friendly with the all-male crew. One even lived with an officer in his quarters and married him later; others gave birth during the long voyage. Convicted Jewish criminals were still preferable to local aboriginal women as wives: what really mattered was that they were white. Some of their offspring formed the first community of Jewish families. Years later, because of a positive immigration policy, their number grew to nearly 100,000, with over 40,000 now living in Sydney.

The local Jewish population and many participants in the

Sydney Games attended a memorial service for the 11 Israelis murdered in Munich. A special stone had been shipped from Israel on which an extinguished Olympic torch was displayed as a symbol of loss. The stone was supported by an 11-cornered plinth, on which the names of those who perished in 1972 were engraved. The special service took place in the presence of various members of the IOC and Walther Tröger, who, as previously stated, had been in charge of the Olympic village in Munich and was a deeply hurt Olympian because of the events there.

The Games

The Governor General of Australia, Sir William Deane, opened the XXVII Games, which was the cue for dance and music. In place of the opera stars who had graced the Barcelona opening ceremony there was *Olivia Newton-John* – the niece of a woman who had come to Australia as a Jewish refugee of Nazi oppression. Her music was chosen by thousands of young athletes. A special composition for orchestra and choir was written by *Elena Kats-Cehrin*. Prominent displays and presentations depicted the life of the Aborigines as an important part of Australian culture and celebrated their participation in modern Australia. Cathy Freeman, winner of two medals at the previous athletic World Championships over 400m, had stepped forward to receive, as the last runner, the flaming Olympic Torch carried in relay many months previously from ancient Olympia in Greece. The public were delighted when they realised that their country had chosen an young Aborigine woman for this high accolade. She became the idol of the people and a symbol of Australian equality. The crowd's reaction to her appearance was a reminder of the 1936 Games in Berlin when Jesse Owens triumphed to the delight of the spectators and the annoyance of Hitler during the Games. Cathy was to become the hot favourite to win a gold medal when Marie-José Perec the French world champion over 400m suddenly retired from the competition. Urged on by over 100,000 spectators, she ended the race triumphantly carrying the Australian flag as well as the colours of her minority; the black, yellow and red of the Aborigine people. Once again, sport had become a springboard for a minority and, no doubt, their successful participation in these Games was an important contribution towards equality.

The number of events was increased to 300 by the inclusion of 29 new events, mainly for women. Still, there were a few dozen

56. Lenny Krayzelburg (USA) won three gold medals in swimming events.

other sports complaining that they had been left out and would continue their demands to become part of future Games' programmes. The number of participants increased to 10,651, including 4,069 female competitors, and the number of the reporting media and recording officials also duly increased.

Thanks to publications such as the London *Jewish Chronicle* and the *Australian Jewish News* edited by *Vic Ahadeff*,[4] I was able to gather more information than ever before about Jewish participation in an Olympics. From these publications I received the names and details of approximately 40 Israeli participants and another 20 from the USA and some from other countries such as Brazil, along with the 5 selected to represent Australia. All in all, over 70 Jewish athletics gathered to compete in Sydney.

The Israeli contingent included many participants who had previously distinguished themselves in various championships but this time managed to gain only one medal – a bronze (in the kayaking – see later). The much smaller American Jewish participation was more successful, perhaps partly because all of its team members had been selected in special qualifying trials.

4   See Appendix.

Out of this field of 70 Jewish participants, the outstanding achievement had to be that of American swimmer Lenny Krayzelburg, who won three gold medals. Lenny was born in the Ukraine, where he had received special training when his talents had been discovered. The family emigrated to America and remain conscious of their Jewish roots, which is not always the case with other Jewish Olympians who recently left Russia and the former states of the USSR; many feel that they would not have an opportunity to be one of the three representatives to be nominated by their country of birth. Lenny won gold in the 100-metre backstroke, broke the Olympic record when taking a second gold in the same stroke over 200 metres and completed his golden trio of medals by swimming his specialist stroke in the victorious American 4 x 100-metre medley relay team. Swimming against Lenny in the final of the 100-metre backstroke was the Israeli *Eitan Orbach*, who finished in eighth position.

Another Jewish swimmer did strike gold, though. Freestyle swimmer *Anthony Ervin* won a gold medal in a dead-heat with another competitor over the sprint distance of 50 metres and a silver medal as part of the American 4 x 100m freestyle relay team. Ervin, the son of a black American father and a Jewish mother, is one of the few black swimmers ever to have won an Olympic medal.

Also posting more than one medal-winning performance was Dara Torres. Following up considerable success at previous Games, Dara took her Olympic medal tally to eight by winning bronze medals in the 100-metre butterfly and the 50- and 100-metre freestyle and gold medals with the American team in the 4 x 100 freestyle and 4 x 100 medley relays. For South African *Sarah Poewe*, though, there was disappointment: she finished in the agonising position of fourth in the 100-metre breaststroke.

One of the most impressive sights of the whole Games was the start – from the steps of the Sydney Opera House – of the triathlon, in which women competed at the Olympics for the first time. Special measures had been taken to protect the swimmers from sharks in the harbour area, where there had been sightings shortly before the Games. In this event, *Joanna Zigler* from America just missed out on a medal by finishing in fourth place.

In the pentathlon, *Natayia Rochupkina* of Russia eventually came sixth, having slipped from second position on the first day. Other Jewish competitors had more success, including Rochupkina's

57. Zhanna Pintusevich-Block (Ukraine), world champion and Olympic medallist.

compatriot *Marina Mazina*, who won gold as a member of the épée team, and *Adriana Behar*, a teacher from Brazil, who took silver with her partner in the beach volleyball, which was played at Bondi Beach and watched by 5,000 spectators. The team's president, *Arthur Nuzman*, was delighted with this achievement.

Israel had great hopes of gaining medals in judo and yachting, where Sabras[5] had done well in previous Olympics and on the international scene at various tennis, swimming, athletics, football and basketball championships. However, the athletics stadium was the scene of one of the greatest disappointments of the Games for Israelis. Pole vaulter *Alex Averburgh*, a former European indoor champion and also a gold medallist in the world championships – where he cleared 5.80 metres – did not reach a similar medal-winning height; neither did team-mate *Danny Krasnow*, who failed to reach the final. In the high jump, the tall Israeli *Konstantin Matousevitch* cleared 2.32, but went on to fail with his final jumps, thereby missing a medal. Triple jumper *Roger Nahum* was also part of the unsuccessful athletics squad.

---

5   A Sabra is a Jew born in Israel or in Palestine before 1948.

Israelis also narrowly missed out in other sports. *Arik Zeevi, Yuri Evseychiv, Shani Kedmi* and *Anat Fabrikant* finished fourth in the sailing, and so just missed a medal. These numerous near misses were very disappointing for the Israelis – and so was the rebuke from Orthodox politicians that the one and only medal winner, *Michael Kolganov*, did not forgo securing his success on a Jewish holy festival day. Michael, who hails from Russia and now lives at Kibbutz Deganyah Bet on the shores of Lake Kinneret, won a gold and a silver medal in the kayaking world championships a short time before the Olympics. At the Games, though, he competed over the longer distance of 500 metres and finished in third place.

There was disappointment of a different kind for Israel when the Ukraine did not release *Zhanna Pintusevich-Block* to represent Israel in spite of having married an Israeli named *Block*. One of the best women sprinters in the world and the only serious rival to American Marion Jones, Zhanna surprisingly failed to reach the 200-metre final and only managed fifth in the 100 metres. The following year, though, at the world championships in Edmonton, Canada, she beat Jones in the 100 metres and became the world champion.

Reading so many Russian names in the list of Israeli competitors, one is reminded of a statement by Israel's 'Diaspora Officer' that two-thirds of Russian immigrants were not Jewish but had married into the faith in Israel. For example, Alexander Danilov, a pistol shooting finalist, remained a Christian and wore a cross on a chain, much to the annoyance of some of the members of the Israeli team.

Whatever the case may be, the enthusiastic Jewish community in Sydney celebrated the Games with the issue of a commemorative medal and endless hospitality. With so many Jewish participants, I could only mention the most successful ones, but there may also be others whose Jewish identity is only now becoming apparent.

The Games closed with an even more exciting spectacle than the opening ceremony and impressive firework display. Finally, the traditional ceremony with the handing over of the Olympic flag to the Mayor of Athens concluded the millennium Games. All in all, this was a fitting end of the 'Midsummer Night's Dream' that became a memorable reality for all who took part and for the millions watching across the world.

The XI Paralympic Games – The Triumph of a Minority

Some four thousand athletes from 121 countries participated in the XI Paralympic Games in Sydney. As with the Olympics, 110,000 tickets were sold in advance for the opening and closing ceremonies. The sporting public and other onlookers had wondered whether these Games would not be an anti-climax after the amazing events of the past 16 days, but now it was for the paraplegics in whose honour Australia's flag rose on the mast, accompanied by thousands singing the national anthem. Just watching the teams or individuals entering the arena either in wheelchairs or walking with the help of support, a stick, or crutches, it was a joy to see the happiness of people who may have been written off in a past age.

Australia's seven-times gold medallist Louise Sauvage lit the fire in the cauldron sitting in her wheelchair and the Olympic Oath was taken by blind competitor Tracy Cross led by her guide dog. A band of Aborigines called the Yothu Yindi moved along a track that was soon to be made ready for competitions.

It was left to Cambridge professor Stephen Hawking, the scholar and sufferer from Motor Neurone Disease, to appear on a large screen to respond to the statement that 'the fire which burns so brightly in you (able bodied athletes) burns in us...in our hearts, in our minds and in our spirits...'

In these Games, less emphasis was placed on 'star' performances compared to the able-bodied version and more on the individual achievements of participants and the Paralympic Movement as a whole. This is what so enthralled the many thousands of spectators. The reporting of the Games also had a different focus. It contained no long lists in the sports pages of national newspapers but, here and there, a special achievement was highlighted, especially when the nation won a gold or even their first medal.

Paralympic competitors are classified in accordance with their disablement. In Sydney, 18 events were staged, but by the very nature of the way the various disabilities are classified for sports purposes – now including those with learning difficulties as well – an extraordinary number of contests had to be arranged. For example, there were 14 classifications for swimmers with impaired vision. Often, only a very small field would compete for the three medals. Of course, the quality of 'equipment', such as an artificial leg or a special wheelchair, favoured the richer and more developed nations, but judging by the many surprise results it was often a case of will power triumphing over all problems. And in overcoming their difficulties, the athletes at these Paralympics proved to millions who watched these Games how much disabled men and women are now able to make a positive contribution to the life and economy of a country.

These competitors were not yet able to share commercial incentives as others – able-bodied sportsmen and women – had in Sydney. But there were other, less tangible, benefits. Twenty thousand enthusiastic spectators were enthralled by the skill and patterns of movements of the disabled basketball players in their hi-tech wheelchairs. Displaying this level of skill and attracting this many people to watch them, the wheelchair basketball players became a symbol for all other competitions for those with disabilities. And let's not forget the volleyball players crouching on the floor who called themselves – having no self pity – 'The Crabs', transforming themselves into another symbol of these remarkable Games.

Israel, which has paid special attention to those victims of violence, had under the guidance of Sir Ludwig Guttmann already participated in The Stoke Mandeville Games some years prior to the Paralympics. In Sydney, they celebrated the victories of the swimmer *Karen Leibowitch*, the rifle-shooter *Doreen Shapiro* and the long jumper *Yorgev Kenzi*.

A British Jew also won medals: blind competitor *Elaine Barrett* swam to a silver in the medley and a bronze in the 100-metre breaststroke.

When both Games closed, Australia returned to a life which

could never be the same. A more important change, though, had taken place. The attitude to the disabled had changed to such an extent that in future, sports festivals and competitions would include some events for the disabled. So, sport on this occasion had really served as a springboard towards normality and against prejudice. The dreams of the founder of the modern Olympic Games, Baron Pierre de Coubertin, and Sir Ludwig Guttmann, whose inspiration began the Paralympic Movement, have been ushered into reality at the start of a new millennium. In their own way, both men assisted minorities in their various stages of recognition.

To place this dream-become-reality in the full, complicated context of life, I turn to the vivid words of Noureddine Morceli of Morocco, the Olympic champion over 1,500m. On receiving his gold medal he said:

> The records and medals are wonderful, but they are mere trinkets in reality. They cannot feed all the people in the world who are hungry, clothe all those who are troubled or bring peace to those who are at war.

Perhaps not, but the Olympics and Paralympics have achieved – and will continue to achieve – progress of real importance. After all, if they had remained a dream, the exploits of Jewish sportsmen and women that I have celebrated in this book – exploits that led to greater recognition for minorities – would never have happened. I, therefore, prefer to leave you with the words of Jesse Owens, one of the greatest and most gracious of all Olympians, reflecting on his famous long jump contest with Luz Long:

> This long jump set an example which has lasted me a lifetime... more clearly than anything else could have done: that free competition between free men does not breed hatred, but friendship, understanding and the fulfilment of one's best effort.

Part V

Appendices

List of all Jewish Olympic Medal Winners, 1896–2000

Explanations:
F = Female; D = Disputed; WR = World Record; OR = Olympic Record
As data given by various Sport Historians differs, the following list is a composite based on all information available to the author. The names of Jewish persons are printed in *italics* on their first mention in the main body of the text.

1896 Athens

Gold	Alfred Flatow	Germany	Parallel Bars
	Alfred Flatow	Germany	Parallel Bars, Team
	Alfred Flatow	Germany	Horizontal Bar, Team
	Gustav-Felix Flatow	Germany	Parallel Bars, Team
	Gustav-Felix Flatow	Germany	Horizontal Bar, Team
	Alfred (Hajós) Guttmann	Hungary	100m Freestyle
	Alfred (Hajós) Guttmann	Hungary	1,200m Freestyle
	Paul Neumann	Austria	500m Freestyle
Silver	Alfred Flatow	Germany	Gymnastics — Horizontal Bar
Bronze	Otto Herschmann	Austria	100m Freestyle
	Gyula Kellner	Hungary	Marathon

1900 Paris

Gold	Myer Prinstein	USA	Triple Jump	OR
Silver	Jean Bloch	France	Football
	Henri Cohen	Belgium	Water Polo

Bronze	Myer Prinstein		USA	Athletics	Long Jump
	Otto Wahle		Austria	Swimming	1,000m Freestyle
	Otto Wahle		Austria	Swimming	200m Obstacle Race
	Siegfried Flesch		Austria	Fencing	Sabre
	Helga Hedwig Rosenbaumova	F	Bohemia	Tennis	Singles
	Helga Hedwig Rosenbaumova	F	Bohemia	Tennis	Mixed Doubles

1904 St Louis

Gold	Samuel Berger		USA	Boxing	Heavyweight
	Myer Prinstein		USA	Athletics	Triple Jump
	Myer Prinstein	OR	USA	Athletics	Long Jump
Silver	Daniel Frank		USA	Athletics	Long Jump
	Philip Hess		USA	Lacrosse	
	Albert Lehman		USA	Lacrosse	
Bronze	Otto Wahle		Austria	Swimming	400 yards Freestyle

1906 Athens

Gold	Henrik (Hajós) Guttmann		Hungary	Swimming	4 x 250m Freestyle
	Myer Prinstein		USA	Athletics	Long Jump
	Otto Scheff		Austria	Swimming	400 yards Freestyle
Silver	Edgar Seligman		Great Britain	Fencing	Epée, Team
Bronze	Ödön Bodor		Hungary	Athletics	4 x 400m
	Hugo Friend		USA	Athletics	Long Jump
	Otto Scheff		Austria	Swimming	1,500m Freestyle

1908 London

Gold	Deszö Földes		Hungary	Fencing	Sabre, Team
	Jenö Fuchs		Hungary	Fencing	Sabre
	Jenö Fuchs		Hungary	Fencing	Sabre, Team

Silver			
Oszkár Gerde	Hungary	Fencing	Sabre, Team
Alexandre Lippmann	France	Fencing	Epée, Team
Eugène Olivier	France	Fencing	Epée, Team
Jean Stern	France	Fencing	Epée Team
Richard Weisz	Hungary	Wrestling	Greco-Roman, Heavyweight
Lajos Werkner	Hungary	Fencing	Sabre, Team
Harald Bohr	Denmark	Football	
Otto Froitzheim	Germany	Tennis	Singles
Alexandre Lippmann	France	Fencing	Epée
Jöszef Munk	Hungary	Swimming	4 x 200m Freestyle
Edgar Seligmann	Great Britain	Fencing	Epée, Team
Harry Simon	USA	Shooting	Rifle, Free-standing 300m
Bertram Solomon	Great Britain	Rugby	
J.C. 'Barney' Solomon	Great Britain	Rugby	
Imre Zachár	Hungary	Swimming	4 x 200m Freestyle
Bronze			
Paul Anspach	Belgium	Fencing	Epée, Team
Charles Jacobs	USA	Athletics	Pole Vault
Eugène Olivier	France	Fencing	Epée
Otto Scheff	Austria	Swimming	400 yards Freestyle

1912 Stockholm

Gold			
Henry Anspach	Belgium	Fencing	Epée, Team
Paul Anspach	Belgium	Fencing	Epée
Paul Anspach	Belgium	Fencing	Epée, Team
Deszö Földes	Hungary	Fencing	Sabre, Team
Jenö Fuchs	Hungary	Fencing	Sabre
Jenö Fuchs	Hungary	Fencing	Sabre, Team
Oszkár Gerde	Hungary	Fencing	Sabre, Team
David Jacobs	Great Britain	Athletics	4 x 100m
Jacques Ochs	Belgium	Fencing	Epée, Team
Gaston Salmon	Belgium	Fencing	Epée, Team

Medal	Name		Country	Sport	Event
Silver	Zoltán Schenker		Hungary	Fencing	Sabre, Team
	Lajos Werkner		Hungary	Fencing	Sabre, Team
	Samu Fóti		Hungary	Gymnastics	Combined Exercises, Team
	Imre Gellert	D	Hungary	Gymnastics	Combined Exercises, Team
	Otto Herschmann		Austria	Fencing	Sabre, Team
	Abel Kiviat		USA	Athletics	1,500m
	Alvah T. Meyer		USA	Athletics	100m
	Ivan Osiier		Denmark	Fencing	Epée
	Jenö Réti – Rittich		Hungary	Gymnastics	Combined Exercises, Team
	Edgar Seligman		Great Britain	Fencing	Epée, Team
Bronze	Jean Hoffmann		Belgium	Water Polo	
	Salomon Nardus		Holland	Fencing	Epée, Team
	Josephine Sticker	F	Austria	Swimming	4 x 100m Freestyle

The Olympic Games awarded to Berlin for 1916 could not take place during the First World War

1920 Antwerp

Medal	Name	Country	Sport	Event
Gold	Morris Fisher	USA	Shooting	Rifle three positions
	Morris Fisher	USA	Shooting	Rifle three positions, Team
	Morris Fisher	USA	Shooting	Rifle prone position, Team
	Samuel Mosberg	USA	Boxing	Lightweight
	Albert Schneider	Canada	Boxing	Welterweight
Silver	Paul Anspach	Belgium	Fencing	Epée, Team
	Gérard Blitz	Belgium	Water Polo	
	Maurice Blitz	Belgium	Water Polo	
	Samuel Gerson	USA	Wrestling	Featherweight, Freestyle
	Alexandre Lippmann	France	Fencing	Epée
Bronze	Gérard Blitz	Belgium	Swimming	100m Backstroke
	Montgomery Herscovitch	Canada	Boxing	Middleweight

Alexandre Lippmann	France		Fencing	Epée, Team
Fredrick Meyer	USA		Wrestling	Freestyle Heavyweight

1924 Chamonix/Paris

No Jewish Medal winners at the first Winter Games

Gold	Harold Abrahams	Great Britain	OR	Athletics	100m
	Louis Clarke	USA		Athletics	4 x 100m
	John (Jackie) Fields	USA		Boxing	Featherweight
	Morris Fisher	USA		Shooting	Rifle, free-standing
	Morris Fisher	USA		Shooting	Rifle, free-standing, Team
	Elias Katz	Finland		Athletics	Cross-Country 3,000m, Team
	Alexandre Lippmann	France		Fencing	Epée, Team
	Ellen Osiier	Denmark	F, D	Fencing	Foil
	John Spellman	USA		Wrestling	Light-Heavyweight
Silver	Harold Abrahams	Great Britain		Athletics	4 x 100m
	Paul Anspach	Belgium		Fencing	Epée, Team
	Gérard Blitz	Belgium		Water Polo	
	Maurice Blitz	Belgium		Water Polo	
	János Garai	Hungary		Fencing	Sabre, Team
	Alfred (Hajós) Guttmann	Hungary		Art	Architecture
	Elias Katz	Finland		Athletics	Steeplechase, 3,000m
	Zoltán Schenker	Hungary	D	Fencing	Sabre, Team
Bronze	János Garai	Hungary		Fencing	Sabre
	Sidney Jelinek	USA		Rowing	Four with Cox
	Umberto Luigi de Morpurgo	Italy		Tennis	Singles
	Zoltán Schenker	Hungary	D	Fencing	Foil, Team

1928 St Moritz/Amsterdam

Medal	Name		Country	Sport	Event
Gold	Estella Agsteribbe	F	Holland	Gymnastics	Team
	János Garai	D	Hungary	Fencing	Sabre, Team
	Sándor Gombos	D	Hungary	Fencing	Sabre, Team
	Hans Haas	WR	Austria	Weightlifting	Lightweight
	George Kojac	F	USA	Swimming	100m Backstroke
	Elka de Levie	F, D	Holland	Gymnastics	Team
	Helene Mayer		Germany	Fencing	Foil
	Ferenc Mezö		Hungary	Art	Literature
	Allie Morrison		USA	Wrestling	Featherweight
	Helena Nordheim	F	Holland	Gymnastics	Team
	Attila Petschauer		Hungary	Fencing	Sabre, Team
	Annie Polak	F	Holland	Gymnastics	Team
	Fanny Rosenfeld	WR, F	Canada	Athletics	4 x 100m
	Judikje Simons	F	Holland	Gymnastics	Team
Silver	István Barta		Hungary	Water Polo	Team
	Lillian Copeland	F	USA	Athletics	Discus
	Isaac Israëls		Holland	Art	Painting in oil
	Attila Petschauer		Hungary	Fencing	Sabre
	Fanny Rosenfield	F	Canada	Athletics	100m
Bronze	Harold Devine		USA	Boxing	Featherweight
	Harry Isaacs		South Africa	Boxing	Bantamweight
	Michael Jacob-Michaelsen		Denmark	Boxing	Heavyweight
	Samuel Rabin		Great Britain	Wrestling	Freestyle Middleweight
	Ellis Smouha		Great Britain	Athletics	4 x 100m

1932 Lake Placid/Los Angeles

Gold	István Barta		Hungary	Water Polo	
	György Brody		Hungary	Water Polo	
	Lillian Copeland	OR, F	USA	Athletics	Discus
	George Gulack		USA	Gymnastics	Rings
	Irving Jaffee		USA	Speed Skating	5,000m
	Irving Jaffee		USA	Speed Skating	10,000m
	Endre Kabos		Hungary	Fencing	Sabre, Team
	Attila Petschauer		Hungary	Fencing	Sabre, Team
	Ellen Preis	F, D	Austria	Fencing	Foil
Silver	Miklós Sárkány		Hungary	Water Polo	
	Philip Erenberg		USA	Gymnastics	Club-Swinging
	Hans Haas	D	Austria	Weightlifting	Lightweight
	Peter Jaffe		Great Britain	Yachting	Star
	Károly Kárpáti		Hungary	Wrestling	Freestyle, Lightweight
	Abraham Kurland		Denmark	Wrestling	Greco-Roman, Lightweight
Bronze	Rudi Ball		Germany	Ice Hockey	
	Nathan Bor		USA	Boxing	Lightweight
	Nikolaus Hirschl		Austria	Wrestling	Freestyle, Heavyweight
	Nikolaus Hirschl		Austria	Wrestling	Greco-Roman, Heavyweight
	Albert Schwartz		USA	Swimming	100m Freestyle
	Jadwiga Wajsowna	F	Poland	Athletics	Discus

1936 Garmisch-Partenkirchen / Berlin

Gold	Samuel Balter		USA	Basketball	
	György Brody	F, D	Hungary	Water Polo	
	Ibolya K. Csák		Hungary	Athletics	High Jump
	Endre Kabos		Hungary	Fencing	Sabre
	Endre Kabos		Hungary	Fencing	Sabre, Team

Silver	Károly Kárpáti		Wrestling	Hungary	Freestyle, Lightweight
	Ilona Elek-Schacherer	F, D	Fencing	Hungary	Foil
	Miklós Sárkány		Water Polo	Hungary	
	Robert Fein		Weightlifting	Austria	Lightweight
	Irving Meretsky		Basketball	Canada	
	Helene Mayer	F, D	Fencing	Germany	Foil
	Jadwiga Wajsowna	F	Athletics	Poland	Discus
Bronze	Gérard Blitz		Water Polo	Belgium	
	Ellen Preis	F, D	Fencing	Austria	Foil
	Em l a Rotter	F	Figure Skating	Hungary	Pairs
	Laszló Szollás		Figure Skating	Hungary	Pairs

Prof. Dr. Günter Dyrenfurth (and his wife) Germany / Switzerland, Mountaineer and Explorer, received a Gold Medal from the IOC (No Competition).

In 1940 and 1944, the Olympic Games were cancelled because of the Second World War

1948 St Moritz / London

Gold	Ilona Elek-Schacherer	F, D	Fencing	Hungary	Foil
	Frank Spellmann	OR	Weightlifting	USA	Middleweight
	Henry Wittenberg		Wrestling	USA	Freestyle, Light-Heavyweight
Silver	Ágnes Kéleti		Gymnastics	Hungary	Team
	Karen Lachmann	F, D	Fencing	Denmark	Foil
	Ivan Osiier		Fencing	Denmark	Epée
	Steve Seymour		Athletics	USA	Javelin
	Fritzi Wulf Natahanson-Carsten	F	Swimming	Denmark	4 x 100m
Bronze	Norman Armitage		Fencing	USA	Sabre, Team

Medal	Name	Code	Country	Sport	Event
	James Fuchs	E, D	USA	Athletics	Shot
	Ellen Müller-Preis		Austria	Fencing	Foil

1952 Oslo / Helsinki

Medal	Name	Code	Country	Sport	Event
Gold	Róbert Antal	D	Hungary	Water Polo	
	Valéria Gyenge	F, D	Hungary	Swimming	400m Freestyle
	Maria Gorokhovskaya	F	Russia	Gymnastics	Combined Exercises, Team
	Ágnes Kéleti	F	Hungary	Gymnastics	Floor Exercises
	Kálman Markovitz	D	Hungary	Water Polo	
	Claude Netter		France	Fencing	Foil, Team
	Mikhail Perelman		Russia	Gymnastics	Combined Exercises, Team
	Éva Székely	F	Hungary	Swimming	200m Breaststroke
	Judith Temes	F, D	Hungary	Swimming	4 x 100m Freestyle
Silver	Ilona Elek-Schacherer	F, D	Hungary	Fencing	Foil
	Leonid Gissen		Russia	Rowing	Eights
	Maria Gorokhovskaya	F	Russia	Gymnastics	Asymmetrical Bars
	Maria Gorokhovskaya	F	Russia	Gymnastics	Floor Exercises
	Maria Gorokhovskaya	F	Russia	Gymnastics	Horse Vault
	Maria Gorokhovskaya	F	Russia	Gymnastics	Balance Beam
	Ágnes Kéleti	F	Hungary	Gymnastics	Combined Exercises, Team
	Aleksandr Moiseyev		Russia	Basketball	
	Grigory Novak	D	Russia	Weightlifting	Middle Heavyweight
	Henry Wittenberg		USA	Wrestling	Freestyle, Light-Heavyweight
Bronze	James Fuchs	D	USA	Athletics	Shot
	Maria Gorokhovskaya	F	Russia	Gymnastics	Combined Exercises, Team
	Ágnes Kéleti	F	Hungary	Gymnastics	Asymmetrical Bars
	Ágnes Kéleti	F	Hungary	Gymnastics	Portable Apparatus, Team
	Karen Lachmann		Denmark	Fencing	Foil
	Lev Vainshtein	F, D	Russia	Shooting	Free Rifle, Three Positions

1956 Cortina d'Ampezzo / Melbourne

		WR			
Gold	Isaak Berger		USA	Weightlifting	Featherweight
	Yevgeniy Babitsch		Russia	Ice Hockey	
	László Fábián		Hungary	Canoeing	Kayak, Pairs 10,000m
	Ágnes Kéleti	F	Hungary	Gymnastics	Floor Exercises
	Ágnes Kéleti	F	Hungary	Gymnastics	Balance Beam
	Ágnes Kéleti	F	Hungary	Gymnastics	Portable Apparatus, Team
	Aleze Kértesz	F	Hungary	Gymnastics	Portable Apparatus, Team
	Boris Raazinsky		Russia	Football	
	Leon Rotman		Romania	Canoeing	Kayak, 1,000m
	Leon Rotman		Romania	Canoeing	Canadian, 10,000m
Silver	Allan Erdman		Russia	Shooting	Free Rifle, Three Positions
	Rafael Gratsch		Russia	Speed Skating	500m
	Ágnes Kéleti	F	Hungary	Gymnastics	Combined Exercises
	Ágnes Kéleti	F	Hungary	Gymnastics	Combined Exercises, Team
	Aleze Kértesz	F	Hungary	Gymnastics	Combined Exercises, Team
	Claude Netter		France	Fencing	Foil, Team
	Éva Székely	F	Hungary	Swimming	200m Breaststroke
Bronze	Yves Dreyfus		France	Fencing	Epée, Team
	Imre Fárkas		Hungary	Canoeing	Canadian, Pairs 10,000m
	Boris Goikhman		Russia	Water Polo	
	Oscar Moglia		Uruguay	Basketball	
	Armand Mouyal		France	Fencing	Epée, Team
	Yakov Rylsky		Russia	Fencing	Sabre, Team
	David Tyschler		Russia	Fencing	Sabre, Team

1960 Squaw Valley / Rome

Medal	Name	Code	Country	Sport	Event
Gold	Leonid Geishtor		Russia	Canoeing	Canadian, Pairs 1,000m
	Vira Krepkina	OR, F, D	Russia	Athletics	Long Jump
	Mark Midler		Russia	Fencing	Foil, Team
	Irina Press	F	Russia	Athletics	80m Hurdles
	Tamara Press	OR, F	Russia	Athletics	Shot
	Isaac Berger		USA	Weightlifting	Featherweight
Silver	Boris Goikhman		Russia	Water Polo	
	Allan Jay		Great Britain	Fencing	Epée
	Allan Jay		Great Britain	Fencing	Epée, Team
	Guy Nosbaum		France	Rowing	Coxed Fours
	Vladimir Portnoi		Russia	Gymnastics	Combined Exercises, Team
	Tamara Press	F	Russia	Athletics	Discus
	Ildiko Ujláky-Réjtö	F	Hungary	Fencing	Foil, Team
Bronze	Albert Axelrod		USA	Fencing	Foil
	Klara Fried-Banfalvi	F	Hungary	Canoeing	Kayak, Pairs 500m
	Moyses Blas		Brazil	Basketball	
	Imre Fárkas		Hungary	Canoeing	Canadian, Pairs 1,000m
	Rafael Gratsch		Russia	Speed Skating	500m
	Robert Halperin		USA	Yachting	International Star
	Leonid Kolumbet		Russia	Cycling	4000m, Team
	Alfred Kuchovsky		Russia	Ice Hockey	
	Kátmáro Markovitz		Hungary	Water Polo	
	Mihály Mayer		Hungary	Water Polo	
	Vladimir Portnoi		Russia	Gymnastics	Horse Vault
	Leon Rotman		Romania	Canoeing	Canadian, 1,000m
	David Segal		Great Britain	Athletics	4 x 100m

1964 Innsbruck / Tokyo

Gold	Gerald Ashworth	USA		Athletics	4 x 100m
	Lawrence Brown	USA		Basketball	
	Vitaly Davidov	Russia		Ice Hockey	
	Boris Dubrovski	Russia		Rowing	Double Sculls
	János Fárkas	Hungary		Football	
	Támás Gábor	Hungary		Fencing	Epée, Team
	Irena Kirszenstein	Poland	F	Athletics	4 x 100m
	Grigory Kriss	Russia		Fencing	Epée
	Mihály Mayer	Hungary		Water Polo	
	Mark Midler	Russia		Fencing	Foil, Team
	Árpád Orbán	Hungary		Football	
	Irina Press	Russia	WR, F	Athletics	Pentathlon
	Tamara Press	Russia	OR, F	Athletics	Shot
	Rudolf Plukfelder	Russia		Weightlifting	Light Heavyweight
	Mark Rakita	Russia		Fencing	Sabre
	Ildiko Ujláky-Réjtö	Hungary	F	Fencing	Foil
	Ildiko Ujláky-Réjtö	Hungary	F	Fencing	Foil, Team
	Yakov Rylsky	Russia		Fencing	Sabre, Team
	Yuri Venherovsky	Russia		Volleyball	
	Nelly Abramova	Russia	F	Volleyball	
Silver	Isaac Berger*	USA	WR, OR	Weightlifting	Featherweight
	Alain Calmat	France		Figure Skating	
	Mihály Hesz	Hungary		Canoeing	Kayak, 1,000m
	Irena Kirszenstein	Poland	F	Athletics	200m
	Irena Kirszenstein	Poland	F	Athletics	Long Jump
	Marilyn Ramenofsky	USA	F	Swimming	400m Freestyle
	Yakov Rylsky	Russia		Fencing	Sabre
Bronze	James Bergmann	USA		Judo	Middleweight
	Yves Dreyfus	France		Fencing	Epée, Team

	Vivian Joseph	F	USA	Figure Skating	Pairs
	Roland Joseph		USA	Figure Skating	Pairs

1968 Grenoble / Mexico City

Gold	Vitaly Davydov		Russia	Ice Hockey	
	Mihály Hesz		Hungary	Canoeing	Kayak, 1,000m
	Yevhen Lapinski		Russia	Volleyball	
	Valentin Mankin		Russia	Yachting	Finn
	Deborah Meyer	OR, E, D	USA	Swimming	800m Freestyle
	Yuri Moiseyev		Russia	Ice Hockey	
	Naum Prokupets		Russia	Canoeing	Kayak, Pairs 1,000m
	Mark Spitz	WR	USA	Swimming	4 x 100m Medley
	Mark Spitz		USA	Swimming	4 x 200m Freestyle
	Irena Szewinska-Kirszenstein	F, WR	Poland	Athletics	200m
	Valentina Vinogradova	F	Russia	Volleyball	
	Eduard Vinokurov		Russia	Fencing	Sabre, Team
	Victor Zinger		Russia	Ice Hockey	
Silver	Semyon Belitz-Geiman		Russia	Swimming	4 x 100m Freestyle
	Grigory Kriss		Russia	Fencing	Epée, Team
	Grigory Kriss		Russia	Fencing	Epée, Team
	Anna Pfeffer	F	Hungary	Canoeing	Kayak, Pairs 500m
	Mark Rakita		Russia	Fencing	Sabre
	Íldiko Ujláky-Réjtö	F	Hungary	Fencing	Foil, Team
	Mark Spitz		USA	Swimming	100m Butterfly
	Yosif Vitebsky		Russia	Fencing	Epée, Team
Bronze	Semyon Belitz-Geiman		Russia	Swimming	4 x 200m Freestyle
	Mihály Mayer	D	Hungary	Water Polo	
	Naum Prokupets		Russia	Canoeing	Canadian, Pairs 1000m
	Íldiko Ujláky-Réjtö	F	Hungary	Fencing	Foil
	Mark Spitz		USA	Swimming	100m Freestyle
	Irena Szewinska-Kirszenstein	F	Poland	Athletics	100m

1972 Sapporo / Munich

Gold	Vitaly Davydov	Russia		Ice Hockey	
	Sandor Erdős	Hungary		Fencing	Epée, Team
	Valentin Mankin	Russia	F, OR	Yachting	Tempest Pairs
	Fan a Melnik	Russia		Athletics	Discus
	Nikolai Melnikov	Russia		Water Polo	
	Irena Rodnina	Russia		Ice Skating	Pairs
	Mark Spitz	USA	WR	Swimming	100m Freestyle
	Mark Spitz	USA	WR	Swimming	200m Freestyle
	Mark Spitz	USA	WR	Swimming	100m Butterfly
	Mark Spitz	USA	WR	Swimming	200m Butterfly
	Mark Spitz	USA		Swimming	4 x 100m Medley
	Mark Spitz	USA	WR	Swimming	4 x 100m Freestyle
	Mark Spitz	USA	WR	Swimming	4 x 200m Freestyle
	Yakov Zheleznyak	Russia	WR, OR	Shooting	Running Game Target
Silver	Bruce Davidson	USA		Equestrian	3 Day Event, Team
	Andrea Gyarmati	Hungary	F	Swimming	100m Backstroke
	Boris Menik	Russia		Shooting	Rifle, Three Positions
	Mark Rakita	Russia		Fencing	Sabre, Team
	Ildiko Ujláky-Réjtö	Hungary	F	Fencing	Foil, Team
	Neal Shapiro	USA		Equestrian	Jumping, Grand Prix, Team
	Eduard Vinokurov	Russia		Fencing	Sabre, Team
Bronze	Peter Asch	USA		Water Polo	
	Donald Cohan	USA		Yachting	Dragon, Team
	Andrea Gyarmati	Hungary		Swimming	100m Butterfly
	Grigori Kriss	Russia		Fencing	Epée, Team
	Yevhen Lapinsky	Russia		Volleyball	
	Vladimir Patkin	Russia		Volleyball	
	Anna Pfeffer	Hungary	F	Canoeing	Kayak, 500m
	Neal Shapiro	USA		Equestrian	Jumping, Grand Prix

	Irena Szewinska-Kirszenstein	F	Poland	Athletics	200m
	Barry Weitzenberg		USA	Water Polo	

1976 Innsbruck / Montreal

Gold	Ernest Grunfeld		USA	Basketball	
	Yuri Liapkin		Russia	Ice Hockey	
	David Rigert	OR	Russia	Weightlifting	Middleweight
	Valery Shary	OR	Russia	Weightlifting	Light Heavyweight
	Irena Szewinska-Kirszenstein	WR, F	Poland	Athletics	400m
	Alexsandr Vinogradov		Russia	Canoeing	Canadian Pairs 500m
	Alexsandr Vinogradov		Russia	Canoeing	Canadian Pairs 1,000m
	Eduard Vinokurov	D	Russia	Fencing	Sabre, Team
Silver	Larisa Bergen	F	Russia	Volleyball	
	Natalia Kushnir	F	Russia	Volleyball	
	Nancy Lieberman	F	USA	Basketball	
	Valentin Mankin		Russia	Yachting	Tempest
	Anna Pfeffer	F	Hungary	Canoeing	Kayak, Pairs 500m
Bronze	Leonid Buryak		Russia	Football	
	Edith Master	F	USA	Equestrian	Dressage Team
	Íldiko Ujláky-Réjtö	F	Hungary	Fencing	Foil, Team
	Wendy Weinberg	F	USA	Swimming	800m Freestyle
	Victor Zilberman		Romania	Boxing	Welterweight

1980 Lake Placid / Moscow

Gold	Nikolai Chernetzky		Russia	Athletics	4 x 400m
	Johan Hamenberg		Sweden	Fencing	Epée
	Valentin Mankin		Russia	Yachting	Star, Pairs
	Shamil Shabrirov		Russia	Boxing	Light-Flyweight
	Eduard Vinokurov		Russia	Fencing	Sabre, Team

	Name	F/D	Country	Sport	Event
Silver	Svetlana Krachevskaja	F	Russia	Athletics	Shot
	Vladimir Novitzky		Russia	Handball	
	Vladimir Nyschkin		Russia	Ice Hockey	
	Nicolai Polyakov		Russia	Yachting	Soling, Team
Bronze	Yuri Gavrilov		Russia	Football	
	Boris Lukemsky		Russia	Fencing	Epée, Team
	Ulf Weinstock		Sweden	Ice Hockey	

1984 Sarajevo / Los Angeles

	Name	F/D	Country	Sport	Event
Gold	Carina Benninga	F	Holland	Hockey	
	Tiffany Cohen	F, D	USA	Swimming	400m Freestyle
	Tiffany Cohen	F, D	USA	Swimming	800m Freestyle
	Mitch Gaylord		USA	Gymnastics	Combined Exercises, Team
	Dara Torres	F, D	USA	Swimming	4 x 100m, Freestyle
Silver	Daniel Adler		Brazil	Yachting	Soling, Team
	Bob Berland		USA	Judo	Middleweight
	Mitchel Gaylord		USA	Gymnastics	Horse Vault
	Jay Glaser		USA	Yachting	Tornado
	Bernhard Rajzman		Brazil	Volleyball	
Bronze	Mark Berger		Canada	Judo	Heavyweight
	Mitchel Gaylord		USA	Gymnastics	Rings
	Mitchel Gaylord		USA	Gymnastics	Parallel Bars

1988 Calgary / Seoul

	Name	F/D	Country	Sport	Event
Gold	David Berkoff		USA	Swimming	200m Medley Relay
Silver	Attila Abraham		Hungary	Canoeing	Kayak, Fours 1,000m
	Karen Josephson	F	USA	Swimming	Synchronised Pairs
	Sarah Josephson	F	USA	Swimming	Synchronised Pairs
Bronze	Seth Bauer	F	USA	Rowing	Eights
	Carina Benninga	F	Holland	Hockey	

	Name	F/D	Country	Sport	Event
	Mark Benninga		Holland	Hockey	
	Brad Gilbert		USA	Tennis	
	Dara Torres	F, D	USA	Swimming	4 x 100m Freestyle

1992 Albertville / Barcelona

	Name	F/D	Country	Sport	Event
Gold	Joe Jacobi	F	USA	Canoeing	Canadian Slalom, Pairs
	Karen Josephson	F	USA	Swimming	Synchronised Pairs
	Sarah Josephson		USA	Swimming	Synchronised Pairs
	Dara Torres	F, D	USA	Swimming	4 x 100m Freestyle
	Yael Arad	F	Israel	Judo	61kg
Silver	Avital Seliger		Holland	Volleyball	
	Attila Abraham		Hungary	Canoeing	200m Pairs
Bronze	Dan Greenbaum		USA	Volleyball	
	Shay Oren Smadga		Israel	Judo	78kg
	Kerri Strug	F	USA	Gymnastics	Combined Exercises, Team

1996 Atlanta

	Name	F/D	Country	Sport	Event
Gold	Lenny Krayzelburg		USA	Swimming	4 x 100m Freestyle
	Brad Schumacher	F	USA	Swimming	4 x 100m Freestyle
	Kerri Strug	F	USA	Gymnastics	Combined Exercises, Team
	Kirsty Thatcher		USA	Swimming	4 x 100m Freestyle
Silver	—		—	—	
Bronze	Gal Friedman	F	Israel	Yachting	Mistral
	Miryam Fox-Jerushalmi	F	France	Canoeing	Kayak, Slalom

2000 Sydney

	Name	F/D	Country	Sport	Event
Gold	Sergei Charikov		Russia	Fencing	Sabre, Team
	Anthony Ervin		USA	Swimming	50m Freestyle

	Lenny Krayzelburg	OR	USA	Swimming	200m Backstroke
	Lenny Krayzelburg		USA	Swimming	100m Backstroke
	Lenny Krayzelburg		USA	Swimming	4 x 100m Medley
	Marina Mazina		Russia	Fencing	Epée, Team
	Dara Torres	F, D	USA	Swimming	4 x 100m Medley
	Dara Torres	F, D	USA	Swimming	4 x 100m Freestyle
	Adriana Behar	F	Brazil	Beach Volleyball	
Silver	Anthony Ervin		USA	Swimming	4 x 100m Freestyle
	Michael Kolganov		Israel	Canoeing	Kayak 500m
Bronze	Jason Lezak		USA	Swimming	4 x 100m Freestyle
	Dara Torres	F, D	USA	Swimming	100m Freestyle
	Dara Torres	F, D	USA	Swimming	100m Butterfly
	Dara Torres	F, D	USA	Swimming	50m Freestyle

Number of Medals Won, 1896–2000

Number of Olympic Medals Won by Jewish Men and Women, 1896–2000

Year	Total	Gold	Doubtful (0)
1896	11	8	
1900	9	1	
1904	7	1	
1906	6	3	
1908	19	8	
1912	17	9	
1920	14	5	
1924	19	8	2
1928	24	14	3
1932	21	10	2
1936	16	8	4
1948	11	3	3
1952	25	9	8
1956	24	10	
1960	26	5	1
1964	31	19	
1968	25	12	1
1972	29	13	
1976	19	8	1
1980	10	3	
1984	12	4	1
1988	8		1
1992	10	4	1
1996	6	4	
2000	17	10	5
Total	**416**	**179**	**33**

Number of Olympic Medals Won by Jewish Women, 1896–2000

Year	Total	Gold	Doubtful (0)
1896			
1900	2		
1904			
1906			
1908			
1912	1		
1920			
1924	1	1	1
1928	9	7	1
1932	3	2	1
1936	6	2	4
1948	4	1	3
1952	15	5	4
1956	8	4	
1960	6	3	1
1964	10	5	
1968	6	2	
1972	5	1	
1976	8	1	
1980	1		
1984	3	3	1
1988	5	3	1
1992	5	3	1
1996	4	2	
2000	8	4	5
Total	**110**	**49**	**23**

Number of Olympic Gold Medals Won by Jewish Competitors (Men and Women) by Discipline, 1896–2000

Fencing	47
Swimming	34
Athletics	22
Gymnastics	19
Canoeing	9
Water Polo	8
Ice Hockey	7
Shooting	6
Weightlifting	6
Wrestling	6
Basketball	4
Boxing	4
Art	3
Football	3
Volleyball	3
Yachting	3
Rowing	1
Hockey	1
Total	**186**

Olympic Games 1896–2000: Number of medals (gold, silver and bronze) won by Jews

	Total	Austria	Belgium	Bohemia = Czech	Brazil	Canada	Denmark	Finland	France	Germany	Gt Britain	Holland	Hungary	Israel	Italy	Poland	Romania	Sweden	South Africa	(former) Russia	USA	Uruguay
1896	14	5								6			3									
1900	9	3	1	2					1												2	
1904	7	1																			6	
1906	6	2									1		1								2	
1908	19	1					1		3	1	3		8								2	
1912	23	2	6				1				2	1	6								2	
1916																						
1920	14		4			2			2												6	
1924	19		3				1	2	1	2			4		1						5	
1928	25	1				2	1			1	2	6	7						1		4	
1932	21	4					1				1		6			1					1	
1936	16	2	1			1					1		9			1					1	
1948	11	1					3						2							2	5	
1952	25						1		1				10							11	2	
1956	24								3				10				2			1	1	1
1960	26			1					1	3			5			1				3	3	
1964	31								2				7			3				7	7	
1968	25												5			2					4	
1972	29												5			1					13	
1976	19	1											2			1	1				4	
1980	10	1																1				
1984	12			2	1								8									
1988	8												1	2						5	5	
1992	10												1	1		2				6	6	
1996	6								1					1						4	4	
2000	16			1	1								1						3	2	11	
Total	425	23	15	5	3	5	9	2	15	10	14	10	95	4	1	9	4	1	4	90	109	1

Changing Patterns

The medal tables tell a story of success for Jewish medal winners who competed for their country at the time. They also mirror a changing world through war and the aftermath which resulted in a shifting population. Evaluation is complex, as on first impressions it may strike the reader that actually only three Jewish communities excelled themselves; America and Russia with the largest number.

The members of the Hungarian team occupied a unique position in the tables. Hungary's achievements are immense seen in proportion to the larger continents, especially when they were part of the Hapsburg Empire.

It should be noted that before the Second World War Jews were excluded from the Soviet teams and that in 1980 America withdrew from the Moscow Games in response to the previous Soviet withdrawal. After the Second World War the picture changed completely, especially for the Europeans because of the decimation and exodus of the Jews through the Holocaust. However, it is quite astonishing how quickly some of the communities managed to recover and how much the movement of Eastern European Jews strengthened Western teams first in Europe, then in the United States and finally Israel. The new State founded in 1948 received many Soviet immigrants whose Jewish background could be difficult to confirm and are now living as part of a population which equals North America in numbering nearly 5 million.

Honours – 'Better late than never'

After the Second World War, it took some time until honours were bestowed on Olympic and other champions in Europe. There was understandable reluctance to rename streets and thoroughfares. Of course people opposed the expense of the schemes, but I am sure that some residents had other reasons for their hostility.

There is a *Helene Mayer* street in Offenbach – a ring road around the Olympic Complex was named after her at the time of the 1972 Games in Munich.

A postage stamp was also issued for the brothers *Alfred* and *Gustav-Felix Flatow*. The former Reichssportfeld Allee has been renamed the *Flatow-Allee,* and a special trophy, the Flatow trophy, is awarded annually to the best performer at the German gymnastics championship. A school is also named after the Flatows

Gretel Bergmann has been awarded the 'Opel Prize', and a sports hall in Berlin and a stadium at her birthplace Laupheim bear her name.

Karlsruhe honoured their Olympic football champion *Juller Hirsch* by naming a new indoor sports hall after him.

Bad-Kreuznach, my birthplace, responded to a request for a 'Gebrüder *Baruch* Strasse' by unveiling a plaque commemorating both brothers who died in concentration camps.

Lilli Henoch, the ten times German champion and holder of two world records, was murdered near Riga. She had a street and sports hall named after her.

The Hungarians honoured *Bela Komyadi* their famous water polo coach, with a bust at the National Swimming stadium in Budapest.

The Americans and Israelis have Halls of Honour with a

detailed catalogue of former American, Israeli and some European champions. These exhibitions are permanent and from time to time new names are added. It will never be too late to honour those as yet unknown champions who were Jewish.

Documents

Letter from Gestapo Chief Reinhard Heydrich

Based on paragraph 1 of the edicts published by the Reich's President for the protection of the German people and State dated 28 February 1933 and published in the German Gazette under IS page 85, I hereby forbid you, until further notice to act as speaker in any public or closed meetings of any kind.

Heydrich
5 April 1935

Einberufung zum Lehrgang

An

Herrn — ~~Frau xx Frl.~~   Paul Y. Meyer

in   Berlin

Sie werden hiermit zu dem vom   16. Juni   bis   22. Juni 1935

stattfindenden   Schulungslager

(genaue Bezeichnung des Lehrgangs)

in   Ettlingen/B.   einberufen.

Nächstgelegener Bahnhof für den Lehrgang   Ettlingen-Stadt

Reisetag   15. Juni 1935

Dieses Schreiben gilt auch als Ausweis für die Fahrpreisermäßigung für Hin= und Rück=fahrt. Es ist bei der Fahrkartenausgabe und jederzeit auf Verlangen vorzuzeigen.

(Vermerke und Tagesstempel der Fahrkartenausgabe)

Stempel
Berlin

Berlin, den   5. Juni 1935 19

(Unterschrift)

Der Inhaber dieses Schreibens wird von dem   Schulungslager
(Lehrgang)

Wilhelmshöhe   in   Ettlingen

zum   den Prüfungskämpfen   23./24.6.
(Lehrgang)

in   Mainz   versetzt.

Nächstgelegener Bahnhof für den neuen Lehrgang   Mainz

Reisetag   22. Juni 35

Ettlingen   den 22. Juni   19 35

Hbf. Karlsruhe Hbf.
22 JUN 1935
4

Fachamt für Leichtathletik
Olympia-
Stempel
i. D. R. L.

...nerschule „Wilhelmshöhe
Ettlingen bei Karlsruhe (Ba.)
(Unterschrift der Lehrgangsleitung)

Der Teilnehmer am   den Prüfungskämpfen in Mainz

(Art des Lehrgangs)

reist nach Beendigung des Lehrgangs nach seinem Wohnort (nächstgelegener Bahnhof

Reisetag   24. Juni 1935   Berlin   ) zurück.

(Vermerke und Tagesstempel der Fahrkartenausgabe)

Fahrkartenausgabe
24. JUN. 1935

Fachamt für Leichtathletik
Olympia-
Stempel
im D. R. L.

Mainz   den   24.6.   19 35

(Unterschrift der Lehrgangsleitung)

Bei Beendigung der Rückfahrt mit der Fahrkarte abzugeben.

V 601 36 A   Einberufungsschreiben zu einem anerkannten Lehr...   DIN A 4 h 6a 1²s München   I 35   100 000 S dk Mal

Call up to Olympia course, Ettlingen 1935.

Maccabi and Schild athletics, men and women.

This watercolor portrait of one of Germany's first Olympians, gymnast Gustav Felix Flatow (1875–1945) was painted on sheet music (the only available paper) in the Theresienstadt concentration camp three weeks before Flatow's death from starvation in January 1945. Flatow had been on the German team that was placed first in the parallel bars and horizontal bar team events at the 1896 Athens Olympics. After Germany invaded the Netherlands in 1940, Flatow, who had fled there earlier, was arrested. He was later deported from the Westerbork transit camp in the Netherlands to Theresienstadt near Prague, Czechoslovakia, on 26 February 1944. He and his cousin Alfred died there of starvation.

AFTER THE GLORY

by Ruud Paauw

About half of the Dutch ladies' gymnastics team which won the Olympic title in Amsterdam in 1928 consisted of girls of Jewish descent: Estella Agsteribbe, Helena Nordheim, Anna Polak, Elka de Levie, and Judikje Simons. Who had survived the war and who had not? Until a few months ago the Netherlands Olympic Committee, of which I am one of the archivists, had tried in vain to know their fate. We had turned a few times to the War Graves Foundation of the Dutch Government Institute for War Documents in Amsterdam, but could find no trace of them. The Foundation supposed they were all married after 1928 and without the married names of the girls it could not help us. The administration of all the Jewish female victims was grounded on German data and these did not mention their maiden names, but only their husband's names. Since the Jewish women had not played an important role in sports after 1928, we had lost sight of them and could not give the married names.

Thanks to an energetic Dutch engineer, living in the United States, 80-year-old Fred A. Lobatto of New York, who as a schoolboy saw the 1928 Games, we now know, sadly, what happened to the Jewish girls of the 1928 Dutch gymnastic team. Lobatto's daughter found a trace of the girls at the Morman Genealogical Library in Salt Lake City. Then he followed the same path we did: the War Graves Foundation in Amsterdam and . . . he came at the right moment. After a work of many years the Dutch Society for Jewish Genealogy had just tracked down the maiden names of many thousands of married Jewish women. Now the fate of the gymnasts became known: **four of the five lost their lives in German concentration camps.**
    1) Estella Agsterribe, later Estella Blits-Agsterribe, born 6 April 1909, deceased (murdered is a better word in all of the following) 17 September 1943 in Auschwitz, together with her 2-year-old son Alfred and 6-year-old daughter Nanny. Since they all died on the same date, shortly after deportation, they must have lost their lives in the gas chambers. Her husband, Samuel Blits, died on 28 April 1944 at Auschwitz.
    2) Helena Nordheim, later Helena Kloot-Nordheim, born 1 August 1903, died 2 July 1943 at Sobibor, together with her husband Abraham and their 10-year-old daughter Rebecca. They were all killed in the gas chambers.
    3) Anna Polak, later Anna Dresden-Polak, born 24 November 1906, died 23 July 1943 at Sobibor, together with her 6-year-old daughter, Eva. Her husband, Barend, died at Auschwitz, 30 November 1944.
    4) Judikje Simons (an alternate who did not compete), later Judikje Themans-Simons, born 20 August 1904, died 3 March 1943 at Sobibor, together with her husband, Bernard, their 5-year-old daughter, Sonja, and their 3-year-old son, Leon.
    5) Elka de Levie, later Elka Boas-de Levie, survived the war. How? - we do not know. Married to a man named Boas, they divorced in 1943. She died on 12 December 1979 without issue.
    One of the two coaches of the Dutch gymnastic team in 1928 was the popular and enthusiastic Gerrit Kleerekoper, adored by all. Gerrit Kleerekoper, born 15 February 1897, died at Sobibor on 2 July 1943, together with his wife, Kaatje, and their 14-year-old daughter, Elisabeth. His 18-year-old son, Leendert, died at Auschwitz on 31 July 1944. So Kleerekoper and Helena Nordheim died on the same day and in the same camp.
    As far as I know, two of the women from the glorious 1928 team are still alive. One of them is Ali van den Bos, who was coach of the Dutch Olympic team which finished 5th at the 1948 Olympic Games.

Unbelievable

The following saga concerns a man called *David Cohen* whose story appeared in the well-informed and reliable *Australian Jewish News*. His daughter, *Anne Marie Cohen*, who works for Jewish Care in Australia, told the story, which I found incredible. I wrote to the editor of the paper but received no reply. Finally I contacted the International Society of Olympic Historians which published the article opposite in the January 2003 issue of its *Journal of Olympic History*.

I give the story as an example of the great difficulties I experienced when trying to ascertain the Jewish background of approximately four hundred medal winners in the first century of the Olympic Games.

A Giant Hoax? Osendarp a Jew

by Tony Bijkerk

Martinus Osendarp

ISOH's oldest member, Dr. Paul Yogi Mayer has mailed me a photocopy of an article published on September 15 2000 in the magazine: *Medals & Martyrs, Australian Jewish News*.

"Two bronze medals in Berlin", written by Shira Sebban, tells the story of a fifteen year old athlete David Cohen, who under the pseudonym of Osendaarp should have won two bronze medals in sprinting (100 and 200 metres) during the 1936 Olympic Games in Berlin.

David Cohen was born in the Dutch East Indies in 1921, brought up in a strictly Jewish home before being sent to boarding-school in Holland.

According to his daughter, Jewishcare community relations officier Annamarie Cohen, David was determined to participate in the Olympics, but knowing Hitler didn't like Jews, decided to change his name into Osendarp. The story continues telling that his mother encouraged him and even paid for the trip. David arrived in Berlin to compete as an independent - ostensibly because at 15 he was too young to be part of the Dutch team. *"The Dutch were worried not only because of his age, which they could have falsified, but because of his Jewishness"*, Ms Cohen stated. *"But when he won the bronze in the 100 and 200, they claimed him as one of their own".*

"He became good friends with Jesse Owens because they were both facing adversity. The Olympics were a chance for Hitler to prove Aryan superiority, and they both proved Hitler wrong."

Cohen returned to Holland after the Games. During World War II, he joined the Dutch Air Force in the Dutch East Indies, escaping the Holocaust. He died in 1993.

When I first read this story, I could not believe my eyes! I never saw a story with a bigger historical lie than this one! I do not know anything about David Cohen. He may have existed and his daughter seems to be the living truth that he did!

However, David Cohen could never scarcely have been more different, just as black is different to white. The real "Tinus" Osendarp died 20 June 2002 in Heerlen. In the August/September 2002 issue of the *Olympic Review*, I published the following OBITUARY on Osendarp.

June 20, 2002, in Heerlen, The Netherlands, "Martinus Bernardus "Tinus" Osendarp (1916–2002), twice bronze medal winner at the Games of the XIth Olympiad in Berlin in 1936, passed away after a short illness at the age of 86 years. In 1986 Osendarp was called 'the fastest white man in the world' because he lost to the famous Jesse Owens and Ralph Metcalfe in the 100 metres and again to Owens and Robinson in the 200 metres, all of them black athletes. In the 4x100 metres relay, the Dutch team [Osendarp] lost the baton and as a consequence was disqualifed. It would have been a possible third medal for Osendarp. During World War II Osendarp became known for his collaboration with the German occupation forces. He became a member of the German SS and took part in the hunt for members of the Dutch resistance. He was sentenced to twelve years jail after the end of the war, but was released from prison in 1952. With the help of the president of the Royal Netherlands Athletic Union Frans Jutte, Osendarp got a job working in the coalmines in Limburg. He literally went underground for a long period After his retirement, he remained incommunicado for the media, but broke his silence a few years ago, when he was interviewed on television. During the interview he showed little repentance for his war past. 'I only did what I was orderqd to do', was his excuse."*

This obituary clearly shows that the real Osendarp persecuted his Jewish countrymen and in fact never repented for his past. Also his appearance is completely different from the photograph shown in the Australian article for David Cohen. Tinus Osendarp was a strapping guy with strawcoloured hair, while David Cohen was darkhaired, as can be seen from the photograph.

David Cohen

I do not know why this story was ever published. Any editor of a serious magazine should have checked the contents of the story first of all. A simple call to the Netherlands Olympic Committee could have informed them about the real facts: that is, that the real Tinus Osendarp was still alive at the time (2002). It is surprising how much Olympic history can be distorted by this kind of false report.

The problem is that this might be the beginning of another *"Genesis of Legends"*!

Bibliography

ABRAHAMS, Harold: XVII. *Olympic Games/Rome 1960*. London, 1960.

ADER, Armin: 'Erlebeter Sport' Sport in Autobiographien des 20 Jahrhunderts, Schriften zur Sportswissenschaft. Band 37. Hamburg, 2000.

ANGRESS, T. Werner: Generation zwischen Furcht und Hoffnung. Judische Jugend im Dritten Reich. Christians, 1985.

ANTHONY, Don: 'Minds, Bodies and Souls.' Manuskript, Selbstverlag (o.O., o.J.).

ATLASZ, Robert (Hrsg.): *Bar Kochba. Makkabi-Deutschland 1898–1938*. Tel Aviv, 1977.

BACHARACH, Susan: *The Nazi Olympics. Berlin 1936*, United States Memorial Museum. Wille, Brown, New York and London, 2000.

BALLARD, Roger: Census symposium. In: Pattern of Prejudice, Jahrg. 32 (1998) Heft 2.

BECK, Peter J.: *Scoring for Britain: International Football and International Politics, 1900–1936*. Frank Cass, London and Portland, OR, 1999.

BECKER, Hartmut: Jüdischer Sport in Displaced Persons Camps. In: Die Grunderjahre des Deutschen Sportbundes. Wege aus der Not zur Einheit, hrsg. vom DSB. Schorndorf 1990, S.161–163.

Ders.: *Antisemitismus in der Deutschen Turnerschaft*. St Augustin, 1980.

BELLERS, Jürgen: *Die Olympiade im Spiegel der auslandischen Presse*. Munchen, 1986.

BENTWICH, Norman: *I understand the risk. The story of the refugees from Nazi Germany, who fought in the british forces in the world war*. London, 1950.

BENZ, Wolfgang: *Integration ist machbar. Ausländer in Deutschland*. München, 1993.

BERGMAN, George: 'Jewish Mountaineers. A study about jewish emancipation in Central Europe'. Manuscript, Sydney.

BERLINER Sportclub: BSC-100 Jahre in Bewegung. 1895–1995.

BERNETT, Hajo: *Der Jüdische Sport im Nationalsozialistischen Deutschland 1933–1938*. Schorndorf, 1978.

Ders.: *Leichtathletik im geschichtlichen Wandel. Hrsg. vom Deutschen Leichtathletikverband*. Schorndorf, 1987.

Ders.: *Untersuchungen zur Zeitgeschichte des Sports*. Schorndorf, 1973.

Ders.: Symbolik und Zeremoniell der XI. Olympischen Spiele in Berlin. In: *Sportwis-senschaften*, Bd. 4 (1986), Schorndorf, S. 357–397.

Ders.: Opfer des 'Arierparagraphen' – Der Fall der Berliner Turnerschaft.

In: M. Lämmer (Hrsg.), Die jüdische Turn- und Sportbewegung in Deutschland 1898–1938. In: *Stadion*, Bd. XV (1989), St Augustin, S.29-43.

Ders.: 'Sportpublizistik im totalitären Staat. 1933–1945', *Stadion* Xl/2 1985, St Augustin, S.263-295.

Ders.: 'Alfred Flatow. Vom Olympiasieger zum "Reichsfeind"', *Sozial- und Zeitgeschichte des Sports* 1 (1987), Heft 2, S. 94-102.

Ders.: 'Die jüdische Turn- und Sponrtewegung als Ausdruck der Selbstfindung und Selbstbehauptung des deutschen Judentums', *Publications of the Leo Baeck Institute, Year Book XXXI*, London, 1986.

BINSFELD, R.D.: *The story of the Olympic Games*. London, 1948.

BLACKMAN, Lionel: *Athletic worldrecords in the 20th century*. Lewes, 1988.

British Broadcasting Corporation: *Olympics 92*. The Official BBC Sportmagazine.

British Olympic Association: *The official reports. of the olympic games, 1936, 1948, 1988, 1992, 1996*.

British Wheelchair Sports Foundation: *Paralympic Special* 1960.

BRÜGGEMANN, Franz Joseph: *'Der Ball ist rund' Zur 100 Jahre, Fussball Ausstellung*, Waterman Druck, Zwickau, 2000.

BUNZEL, John: *Hoppauf Hakoah. Jüdischer Sport in Österreich. Von den Anfängen bis zur Gegenwart*. Wien, 1987.

BÜTTNER, Ursula: Die Verfolgung der Judenchristen im Dritten Reich, in *Krisen und Umbruche in der Geschichte des Christentums, hrsg. von der Forschungsstelle für Zeitgeschichte*, Hamburg, 1994.

CESH: 'Committee for the history of Sport' Band II Kruger, Teja, Trangbæk, Tischler Verlag, Berlin, 2000.

COOTE, James: *The Games since 1896. A pictorial report*. Brighton.

Deutsche Sporthilfe: *Sapporo und München. Text und Resultate, 2 Bde.*, München, 1972.

Deutsch-Jüdische Soldaten 1914–1945. Katalog zur Wanderausstellung des Militärgeschichtlichen Forschungsamtes, Herford/Bonn, 1987.

DIEDERIX, Claudia: Die Judenfrage im Sport. Eine Untersuchung am Beispiel des Lebensweges der deutschen Sportlerin Gretel Bergmann. Magisterarbeit, Stuttgart, 1993.

DUNKER, Ulrich: *Der Reichsbund jüdischer Frontsoldaten. Geschichte eines jüdischen Abwehrvereins*. Düsseldorf, 1977.

EISEN, George: 'Jews and Sport. A century of retrospect', *Sport History*, 26/2 (1999), 225–239.

English Sports Council: *Black and Ethnic. A minorities report, 15/1977*.

English Sports Council: *People with Disabilities, 11/1977*.

Encyclopaedia Judaica: Sports, Vol. 15, 292–306, Jerusalem.

GEHRMANN, Siegfried: 'Symbol of National Resurrection: Max Schmeling, German Sports Idol', in J. A. Mangan et al. (eds.), *European Heroes: Myth, Identity, Sport*. Frank Cass, London, Portland, 1996.

Gewerkschaftliche Monatshefte: *'Sport-Spiel Sport' Tulle, Harder, Waffen SS*. KZ Sachsenhausen und Neeugamme. Bund Verlag, Berlin 1947.

Ders.: Olympia am Ende?, Nr. 47/96.

GILLMEISTER, Heiner: 'The tale of little Franz and big Franz: The founding of Bayern Munich FC', *Soccer Society*, Vol.1, No.2 (Summer 2000).

GREENBERG Stan: *The Guinness book of olympics facts and feats*. Enfield, 1996.

GREENBERG, Stanley: *Whitaker's Olympic Almanac: An encyclopaedia of the Olympic Games*. Stationery Office, London, 2000.

GUIDE JUIF DES FRANCE: *Sport*, Paris.

Ders.: *Sport and the Disabled*. London.

HANAK, Arthur: *Leibesübungen der Juden im Mittelalter und in der frühen Neuzeit*. Tel Aviv, 1986.

HÄNDLER, Andrew: *From the Ghetto to the Games*. New York, 1985.

HART-DAVIS, Duff: *Hitler's Games, 1936*, Century, Hutchinson Verlag Ltd, 1986.

HANNUS, Matti: 'The story of Elia Katz', *Quarterly National Union of Track Statisticians*, Vol.39, No.3 (1995).

HEIBER, Helmut: Der ganz normale Wahnsinn unterm Hakenkreuz. Triviales und Absonderliches aus den Akten des Dritten Reiches.

HOBERMANN, John: *Darwin's Athletes. How Sport has damaged Black America and preserved the myth of race*.

HOLMES, Judith: *Olympia 1936. Blaze of Glory for Hitler's Reich*.

ISOH: *Journal of the International Society of Olympic History* (2000–2003).

ISOH: INDEX of contributions since 1992 Ture Widland 2003.

ISOH: Also INDEX 1992–2003.

Jewish Yearbook: *Who is Who*, Jewish Chronicle, London, 1992.

Jews in Hungarian Sport: Museum of physical cultur Budapest, Tel Aviv, 1993.

JOKL, Ernst: Salomon Mendelsohn. Leo Baeck institute XII, 1960.

KILLANIN, M. N./RODDA, John: *The Olympic Games. 80 years of people, events and records*. New York, 1976.

KIRKOW GULDENPFENNIG: *Deutsches Olympische Komitee*, Meyer and Meyer, Aachen, 2000.

KRÜGER, Arnd: Die Olympischen Spiele 1936 und die Weltmeinung. Ihre außenpolitische Bedeutung unter besonderer Berücksichtigung der USA, Berlin, München, Frankfurt am Main, 1972.

Ders.: '100 Jahre und kein Ende? – Postmoderne Anmerkungen zu den Olympischen Spielen', in DIEKMANN, Irene/TEICHLER, Hans Joachim (Hrsg.), *Körper, Kultur und Ideologie. Sport und Zeitgeist im 19. und 20. Jahrhundert*, Bodenheim, 1997.

Ders: Theodor Lewald. Sportführer ins Dritte Reich (= Tum- und Sportführer im Dritten Reich, Bd. 3). Berlin, Munchen, Frankfurt am Main, 1975.

Ders.: 'Wenn die Olympiade ist vorbei schlagen wir die Juden zu Brei!' Das Verhältnis der Juden zu den Olympischen Spielen von 1936, in *Menora. Jahrbuch fur deutschjüdische Geschichte*. Bd. 5, München, Zürich, 1994, S. 331–346.

KRÜGER, Arnd/PEIFFER, Rolf: Theodor Lewald, Eine Karriere im Dienste des Vaterlandes oder die vergebliche Suche nach der jüdischen Identitat eines 'Halbjuden'.

LABANOVICH, Stan: *The Paralympic Games. A retrospective view*.

LÄMMER, Manfred: *Stationen der deutschen Turnbewegung 1898–1938*. St

Augustin, 1989.

Ders. (Hg.): Die Judische Turn- und Sportbewegung in Deutschland 1898–1938. Sonderdruck aus Stadion, Bd. XV (1989).

Leo Baeck Institute (Hrsg.): Die Juden im Nationalsozialistischen Deutschland 1933–1943. Sonderdruck, Leo Baeck Institute Year Book 25 (1980).

LEYENBERG, Hans Joachim: Offenbachs Blonde HE. Olympiasiegerin und Kronzeugin eines deutschen Schicksals, F.A.Z.

NATIONALES OLYMPISCHE KOMITEE in Deutschland: *Zehn Jahre Wiederbegin der Olympischen Einheit Deutschlands*. Berlin, 2000.

MAIS, Edgar: *Die Verfolgung der Juden in den Landkreisen Bad-Kreuznach und Birkenfeld 1933–1945*, Bad Kreuznach, 1988.

MANDELL, Richard: *The Nazi Olympics*. New York, 1971.

MASSIL, Stephen W: *The Jewish Year Book*, Vallentine Mitchell, London Portland, 2002.

MAYER, Paul Yogi: 'Deutsche Juden und Sport', in Irene Deckmann, Hans Joachim Teichler (eds.), *Körper und Kultur*, Philo Verlag, Mainz, 1997.

Ders.: *Jugendbewegung und Sport. Deutsche Juden, ihre Leistungen ihre Schicksal*, Menorah Institute fur Deutsch-jüdische Geschichte, Piper München 1999.

McGEOCH, Rod/KORPORAL, Glenda: *The BID. How Australia won the 2000 games*, 1994.

MEISL, Willy/PINCZOWER, Felix: *Juden im deutschen Sport*. Tel Aviv, 1968.

MENZEL, Robert/MENZEL, Friedrich: *Weltmacht Tennis. Jubilaumsbuch des Deutschen Tennisbundes. Tabellen und Ranglisten*. München, 1951.

MEDEWARS, John et al., *Hitler's Gift: Scientists who fled from Nazi Germany*, Richard Cohen Books, London, 2000.

NAUL, Roland: *Contemporary studies in the National Olympic Games Movement.*

Olympische Spiele; *Barcelona and Albertville 1972*, Copress Verlag, München

Olympische Spiele 1936, 2 Bände, Berlin und Garmisch-Partenkirchen. Cigarettendienst Hamburg-Bahrenfeld 1936.

PAUKER, Arnold: 'Jüdischer Widerstand in Deutschland', in Beiträge zum Widerstand 1933–1945, Heft 37, Berlin 1991.

PELLMANN, Alfred: *Sportlexikon*.

PFISTER, Gertrud: 'Die Rolle der jüdischen Frauen in der Torn- und Sportbewegung (1900–1933)', *Stadion* XV (1989), Bd. 1, S. 65–89.

PFISTER, Gertrud/STEINS, Gerd: *Sport in Berlin. Vom Ritterturnier zum Stadtmarathon*. Berlin, 1987.

Philolexikon, Handbuch des jüdischen Wissens. Wertheimer, Martha/Goldschmidt, Sidi/Mayer, Paul Yogi, Philo 1937, Suhrkamp 1992.

POSTAL, B./SILVER, R.: *Encyclopaedia of Jews in Sport*. New York, 1965.

PRUSCHNOWSKI/ITZCHAK: *Dornen am Lorbeer. Ein Filmdokument des Senders Freies* Berlin, 1987.

REEVE, Simon: *One day in September*. Faber and Faber, London, 2000.

RIBALOW, H./RIBALOW, M.: *Jews in american sports*. 4th edition, 1985.

RODDA, John/BRIERLY, Steve: *Olympic games in questions*.

ROLFES, JOACHIM: *Juden in den Vereinigten Staaten*. Friedrich-Ebert-Stiftung, 1990.

RÜRUP, Reinhard: *Die Olympischen Spiele und der Nationalsozialismus. Eine Dokumentation zur Ausstellung*, Berlin, 1986.

SCHILDE, Kurt: Mit dem Davidstern auf der Brust. Spuren der jüdischen Sportjugend in Berlin zwischen 1898 und 1938, Berlin 1988.

SCHOEPS, Hans Joachim: Bereit für Deutschland. Der Patriotismus deutscher Juden und der Nationalsozialismus. Frühe Schriften 1930-1939. Eine historische Dokumentation. Berlin, 1970.

SEGAL, Eric: 'Greek athletics and the Jews. Referat zur Olympiaausstellung 1986'. Institute of Contemporary History. Manuscript.

SEGEL, Richard/RHEINS, Carl J.: *Jewish Almanac – Sport. Traditions, History, Religion, Wisdom, Achievements*. Bantam/USA, 1980.

SIEGMAN, Joseph: *The international jewish sporthall of fame*. New York, 1992.

SIMMENNAUER, Felix: *Die Goldmedaille. Erinnerungen an die Bar Kochba-Makkabi Turn- und Sportbewegun*, Berlin, 1989.

SIMON, Sven: *'Sydney 2000' Express Sport*, Copress Verlag, München, 2000.

SLATER, Robert: *Great jews in sports*. Jonathan David, New York, 1992.

SOZIAL GESCHICHTE DES SPORTS: *Jahrgang 1996*, Stellungnahme zu Carl Diem, Jahrgang II, Heft 1997.

Sportmuseum Berlin: *Sport in Berlin und sporthistorische Blätter*. 1991.

Staatslexikon: Minderheiten in Band 5 S. 716-724, 1160-1166, Basel.

STENGER, Harald: Bewegender Augenblick. Margaret Lambert kehrt an die Stätte des Leidens zurück. Frankfurter Rundschau 11.11.1999.

STOOP, Paul: *Geheimberichte aus dem Dritten Reich*. 1990.

TATZ, Colin/TATZ, Paul: *Black Diamonds. The Aboriginal and Islander Sports Hall of fame*, Australia, 1986.

TEICHLER, Hans Joachim: *Internationale Sportpolitik im Dritten Reich*. Schorndorf, 1991.

Ders.: '1936 – ein olympisches Trauma. Als die Spiele ihre Unschuld verloren', in M. BLÖDORN (Hrsg.), *Sport und Olympische Spiele*, Reinbek, 1984, S. 47–76.

Ders.: 'Berlin 1936 – ein Sieg der NS-Propaganda? Institutionen, Methoden und Ziele der Olympiapropaganda Berlin 1936', *Stadion* 2 (1976), S. 265–306.

Ders.: 'Sport unter der Herrschaft der Ideologie – Sport im Nationalsozialismus', in DIEKMANN, Irene/TEICHLER, Hans Joachim (Hrsg.), Körper, Kultur und Ideologie. Sport und Zeitgeist im 19. und 20. Jahrhundert, Bodenheim, 1997.

Ders.: 'Die olympischen Spiele Berlin 1936. Eine Bilanz nach 60 Jahren', *Politik und Zeitgeschichte*, Bd. 29 (1996).

TEILHABER, Felix: *Jüdische Flieger im Weltkrieg*. Berlin, 1935.

TIMES, THE: Sir Ludwig Guttmann, Issue 2-3-1980.

TYLER, Martin/SOAR, Paul: *The history of the olympics*. 1980.

WALLECHINSKI, David: *The complete book of the olympics*. London, 1996.

WERTHEIMER, Martha: 'Eine Frauensorge zum jüdischen Sport', in *Die Kraft*. Sportbeilage, 1934.

WERTHEIMER, M./GOLDSCHMIDT, S./MAYER, P.Y. (Hg.): *Das Jüdische Sportbuch*. Atid 1937.

WIESENTHAL, Simon: Segel der Hoffnung. Christopher Columbus auf der Suche nach dem gelobten Land, 1991.

Wingate Institute: *Physical education and sports in the jewish history and culture*. Seminarbericht, 1973.

ZEHMER, Kestrin: 'Zwischen Ruhm und Verfolgung. Hermann und Julius Baruch, zwei jüdische Sportler', *Sachor* Nr. 19 (1999), Bad Kreuznach.

ZEIT, Die: *Muskelspiele. Hundert Jahre Olympics*. 19.07.1996.

Index

Numbers in **bold** refer to illustrations.

timekeeping 50, 70
Torbay 138
Torres, Dara 179, 184, 187, 200
Trenker, Louis 117
triathlon 200
triple jump 42, 201
Triumph des Willens (film) 117
Tröger, Walther xiii, 161, 164, 198
Trollmann, Johann **122**, 125
Tschammer von Osten, Hans 78, 82, 97, 102, 114
tug of war 48
Turkey 58
Tyschler, David 147
Tyson, Mike 23

Ujláky-Réjtö, Íldiko 149, 154, 157, 167
Ukraine 30, 155, 190, 202
Ulanov, Alexei 159
United Kingdom 123, 135, 145
see also Great Britain
United States 83n, 124
  and 1896 Olympics 35
  and 1904 Olympics 42, 43
  and 1906 Olympics 44
  and 1908 Olympics 48
  and 1928 Olympics 65
  and 1932 Olympics 69, 70–1
  and 1936 Olympics 83, 93, 94, 98, 104, 109, 113, 114, 115–16, 118
  and 1948 Olympics 140
  and 1952 Olympics 144
  and 1956 Olympics 147
  and 1960 Olympics 148, 149
  and 1964 Olympics 152, 153, 154
  and 1968 Olympics 155, 156, 157
  and 1972 Olympics 161, 165, 167
  and 1976 Olympics 171, 172
  and 1980 Olympics 173–4
  and 1984 Olympics 177, 179–80
  and 1988 Olympics 182, 183, 184
  and 1992 Olympics 187, 188
  and 1996 Olympics 191
  and 2000 Olympics 199, 200
  and Japan 153n
  and Suez crisis (1956) 145
  Hall of Honour in 231–2
  Jewish emigration to 79, 123, 135
  Jewish sportspeople in 233
  Jews in 30, 94–5
Uris, Leon 130
USSR *see* Soviet Union

Vainschtein, Lev 144
Van den Bos, Ali 239

Venherovsky, Yuri 154
Via Appia 148
Vikelas, Demetrius 13, **36**
Vinogradov, Aleksandr 171
Vinogradova, Valentina 158
Vinokurov, Eduard 157, 167, 171, 175
Vintus (sports association) 82
Vitebsky, Yosif 157
Volkholz, Burkhard 90, 91
Völkische Beobachter (daily newspaper) 22, 94, 117
volleyball
  in 1964 Olympics 154
  in 1968 Olympics 158
  in 1972 Olympics 167
  in 1976 Olympics 172
  in 1984 Olympics 180
  in 1992 Olympics 187
  in Paralympics 204

Wagner, Richard 22
Wahle, Otto 41, 43
Wajs, Jadwiga 127, 153n
Wajsowna, Jadwiga 70, 109
Wallace, Edgar 108n
Wallechinski, David 108, 109, 188
Walston (or Waldstein), Charles 9n, 38
Warsaw 127
water polo
  in 1920 Olympics 57
  in 1924 Olympics 60, 109
  in 1928 Olympics 66
  in 1932 Olympics 70
  in 1936 Olympics 107, 109
  in 1952 Olympics 143–4
  in 1956 Olympics 146–7
  in 1960 Olympics 149, 151
  in 1964 Olympics 154
  in 1972 Olympics 167
Wa-Tho-Huck *see* Thorpe, Jim
Wehrpflicht 120
Wehrsport 119
weightlifting
  in 1936 Olympics 109
  in 1948 Olympics 138, 140
  in 1952 Olympics 144
  in 1956 Olympics 147
  in 1960 Olympics 149
  in 1964 Olympics 154
  in 1976 Olympics 171
Weinberg, Moshe **160**
Weinberg, Wendy 172
Weinstock, Ulf 173, 176
Weisse Holle vom Piz Palü, Die (film) 117
Weisz, Richard **47**, 48
Weitzenberg, Barry 167
Wembley Exhibition Halls 138
Wembley Stadium 138
Werder Bremen football team 51

Werkner, Lajos **47**, 48
West Central (Jewish girls' club) 17
Westerbork 238
White City (London) 46
Wiesenthal, Simon 187
Wilhelmina, Queen of the Netherlands 68
Wilhelmshöhe, 82, 83
William II, German Emperor 87
Wimbledon 46
Wingate Institute (Israel) 143
Wittenberg, Henry 140, 144
Woellke, Hans 119
Wolfesson, John 196n
women 14–19, 40, 149
Women's Swimming Association (US) 17
Woods, Tiger 23
Workers' Olympics 6
workers' sport movement 6, 13, 78, 83, 126
wrestling
  in 1920 Olympics 57
  in 1928 Olympics 68
  in 1932 Olympics 70, 71
  in 1936 Olympics 108
  in 1948 Olympics 138, 140
  in 1952 Olympics 144
  in 1960 Olympics 148
Wulff-Nathansen, Fritze 139
Wyckoff, Frank 116

yachting
  in 1932 Olympics 71
  in 1948 Olympics 138
  in 1960 Olympics 149
  in 1968 Olympics 158
  in 1972 Olympics 167
  in 1976 Olympics 172
  in 1980 Olympics 175, 176
  in 1984 Olympics 180
  in 1996 Olympics 190
  in 2000 Olympics 201
Yothu Yindi 203
Young Men's Christian Association 17
Young Men's Hebrew Association 17
Yugoslavia (former) 177, 186

Zachár, Imre 49
Zappas, Evangelis 12
Zappeion 44
Zeevi, Arik 202
'Zeus Throwing the Javelin' (sculpture) 88–9
Zhelesnyak, Yakiv 167
Zigarretten Bilder Dienst 117
Zigler, Joanna 200
Zilberman, Victor 172
Zinger, Victor 155
Zola, Émile 41n

Paul Yogi Mayer was born in 1912 in the Rhineland-Pfalz region of Gerrnany.

He was involved in the German-Jewish youth movement and was active in sport. For a short time he was an assistant teacher in a Jewish school and then left to take charge of the youth department of the Jewish ex-Servicemen's Association in Berlin. He evaded arrest in the November 1938 pogrom and eventually managed to emigrate to England with his wife and baby son in May 1939.

At the outbreak of war, Yogi, a refugee from Nazi oppression, joined the British army and later volunteered for the Special Operations Executive (SOE). He saw service in Europe and in England unil his demobilisation in 1946. Within a year he was involved in youth work, taking charge of a club for young survivors of the concentration camps. After their resettlement, he became Youth Director of the Brady Clubs in East London and then the Inner London Education Authority appointed him Youth and Community Officer for the Borough of Islington.

He received an MBE from the Queen at Buckingham Palace in recognition of 'his services to youth', and an Honorary Doctorate from the Faculty of Philosophy of the University of Potsdam for 'his scientific, journalistic and pedagogic achievements'.